W9-BSQ-818

DISCARD

A Dark Rose

SOUTHERN LITERARY STUDIES
Scott Romine, Series Editor

A Dark Rose

Love in Eudora Welty's Stories and Novels

Sally Wolff

LOUISIANA STATE UNIVERSITY PRESS
BATON ROUGE

Published by Louisiana State University Press
Copyright © 2015 by Louisiana State University Press
All rights reserved
Manufactured in the United States of America
First printing

DESIGNER: Michelle A. Neustrom
TYPEFACE: Whitman
PRINTER AND BINDER: Maple Press

Chapter nine, "'Like the Stamens in a Dainty Bess Rose,'" is based in part on the chapter "'Foes well matched or sweethearts come together': The Love Story in *Losing Battles*" that appears in *The Late Novels of Eudora Welty*, edited by Jan Nordby Gretlund and Karl-Heinz Westarp, published by the University of South Carolina, Columbia, S.C. (1998). Used with permission.

LIBRARY OF CONGRESS CATALOGING-IN-PUBLICATION DATA

Wolff, Sally, author.
   A dark rose : love in Eudora Welty's stories and novels / Sally Wolff.
      pages cm. — (Southern literary studies)
   Includes bibliographical references and index.
   ISBN 978-0-8071-5827-2 (cloth : alk. paper) — ISBN 978-0-8071-5828-9
(pdf) — ISBN 978-0-8071-5829-6 (epub) — ISBN 978-0-8071-5830-2 (mobi)
1. Welty, Eudora, 1909–2001—Criticism and interpretation. 2. Love in
literature. I. Title.
   PS3545.E6Z977 2015
   813'.52—dc23

2014019893

The paper in this book meets the guidelines for permanence and durability of the Committee on Production Guidelines for Book Longevity of the Council on Library Resources. ∞

For my mother, Elaine Wolff,
and my brother, Sam Wolff

Birds came down low into the althea bush . . .
as silent as petals shedding from a dark rose.
—EUDORA WELTY, *Losing Battles*

Contents

Preface

Reminiscences

I *hope* there will be another *occasion*.
—EUDORA WELTY, telephone communication with Sally Wolff, July 1982

Eudora Welty came to Emory University to receive an honorary degree in June 14, 1982. At that time, I was completing a dissertation on her work. Dr. Floyd C. Watkins, professor of southern literature at Emory and my thesis director, held a welcome party at his home in her honor. I attended the party and met Eudora Welty for the first time.

The evening was typical of faculty parties at Emory. Other English Department professors, graduate students, and a few other friends were talking in the living room and dining room, and extra chairs were scattered here and there for guests. Miss Welty was seated on the sofa, in modest pose, legs crossed at the ankle. She wore a soft, mauve silk dress that was sophisticated but not flashy. Her face had an expression that reflected her characteristically serene composure and even-temperedness as she greeted and conversed with a full house of academicians and other guests who swirled around her.

After a decent interval I approached Miss Welty. She saw me coming, and she held a still but graciously inviting expression on her face. Nervous about meeting the author whose work I had been reading and studying for years but encouraged by her small indication of welcome, I introduced myself. She spoke softly to me and invited me to sit beside her. We talked for twenty minutes. I said I had seen a televised interview in which she talked about unusual southern names that she had heard. I asked her to say again a long name that she had recited that night. She gave it to me in one long rhyming burst: "Ta-li-tha-Ta-bi-tha-Ta-mil-ity-Jane-Ta-ka-ta-line-Ta-ca-ta-line-Ruby-Fisher-Valentine," and then she added "the last name is

Eudora Welty received an honorary degree at the Emory University commencement held June 14, 1982. Sally Wolff met her that night at a faculty party hosted by professor Floyd C. Watkins. Reprinted by permission of Emory University.

Floyd." I am not sure about the spelling of this name and regret not asking about that too, but the lilting cadence in her voice as she said that name, performed like a chant or a song or a poem, in the deep register of her normal speaking voice, is unforgettable.

I asked for other southern names that intrigued her. "I have another one," she said. This one carried more facts: "Elder-Brother-Come-to-Tell-You-All-Your-Friends-Are-Dead-and-Gone." She waited for my reaction. I laughed without fully grasping the underlying serious tone. My reaction was too quick and inappropriate—I was wrong to laugh at this one. This one was deadly serious. After the Civil War, she said, someone had been told this message—that all his friends were dead and gone. The serious-ness of the name is reminiscent of "The Rime of the Ancient Mariner," in which the protagonist lives only to tell the horrific story of what has befallen him. In Welty's example the name recounted the aftermath of the Civil War. Fallen soldiers could be commemorated not only in the tall statues that would appear in town squares across the region but also in the simple act of naming in honor of the terrible loss. The name commemo-rated such a somber story.

In our brief encounter Welty had given me two examples of the south-ern penchant for naming—to celebrate the amusing and to mark the mo-mentous. Also, she had given me perfect samples of her two most famous fictional voices: light and comic, the touches for which Welty is so well known, but also by contrast, the haunting and tragic.

That same evening I asked about her current writing; she demurred and instead asked about my writing. I said I was writing about her fiction and wanted to meet with her at her home in Jackson, Mississippi, for an interview. She said, "All right, that would be fine," and I was pleased with the prospect of a chance to talk with her longer and more thoughtfully at her home. A month later I telephoned her and reminded her of our hav-ing met at the faculty party at Emory. She said she remembered. I asked if I could travel to see her in Jackson to discuss her work and ask her some questions. She startled me with her answer, which was delivered, as if it were a yes, wrapped in the deep tones of her sweet voice, with its dis-tinctively southern charm. Her emphasis on the second and last words of her reply belied her true meaning, however: "I *hope* there will be another *occasion*."

In hindsight I see that this reply reveals two of her strongest and most attractive characteristics. On the one hand, she responded with the utmost graciousness of manner. On the other, the answer was a determined no. Eventually, after a period of waiting, I tried again to visit her, and she de-clined again. I wrote her a letter, described my research project, and asked again to meet with her. She did not reply. Then, thankfully, I described my difficulty to Dr. John Stone, Emory cardiologist and poet, who was also a native of Jackson and knew Miss Welty and her circle of friends. He wrote a letter of introduction that he thought would help. He addressed the letter to Dr. Patti Carr Black, who was at the time director of the Mississippi State Department of Archives and History and a very good friend of Eudora. His letter, he later said, attested to my earnest interest in Miss Welty's work, and I believe it helped my cause.

When I visited Jackson that summer, my main goal was to work on an article in the Mississippi State Archives, and I had almost lost hope of meeting with the author. After weeks of reading Miss Welty's manuscripts and enduring rather cold archival temperatures, along with the solitary life of an academic in a strange town, I gathered the courage to telephone Miss Welty again. She seemed more receptive and asked why I was in town. I explained that I was studying her manuscripts at the archives and renewed my request to meet her. This time she agreed.

An Octet of Cosmonauts

We decided to go to lunch. Miss Welty chose the location—a local, upscale grill—and as we walked into the restaurant, her power of observation became immediately apparent to me. She said in a deep-toned, soft aside: "Look at that!" and nodded her head toward a table of eight ladies seated for lunch: four on one side and four, facing them, on the other side. They had identical coiffures, teased up high in perfectly round, blonde bubble shapes. We both smiled. In retrospect I see that she had noticed what I had missed. The ladies looked like an octet of identical cosmonauts about to ascend into outer space. Welty had such an eye for the comic. Her stories are rich with these wry moments. Had she still been writing fiction at the time, no doubt she would have landed those bouffants in a hilarious tale.

Her extraordinary receptiveness of the world was attuned not only to simple, ordinary, hilarious, or sad observations but also to the deeply disturbing, complex, and tragic. She transformed what she saw and what she heard in the world into remarkable fiction. One of her best short stories, "A Worn Path," is a good example. The title is a concise and clear indicator of the story's main image and theme. An old woman walks through woods filled with obstacles and on to town to procure medicine. What at first seems to be a story describing the vicissitudes of old age becomes in the final moments a dark political comment. When the woman, Phoenix

Jackson, arrives at the clinic, a nurse patronizes her in a condescending voice. Phoenix stiffens in response to the insult, but fairly quickly she recovers her dignity and begins her long walk home. A short story, Welty said, should be "like a string pulled taut," and in this one, like so many of her others, she pulls "taut"—at the end—by giving the reader a startling realization: what might at first seem familiar and reliable is instead tightly knotted ethically, morally, and politically.

Tellingly, a biographical note illuminates "A Worn Path": during her long walk Phoenix Jackson mentions to a stranger, although she does not explain exactly what she means, that "I was too old at the surrender." Welty once heard an old woman utter this phrase, and it caught Welty's acute ear. She asked the old woman what it meant, and the reply was that she was too old at the surrender that ended the Civil War to learn to read. This very phrase set Welty on her course to compose the story. Here is Welty's power—the moral tale of an old woman who is free yet still shackled by age, illiteracy, poverty, and prejudice.

Our lunch continued. She ordered shrimp remoulade and drank two bourbons. The drinks had no visible effect on her. We talked for almost an hour about politics and nonliterary matters. As I listened to her describe her life, I realized that I was in the presence of an artist whose command of verbal language was as sophisticated as the written. Somehow this phenomenon surprised me. I had imagined that Welty spent long, agonizing hours laboring to find the right metaphor and simile. While that may or may not have been true, what I witnessed that day is that she created metaphorical language seemingly without any effort whatsoever. The metaphors flowed from her speech with the same easy proliferation as in her writing. For example, I brought her a hibiscus with large orange blooms. She said immediately and with another broad smile "It's a sunrise."[1] She described having seen a woman on television who had on a large hat with long panels draping down the sides of her temples. The woman had fastened campaign buttons all the way down the panels. Welty's hands showed with a sweeping motion down the sides of her head where the woman's hat lapels had flowed and said effortlessly, "It is a waterfall."

Finally, she fixed her clear, blue-eyed gaze on me with a pointed question: "Why are you here?" I asked her for an interview. She said, "All right, but we'll have to go to your apartment. My house is not air-conditioned." Her house, as I would eventually be invited to discover, although un-air-conditioned, was blissfully cool in summer because of shade afforded by an enormous old oak tree. The heat of the day was not the reason, then. She must have had another reason for conducting our first meeting elsewhere.

"I Couldn't Bear It Either": Losing and Finding the Climbing Rose

After our meeting at the restaurant, Eudora Welty allowed me to visit her at her home almost every summer, and our friendship lasted until her death. On one occasion in the mid 1980s, I asked to see the backyard. I asked because I imagined that the climbing roses would be there. She had written about them in *The Optimist's Daughter* with deep poignancy, and she mentions roses many times in her gardening letters (see, e.g., Eichelberger, *Tell about Night Flowers* 15, 27, 37, 42). The roses in her novels are symbolic of love, as is common in literature, but for Welty the rose also implies home, memory, grief, and longing: "a heart that can empty, but fill again." I knew the roses were real.

She agreed to show me the backyard. We emerged from the old, Tudor-style house into the yard by passing through the back screened door. As we walked, Welty pointed to bearded irises, the lemon daylilies, and a mimosa tree. It was a hot day in July. Mosquitoes quickly surrounded us. As we swatted them, we talked about the climbing rose canes that had migrated through the fence in front of us and into the neighbor's yard.

"Oh, something awful happened," Welty began. "The man who has been helping me in the yard"—she paused, as in her fiction, to impersonate the voice of the speaker—"he has a deep, gruff voice like this"—she lowered her voice even more to mimic his low tones—"because something is wrong with his throat. He says, 'I can do *anything*,' but the truth is, he *can't* do anything! He grew tired of caring for the roses, so he took the climbers and pulled them through the fence into the neighbor's yard. If they bloomed, I haven't seen them for years."

"Did you ask him to pull them back through to your side of the fence?" I asked her.

"Well," Welty said, "I asked a friend of mine, and she said that the canes have become too inflexible to bend back through to my side." The climbing roses thus had been lost.

"Let me look at them," I offered. "My mother is a rose grower, too, and I'm handy in the garden."

"Oh, I couldn't ask you to do that," she said generously. "It's too hot, and the mosquitoes will eat you alive, and the poison ivy is everywhere." I sensed that even though she once again had graciously demurred, she wanted me to try my hand with the roses. Modesty and politeness, two of her most essential and charming qualities, were all that stood between the roses and me. I headed for the fence and hoped that I had not misinterpreted her reserved southern manner.

Then I found the climbers, planted long ago along the old wooden fence that divided one side of her yard from the neighbor's. The wood railings were tightly knit with less than an inch separating them. The rose vines, gnarled and interlocked with the planks of the fence, had long since grown through the fence into the neighbor's yard. To complicate matters further, honeysuckle vines crisscrossed everywhere and held the rosebushes in place with heavy growth and thick knots. The climbers bound themselves fast to the neighbor's azaleas. My first task was to pull hard with both arms out straight and all my weight against the honeysuckle vines, to snap them and yank them away.

Miss Welty had long since walked back inside her house to escape the heat and the mosquitoes, but while I was in the her garden, she perched herself at the kitchen window and watched me carefully and steadfastly, and whenever I turned back to look, she was still sitting there, her white hair almost ghostly visible through the darkness of the screened window. Her watchful gaze and her steady position at the window were all the encouragement I needed to see me through three hours of hard work in the July heat among the tangled honeysuckle webs of the rose garden.

Eventually, the roses sprang free, and long green tendrils of the canes whipped high into the air. With coaxing, the thick canes came back through small cracks in the fence railing. From her post in the kitchen, Miss Welty clapped her hands when the vines came home. The last bush, the farthest away, seemed to be the oldest. She called its name "Banksia" and said it

Chestina Andrews Welty, Eudora Welty's mother, in the rose garden at her home in Jackson, Mississippi. Reprinted by permission of Russell & Volkening as agents for the author. Copyright ©Eudora Welty, LLC.

was the first one her mother had planted, years ago.[2] "It still has the most blossoms and the sweetest fragrance," Miss Welty said. The trunk of the rose was thick with age, twisted with honeysuckle, and crusted with bark.

The old trunk, three inches in diameter—thick and wide for a climbing rose and a testament to its age—resembled the wood trunk of a tree. This climber still remained trapped between two boards, a job for tomorrow and a good carpenter. This oldest climbing rose, grand even with few blooms that day, with deeply colored, holly-shaped leaves, called to mind the metaphorical prominence that Welty gave the climbers in her novel *The Optimist's Daughter:* "Memory returned like spring. In some cases it was the old wood that did the blooming."

"My mother was an avid rose gardener," Welty said to me later, after the gardening work. "She had thirty bushes in the far garden at the back of the yard. They succumbed to a blight of nematodes before her death. Nematodes destroy the entire inner system of the plant and can kill a whole garden in a matter of days. That's what happened to hers. But by then her sight was so dimmed that I moved the old crabapple tree up to the middle of the yard. That was twenty years ago." She pointed to a great, spreading tree between the front and farthest gardens, where the roses had been. "She couldn't see past that tree. She assumed the rose garden was there. Now I'll have to get out the book and look up the fertilizing time for the climbers," she said in a hopeful voice.

"I still can't get over what you did out there," she said. "When I saw those canes coming over the fence, I just couldn't believe my eyes. You did exactly what my mother would have done—she would have just gone out there and done it!"

We stood in the dark, cool hallway of her house and talked. She was pensive and quiet. "My thanks to you go back many years."

"I couldn't bear it that the climbers were in the neighbor's yard," I said.

"I couldn't bear it either," she said.

The pain may have seemed unbearable to her, but she did endure it, and for a long time.

Honoring Our Mothers' Rose Gardens

Welty's memories of her mother's rose garden, to which both she and her mother contributed years of careful attention, find their way into her stories and novels. Roses take on symbolic and imaginative power in these works. The rose for Welty represents devotion, home, love of family, lost youth—and grief. In "A Curtain of Green," for example, the widow's garden work prompts her mind to roam across the emotional hardscape of doubt, loneliness, and oblivion. For years following her mother's illness and death, Eudora Welty maintained the garden as she and her mother always had. In her own late age, however, Welty eventually found herself unable to keep the garden as she and her mother faithfully had done for decades. That the climbing roses languished in the neighbor's yard for so long indicates the extent of the ravages of time and old age on the writer and her garden. The degree of distress apparent in Miss Welty's voice and on her face, just in describing the displaced climbers, attests to their importance to her, her inability to reclaim them, and the pain she felt, even a decade later, in having had to let them go.

In the year of the nematodes Miss Welty planted a large apple tree in the forward part of the garden to shield her mother from the truth—that the rose garden was lost. Welty's action in planting the tree was one of protection. She spared her mother the pain of knowing about the lost rose garden. Just as Mrs. Welty had protected and overprotected her daughter, so much so that Welty would later write that she "came from a sheltered life," now it was her turn to shelter her mother. She did so by caring for her mother, physically and psychologically, throughout her mother's elderly years. The apple tree, which hid the diseased rose garden from her mother's failing sight, is a powerful testament of the need of this daughter to guard her mother from hurt and despair. The blight of nematodes and the destroyed rose garden, Welty feared, might crush her mother, psychically. The loss of the rose garden, which they had both worked hard together over many years to preserve and had enjoyed so much, would be too much to bear.

My own mother is also an experienced rose gardener. She has successfully nurtured a rose garden in our home in Arkansas that was planted by my Romanian immigrant grandfather in 1926. She cultivates, among other varieties, the same beautiful and highly prized hybrid tea roses, and even a few climbers, that Miss Welty and her mother enjoyed. Early in the morning, before I departed each summer on trips to see Miss Welty, my mother would say, "Wait a minute," and she would walk out into her garden to cut a fresh bouquet of roses. She prepared them for the three-hour car trip from our home to Miss Welty's in Jackson, Mississippi, by pouring water into a simple but ample tin bucket and setting them on newspapers on the back floorboard of the car. Then I went on my way to Jackson with the wonderfully aromatic scent of fresh roses on board.

Upon my arrival at Miss Welty's house each summer, I presented her with my mother's bucket of freshly cut roses. I always apologized for not presenting them in a crystal vase. With a warm smile, Miss Welty would gather the roses up in her arms and say how pleased she was to have them—

Elaine Wolff in her rose garden in Dumas, Arkansas, 1976. Photo by Haskell Wolff. Photo courtesy of Sally Wolff.

and how pleased her mother would have been. She and I established a friendship that would last for nineteen years, until her death. We were linked partly by the literature she had written and which we spent long hours discussing, but we also were closely linked by the hybrid teas and the climbers—from my mother and her mother, as the generation turned, to her and me. She would lift the roses from the bucket, take them inside to find a proper vase, and place them on the living room mantelpiece. Then she would turn around, face me, and break out into a glorious smile. We had honored our mothers' rose gardens.

Much later I learned that as a younger woman, Welty's signature gift to others was the rose—taken as gifts to friends (Marrs 225). Although Miss Welty never mentioned that tradition to me, the joy she expressed in receiving my mother's annual summer gifts may have reminded her of her own years in rose giving. Miss Welty was not always happy with the gifts people gave her, and I witnessed that on occasion, too, in her wry comments, but the pleasant reactions she always had on receiving my mother's roses was prompted—I like to think—by our mutual participation in the fragrant tradition of giving and receiving roses.

A personal signature of the author, roses appear in almost all of Welty's stories and novels. She describes their various characteristics with detail and admiration. In her life roses clearly provided the author with pleasure and were her prized gifts. For Welty roses are inimitably beautiful, but they come with accompanying pain. Thorns catch the harvester unaware—with a torn shirtsleeve or a pricked finger—and yet roses were the ultimate gift for those she loved. In her art the roses hold transcendent, symbolic power, offered as a sign of the charm of the garden and the warmth of home, a gift to those who find them flowering in splendor—as they thumb through her pages—with a pricked finger.

The climbing rose achieves heightened symbolic importance in *The Optimist's Daughter,* and once again the traditional senses of the image are present but at Welty's hand, combined with a darker reality. Like her short stories, Welty's Pulitzer Prize–winning novel has that same succinct, ironic edge; the same keenly drawn psychological depiction of one main character; and the profound insights into death, loss, and grief, ameliorating into a lighter tone of healing. This brooding, highly autobiographical work concerns a child's relationship with parents, the vagaries of love relationships, and the difficult decision of whether to leave home. An aide-mémoire, the novel reaches its transcendence near the end—her parents dead, the daughter confronts her keen personal loss and grapples with somber realities. Memory is the faculty that at once connects her to her past but simultaneously transmogrifies into the blind and threatening "somnambulist," who harrows her nights and dreams and demands "its rightful tears." For this terror, moreover, religion offers no salvation.

Her answer comes in *One Writer's Beginnings:* "Memory is a living thing—it too is in transit. But during its moment, all that is remembered joins, and lives—the old and the young, the past and the present, the living and the dead." Neither Welty's intellectual existence nor her moral/ethical stance is sheltered, removed, or contrived. She wrote that "a daring life starts from within," and her subtle, complex, and daring expression of life deserves full and careful attention. The rose, finally, is her symbol, for the human power of memory to connect us all—in love and grief.

Sally Wolff, amid her mother's roses, preparing her first article about Eudora Welty in 1983. Photo by Haskell Wolff. Photo courtesy of Sally Wolff.

Recently, in honor of Miss Welty and our mothers, I planted my first rose garden. Like Miss Welty—who once said of herself, "I was my mother's yard boy"—as a young girl, I labored in my mother's rose garden. While I was planting my new hybrid teas lately, my mother's quietly delivered instruction came back to me. I could hear her voice in my memory: remove the leaves yellowed with the black spot fungus; water only at the base—don't wet the leaves; cut a blossom above the five leaf, not above the three; prune in February, fertilize March through June; rest in the hot summer months of July and August but keep them watered. Fertilize in September, and then that's all for the year.

Memories surround me as I work in the new rose garden. I see the old climber in Miss Welty's yard, with its thick, woody trunk. I hear again her story of protecting her nearly blind mother from the sadness of losing her vibrant and colorful garden of thirty roses. I see my own mother's garden, thriving even in her eighty-second year, in the full heat of the July sun. She still delivers freshly cut roses to friends and others—to the sick as well as to those who are celebrating. I hear my father's voice as he comments with pride that my mother sustained his father's rose garden for so long. He was amazed at the strength of the thorns and also the size of the blooms on her roses: "big as moons." My mother calls the names of her favorites: Tropicana, Double Delight, Peace, Love, Taboo, and Mr. Lincoln. In the garden, surrounded by new roses, old lore, fragrance, and memory, I hear, too, Miss Welty's voice reading aloud from *The Optimist's Daughter*, its metaphor fully resplendent now: "Memory returned like spring. In some cases it was the old wood that did the blooming" (115).

Eudora Welty, Sally Wolff, and Elaine Wolff at the Old Capitol House Chamber in Jackson, Mississippi, 1994. Photo courtesy of Sally Wolff.

Acknowledgments

My late husband, Dr. Frederick A. King, offered unending patience and support, especially during late-night hours, when this book took shape. My brother, Dr. Sam Wolff, has been a constant source of strength. Thank you for helping me persevere. To Dr. William B. Dillingham I owe deep and lasting gratitude for his tireless efforts on my behalf in reading and editing the manuscript, mentoring, and advising me. To Drs. Conrad DeBold, Virginia Ross Taylor, and Helen Hurt Tiegreen, I offer thanks for their caring and help with the manuscript in its various stages of development. My appreciation goes also to Ms. Forrest Galey of the Mississippi Department of Archives and History and Derek Parsons at Lippincott Massie McQuilkin for their help in locating and obtaining permissions for the photographs of Miss Welty and her mother. To Erin Mooney, Marie and Eric Nitschke, Nancy Bossert, Samantha Reid, Kathleen Carroll, and Kevin Rodriguez, I offer thanks for expert research assistance. To my mother and late father, Elaine and Haskell Wolff, my thanks to you go back many years.

A Dark Rose

Introduction

Wolff: You have written a great deal about love.

Welty: I suppose I have. What other kind of story is there? It's the basis for any kind of structure of the story—narrative and plot—the drive, the spirit, what makes the human. It's the center of all the stories. Human relationships are all that matter. What other human relationship would be as complex, as true, as dramatic an emotion?

　　　　　—EUDORA WELTY and SALLY WOLFF, "Domestic Thread"

Wolff: Why do murders, rapes, and other bleak events occur in your love stories?

Welty: That's the dark side.

　　　　　—EUDORA WELTY and SALLY WOLFF, personal communication, July 1994

Returning on foot through a hot, dusty field to her estranged husband in *Delta Wedding,* Robbie Fairchild muses about the upcoming marital reunion and asks herself a powerful question: "What do you ask for when you love?" (146). What follows in the omniscient narrative voice indicates that the answer to her question must remain ambiguous: "so much did Robbie love George, that that much the less did she know the right answer." Questions about love lead inevitably in a Welty story to ambiguity, complexity, uncertainty, and perhaps above all, mystery. Always realistic, never sugarcoated, but always with a dark side, Welty pens stories of love, from the heartbroken salesman of her first published story, "Death of a Traveling Salesman," and the infidels of *The Golden Apples* to the reflective widow of *The Optimist's Daughter.* She juxtaposes the tragic and comic faces of love as she seeks to understand love as a vital, emotional force. The Natchez Trace, a boat landing, or the post office—and often the woods—are the landscapes of Welty's love stories.

From her earliest story to her latest novel—some forty-five years later—Welty focuses much of her work on the subject of love and on both the light and dark side. She explores a wide range of communing, both physical and spiritual. More often than not, her stories revolve around the movement of characters toward love and away from it. Weddings, brides, bridegrooms, widows, matrons, seasoned spouses, and spinsters occupy her pages in surprising numbers. The murder of a wife, seduction, and divorce are topics she does not ignore. Rape—both that which is unwelcome and that which almost seems mutually consensual (and as such maybe misnamed)—also takes place. Titles, too, reflect her focus. *The Robber Bridegroom, Delta Wedding,* and *The Bride of the Innisfallen* are obvious examples, but other stories such as "A Piece of News," "Asphodel," "Shower of Gold," *The Ponder Heart, The Optimist's Daughter,* and others also address the topics of love, marriage, and sexuality.

Welty's preoccupation with romance and love is perhaps even more intriguing in view of her closeness to and distance from them at several points in her own life. Although Miss Welty was in love on more than one occasion, she did not marry. Her particular viewpoint gives the perspective from which to examine love both from within and without. She creates autobiographical characters who view different kinds of love—for example, a daughter remembering her parents' marriage or a cousin at the wedding. Welty considers the dynamics of marriage in works such as "A Piece of News," "Death of a Traveling Salesman," *Delta Wedding,* and later in *The Optimist's Daughter.*

Biographers and critics have commented on love in Welty's work, but her complex art deserves further consideration. Robert Penn Warren's landmark essay "The Love and the Separateness in Miss Welty" has sounded an enduring keynote (249). Her stories, he says, "deal with people" who love but "in one way or another, are cut off, alienated, isolated from the world." Warren concludes that isolation "provides the basic situation of Welty's fiction" and alienation brings characters from "innocence to experience" and from "love to knowledge" (250, 256). Cleanth Brooks, Ruth Vande Kieft, William Stuckey, Ruth Weston, James Boatwright, Louise Westling, Mary Catherine Buswell, Peter Schmidt, Gail Mortimer, Rebecca Mark, and Suzanne Marrs have written about love in Welty's works. Brooks points to love, memory, and the past; Boatwright discusses the "continuity" that love provides for Laurel, the protagonist in *The Optimist's Daughter,* and sees the novel as a "brooding on the nature of family and the relationship itself." Ruth M. Vande Kieft's chapter "The Comedy of Love" concludes that "on the whole" the vision of love Welty expresses there is not a "tragic" one (*Eudora Welty* 103). In her overview of Welty's stories Mary Catherine Buswell points to the preponderance of old maids, young maidens, and married women in several of the works and argues that "one of the tragedies of marriage" in Welty's writing is that "the husband and wife have no real communion" (101). Gail Mortimer argues that Welty's characters experience an isolation that is exacerbated by their inability to communicate meaningfully with one another (18). Louise Westling notes that while Welty "celebrated the joy" of marital unions and family life, "she also explored the causes and consequences of the failure of these bonds" (25). The polarity between love and isolation still seems especially prominent for Neil Corcoran, who points out that "the possibility of love . . . lies on the other side of isolation" (31). Rebecca Mark's landmark study considers intertextuality in Welty's writing and revisions her fiction in important ways.

In her tales of days on the Natchez Trace or of great family reunions, moments of reflection occur as Welty's characters mull the question that Robbie Fairchild ponders in the dusty field: "What do you ask for when you love?" For characters in difficult relationships, such as in "Death of a Traveling Salesman," "A Piece of News," and "The Key," cooperation and contentment can but do not always emerge. Jack's private moments with Gloria in *Losing Battles* are initially unsettled, but eventually a calm overtakes them; the same is true for Jamie and Rosamund in *The Robber Bridegroom*, Robbie and George Fairchild in *Delta Wedding*, and in the central marriages of *The Optimist's Daughter*. The majority of Welty's forty-five short stories and five novels focus on love or its absence. "Love," Edna Earle opines in *The Ponder Heart*, is always "banked up somewhere." Her words stand true for much of Welty's canon.

Rarely does Welty write of the devastation of divorce, but more often she grapples with the effect of death on love. In his historic study of romantic love Denis de Rougement argues that "marriage is the grave of savage love" and passion, by its very definition, "stands for a radical condemnation of marriage" (325, 66). In his view passion and marriage are "essentially irreconcilable," and misery inevitably accompanies intense happiness (287). Cleanth Brooks makes a similar argument in his analysis of Faulkner's 1939 novel *The Wild Palms* [*If I Forget Thee, Jerusalem*]. He states: "Gavin [Stevens] not only regards love as something that transcends mere sexuality; he identifies its highest levels with loss, suffering, and lack of possession. Such is what he believes the true heroes and heroines of love must endure. . . . For Gavin, marriage is a good dog, but tied to its tail is the inevitable and necessary tin can of respectability. Marriage simply is not consistent with the high martyrdom that passionate love entails" ("Tradition" 267). Weston's interpretations add immeasurable insight.

Eudora Welty does not usually share these observations about life and literature. She writes much about the pain and conflict that love engenders, yet she also finds her way back to the comfort of familiar relationships, mostly within but sometimes outside of traditional marriage. She occasionally ventures into the realm of sentimentality and heightened romanticism, but usually she elucidates the more subtle psychological complexities and mysteries of the heart, such as those Robbie Fairchild confronts in her long discussion with herself in the searing and chastising summer heat of her walk back to her husband, George.

Welty's love stories often focus on both the tragic and comic states—the light and dark sides—the lovely, scented petals of the relationship and its thorny underside. Exploring love in this full, varied, and complex way is the main task of a Welty love story. As she tests the hearts of couples and solitaires for clues, she identifies factors that cultivate or destroy. In portraying a vast array of relationships, she occasionally idealizes love but more often characterizes it in a more practical and realistic way. Some of her protagonists, too, seek love they never find, dream dreams they will never realize, imagine lovers they will never know, and live, sometimes as widows or widowers, in a tortured solipsism that can lead to early despair, death, and suicide.

The private, sometimes secretive nature of sexual intimacy that excludes outside forces distinguishes some of Welty's fictional lovers and binds them together. The personal life of such couples depends upon a crucial separateness but not of the isolated kind Robert Penn Warren describes. Gail Mortimer asserts that "in Welty's fiction the experience of love and knowledge are closely linked in meaning, because they both involve a willing assumption of the other's similarity with self" (34). Welty's fictional lovers must, at least for a time, remain apart from the community to protect themselves and to resist infringement by others. Respecting the privacy and integrity of this personal sphere, while protecting it from envy and the intrusion of social life, requires a careful balancing of the romantic and the practical. Communal life is a fundamental social component of life in Welty's stories. For pairs to become well adjusted in society, they must eventually leave their privacy behind, join the crowd, enter maturity, embrace a heightened sense of responsibility, and tackle challenging familial and social tasks. Welty's love stories illustrate the potentialities of love along with the complicated, dark, painful, futile, and even fatal consequences of its loss and absence.[1]

The "dark rose" metaphorically illustrates the dichotomies and contradictions Welty sees in love—faithfulness, hope, joy, and sharing balanced against loss, grief, and aloneness. In *Losing Battles* she describes with the image of the petals of a dark rose the quietness of a bird moving in a bush: "birds came down low into the althea bush . . . as silent as petals shedding from a dark rose" (290). Close observation and acute powers of listening are classic attributes of Welty's sensibilities, and her complex description in this passage of the bird moving almost inaudibly—but not quite so—in a bush comes as an expected pleasure. The simile "as silent as petals shedding from a dark rose," then, carries the synesthetic play of both the auditory and visual senses that is highly characteristic of Welty's writing and aptly describes her dichotomous approach in her love stories.

Welty's choice of a word to describe the quiet movement of a bird in this passage is the inaudible *silent*. The rose petals falling make a softly audible sound. The bird, in Welty's brilliant metaphorical comparison, is so quiet that its movements among the leaves in the bush, almost inaudible, are as faintly heard as softly falling petals of a dark rose. The color and movement of the rose petals merit even closer attention. A dark rose has a deep color, and some red roses can be especially dark in hue—and even velvety black in appearance. Rose specialists have names for several dark roses, such as "Taboo" and "Black Magic," with obvious connotations. A dark rose may be even more beautiful than those with less rich color. Red roses turn dark prior to losing their petals, and a rose shedding its petals is certainly dying. Taken together, the images suggest sadness or perhaps the silence of old age. "A dark rose," then, must be a complex, autobiographical image of the author and a metaphor for the provocative commingling of the comic and tragic in Welty's life and art.

CHAPTER 1

"A Fruitful Marriage. That Simple Thing"

Early Stories of Rural Love

Eudora Welty frequently represents the comic and tragic in images that are dichotomous, such as light and dark. Love may be pervasive thematically in her stories, but she offers greatly multifaceted depictions and coequivalencies of the dark and light sides. These topics are consistent over the long years of her writing life. She considers the "dark side," in which her characters and fictional situations range from disappointment to the grim and even ghastly, but then alternately, she depicts those whose love relationships defy obstacle and overturn expectation as they achieve joy, trust, and satisfaction. *A Curtain of Green* and *The Wide Net*, two volumes of stories published within four years of each other, for example, illustrate this pattern. In these volumes Welty offers portraits of successful relationships and marital situations, but she positions them alongside their dark twin of loss. Welty's major fiction supports this essential dichotomy over time. The early stories and late novels alike may shelter a love story at the center, but a dark fate inevitably hovers perilously close at hand.

Welty's short stories often present characters in search of love of one kind or another. The traveling salesmen, Bowman and Harris; Leota, the garrulous but chronically bored and unhappy hairdresser; the artist in "A Memory"; and others reach in vain toward their dream of ideal love—or even a sustaining relationship. Others anticipate sexual awakening and find but then lose it. Some secure permanent attachments, while others miss the opportunity to love or even experience it vicariously.

Stories in these volumes share other compelling characteristics. "A Piece of News," "The Wide Net," and "Death of a Traveling Salesman," among others, center on couples who live out in the country—sometimes deep in the woods—in cabins and dogtrot or shotgun houses. In these relationships Welty explores both the joys and hardships of country life. Her works are often contextually accurate, and autobiographical representations of the author emerge in them as well. She develops subjects and characters from the people she knew or observed, but often, too, depictions of herself emerge in her fiction.

Welty focuses on rural life, and she found good people there during her travels around her home state. During the Depression Welty worked for the Works Progress Administration (WPA), and this experience influenced both the themes and locales of her early works. For the WPA, she drove by car around the state of Mississippi, county by county, to evaluate programs and write reports. She observed and learned from the people she met during these times: "I learned a great deal about Mississippi when I worked for the W.P.A. and traveled around the State. For the first time I saw that Mississippi was a rural world. [The country is] easier to write about than a town. It's a simpler society to describe. It was a different world if you went outside the city. I got to know it pretty well with my journalistic jobs and work with the W.P.A. . . . What I discovered were the people in their rural setting. Their lives didn't change with the times. They were poor. Their conditions didn't change and were really terrible. It was all so much worse than I could have imagined. . . . A friend of mine also had to go into rural areas to buy land for the roads, and oh! the tales he told me of poverty he saw" (Wolff, "Domestic Thread" 20).

Welty saw some rays of light in the attitudes of the people she met, even within the context of deep poverty: "These people were the opposite of what they easily might be—pinched and bitter." When she attended Mississippi State College for Women (MSCW), she came in contact with students from "poor homes." They, too, she thought, found some happiness even amid what some might call adverse conditions. She saw them as "good country people": "I discovered still more by visiting all the county seats. It was an education that I had again when I attended M.S.C.W. It was the first state college for women in the country. At the time, everybody could come to school there, and it was cheap to go there. Some students were ill-educated. The teachers were the best educated people around. The school had a cross-section of girls from the rest of the state and many from poor homes. But their families were happy. Their mothers sent them baskets of fried chicken on Sunday from home. They had happy lives despite terrible conditions. They were good country people.[1] It was a poor, poor time in history, when I look back" (Wolff, "Domestic Thread" 20–21).

Rural landscapes contrast with cityscapes and illustrate Welty's observations about the goodness in the country people around her. She found the human spirit thriving even in rural and impoverished conditions. Her stories of the rural South illustrate that families can survive and even prosper, emotionally and spiritually, even in what may seem to others stark and difficult circumstances. Unlike the more sophisticated and sometimes rootless counterparts, accustomed to spiritually barren conditions in city life, the country life, in a Welty story, sometimes can be sustaining even given harsh conditions.

Biographer Suzanne Marrs notes that the converse is also true, however—that Welty's photographs and stories "document" and "characterize" the consistent and often devastating poverty that she encountered when she worked for the Works Progress Administration in the 1930s: "Welty's photographs of this period document the tattered clothing, shabby housing, hard work, and unbroken spirits that characterize rural Mississippi in the thirties. Her stories, like 'Death of a Traveling Salesman,' 'The Hitch-Hikers,' 'Clytie,' 'A Worn Path,' 'A Piece of News,' and 'The Whistle' tell us of the primitive roads, ramshackle hotels, dogtrot houses, oil lamps, open hearths for cooking and heating, and desperation that were often typical of rural and small-town Mississippi life" (*One Writer's Imagination* 12).

Welty's stories about rural love often follow the traditional narrative form: couples encounter a crisis, work to resolve it, then succeed or fail as the denouement and the resolution occur. By means of a test or an absence, forced, accidental, or intentional—a lovers' quarrel, for example—the crises elicit emotional reevaluation and increased potential for communication, intimacy, and understanding. In some cases, however, the darker portraits emerge, and poverty takes its inevitable and "terrible" toll.

Violence and Love in "A Piece of News"

One of Welty's rural couples, Ruby and Clyde Fisher of "A Piece of News," live in what may seem like strained circumstances: a small cabin within walking distance of Clyde's whiskey still deep in the Mississippi woods.

Their lives, however, fall into the category of those who make a life for themselves without much money or worldly goods, and their relationship, in the main, prospers—out in the country.

Welty stated in an interview that this story emerged in her mind as a result of her reading county newspapers: "[These] stories are all part of the same rural setting. You have to set the stage for a story. You have to have something to identify it. I decided to take all the county newspapers, and I read them all. That's what got me interested in what went on in the State of Mississippi. Just the naked news." The newspapers provided Welty with a good understanding of the local people around her and their settings as well as, in this case, the central idea and some particular language for her story "A Piece of News," in which a character "became shot": "The newspapers back then would have letters from little towns in the paper, by the family of the reporter or the correspondent. What Ruby Fisher reads in the newspaper was the kind of thing that would be in these newspapers: 'So and So became shot' and 'The Sunday visitors in town were. . . .' That gave me a picture of what life was like, much as I think it did for Faulkner. I did know people like that. . . . Jackson was not typical of Mississippi at the time because of its size" (Wolff, "Domestic Thread" 21).[2]

The county newspapers gave Welty a "picture of what life was like," and she found a rich source for her rural stories. Typically, the inspiration for Welty's stories came from a phrase she heard or a particular image she saw, such as the eight bubble-haired ladies she noticed who were seated together at lunch. In "A Piece of News" the county newspaper articles enlivened the muse and provide a narrative tale. Her recollection from the county newspaper—"So and So became shot"—offers the author a premise for her story in which the psychological action focuses on Ruby Fisher, a country wife, who in her partial literacy struggles to understand why her name appears in the newspaper as someone shot by her husband. Although she does not realize that this article refers to another Ruby in another town and in another state—Tennessee—she apprehends the news as applicable to her and imaginatively embraces its implications for her life.

Although the tone of this work seems predominantly light, a shadow of violence hovers ominously, as might be expected in a story in which the hero is a large man with a whiskey still, the heroine an unfaithful wife, and the main symbol a shotgun. A marital eruption does indeed occur, but in this case resolution and reconciliation eventuate for Ruby and Clyde Fisher. After the provocation initiated by the news story, they find a return to marital accord, peace, coexistence, and love, even though they are situated in rural circumstances. Ruby and Clyde are close to the natural world and as such reflect the values of Romanticism. The couple is of meager means but not, as they might easily have been, violent, or "pinched and bitter" (Wolff, "Domestic Thread" 20).

In "A Piece of News" Welty describes Ruby and Clyde Fisher, the people in one isolated house in the country, and she depicts their marital relationship. Ruby is a plain woman who seems physically idle too much of the time, and her bootlegger husband, Clyde, is frequently away at his whiskey still in the woods. Carol Hollenbaugh, Michael Kreyling, and others have noted Ruby's vital, sensual nature. Peter Schmidt sees "Ruby's imagination as associated with the 'natural' powers of 'rain and fire'" (34). The action rises when Ruby, lazing about by the fire, almost illiterate, haltingly reads in the newspaper about a woman with her name, Ruby Fisher, who was shot in the leg by her husband. Unaware that this news article describes another Ruby in another, nearby state, she panics, imagining that Clyde may have shot her. Her emotions rise, in contrast to those of Clyde, who usually seems unemotional.

Previously, Ruby has had time during the lazy days to fantasize sexually about her husband and to infuse him, at least imaginatively, with a passion that this couple, no longer young, seems to have lost: "the fire might have been a mirror in the cabin, into which she could look deeper and deeper as she pulled her fingers through her hair, trying to see herself and Clyde coming up behind her" (24). Suzanne Marrs points out that "the newspapers story reaches her imagination, as Cleanth Brooks has noted, just as Welty's story reaches ours" (*One Writer's Imagination* 31). Now home alone with her desire and news of the violent shooting, Ruby dramatically imagines sex and death as she considers that having been shot by Clyde, she will appear to him "beautiful, desirable, and dead" (25).[3] Her death, she envisions, would elicit in Clyde passion, longing, and regret: he would be "wild, shouting, and all distracted, to think he could never touch her one more time" (26). In her mind's eye his emotional outpouring at her death exemplifies his passionate love for his departed wife.

Although Clyde is now bald, Ruby remembers him with his "wild black hair hanging to his shoulders," a look, and a time in life, she longs to recover. Marrs sees Clyde as an "unromantic man" who is "scarcely the man Ruby sees in her imagination" (*One Writer's Imagination* 33), and while that may be true now, through memory Ruby recovers their sexual past. Although she seems slow-witted and almost illiterate, Ruby's recollections here flare as brightly as the cabin fire. She recalls Clyde "as he once looked" in former days (25), before his baldness began and with it a possible loss of virility or at least a loss of passion in their relationship. The older Clyde is sluggish. Mostly, he is interested in when his dinner will be ready. Ruby wants the old Clyde back. That feeling is not unusual in a marriage, especially as partners age. Her clear memory of his "wild black hair" implies her longing for the vitality that once must have kindled their lives—with a brightness that seems diminished.

Ruby's apparent afternoons of adultery with the coffee salesman are a somewhat unexpected component of the story: "When Clyde would make her blue, she would go out onto the road, some car would slow down, and if it had a Tennessee license, the lucky kind, the chances were that she would spend the afternoon in the shed of the empty gin" (24). Perhaps even more surprising is that her infidelity does not seem particularly problematic for her marriage. When Clyde returns home from a day at the still, initially he seems aware of her afternoon's activity. A Mississippi man, he does notice that the coffee can Ruby obtains is wrapped in a Tennessee newspaper. Clyde wants to know how Ruby came by this out-of-state newspaper. His response is not angry, abusive, or wild, however, when he realizes that a coffee salesman must have given her a tin of coffee wrapped in newspaper—apparently in return for favors. Ruby also seems to know instinctively that Clyde might slap her playfully and call her "Hussy" but that he would never shoot her (28). She and Clyde talk about her illicit afternoon, but then the moment dissipates without incident. Daniel Curley sees their silence as "a force" in itself: "Miss Welty uses silence merely as a device for eliminating one major source of error in communication, that is, speech. With speech out of the way, she lays open the approaches to communication through a simple vocabulary of gesture" (210). Clyde has not, in a tirade or fit of jealousy, shot Ruby, and she is not "dead at his hand."

Clyde's casual attitude about his wife's infidelity may reflect his personality, his values, or perhaps even his own diminished vitality or caring. The couple lives in relative isolation in the country. In what may be a rural custom, she defers to him at dinner: she serves his meal, waits while he eats it, and goes to her dinner later. Clyde spends whole days at his whiskey still—shotgun by his side—and he simply may not pay attention to his wife's activities because he is busy watching for unwanted visitors. He may regard her mental state as too simple to impose upon her a standard of marital fidelity. He may be older and tired.

Although some see Clyde as violent, the textual evidence does not support that claim. In the kitchen with her husband at home, Ruby is "filled with happiness" to be in Clyde's presence, and she makes "many unnecessary trips back and forth across the floor, circling Clyde," while serving his dinner (27). Clyde is playful in return, and he "almost chuckles" at her activities. He swats at her but does not strike her: she dodges "mechanically"— these maneuvers between them are familiar and friendly. Later he spanks her "good-humoredly across her backside" (29), not an act of violent abuse. He shows little emotion, even after he questions her about her afternoon encounter with a coffee salesman from Tennessee.

Ruby's fantasy of her own death reemerges and intensifies, however, after she haltingly reads and erroneously interprets the newspaper article describing a woman named Ruby who was shot in the leg by her husband. The newspaper story startles Ruby into a momentary shift of reality—a ruthless version of her own life. In her fantasy Clyde fully exhibits latent but violent potentiality and makes her ask the question: could Clyde do this to Ruby? Scholars have focused intently on this narrative question. "For an instant," writes Ruth Vande Kieft "they have had a vision of each other in alien fantasy roles—an experience which is pleasing, exciting, and rather frightening" (*Eudora Welty* 45). Schmidt calls Ruby's mistake "superb comedy" and a "case of mistaken identity" (32). Marrs's assessment is that "the power of the imagination, the power that was Eudora's lifeblood, had become the subject of the story" (*Eudora Welty* 55).

One dependable hallmark of a Welty love story is the weather, which typically mirrors the emotional states of her characters. In "A Piece of News" the weather reflects the tension in the story that Welty is developing. In an interview she described this pathetic fallacy, in which the weather functions in two ways, both that "the crisis is coming out of the weather" and "the crisis is the cause of the weather": "I plan a story by its dramatic sense, not by a particular pattern. That's the dramatic end of writing. . . . [In my love stories] the weather depends on the [emotional crisis of the characters]—the crisis is coming out of the weather—the crisis is the cause of the weather" (Wolff, "Domestic Thread" 24).

Welty achieves the "dramatic sense" when she gives full theatrical play to the psychological action of the story: the marital crisis both generates and reflects the weather, which escalates throughout the story from an initial, quiet, soft falling rain to a violent, thunderous storm that scares Clyde, even though he otherwise seems fearless. While the quiet rain initially dampens Ruby's mood, her emotional crisis builds with the developing thunderstorm outside. At first she sings to herself a simple song, "The pouring-down rain, the pouring-down rain," as she calmly dries her hair by the fire. The more she ponders—and misconstrues—the import of the news article that she has read, however, the more the storm intensifies. As Welty noted, the crisis both causes and reflects the weather. Images of sex and death dramatically commingle in Ruby's mind like the fierce tangle in her hair.

As Ruby contemplates whether Clyde might indeed shoot her, the storm generates increasing intensity outside. She screamed for him and "ran straight to the door. . . . There was a flash of lightning, and she stood waiting, as if she half thought that would bring him in, a gun leveled in his hand" (24). The human world empowers the natural one, and vice versa, as the lovers' gathering emotional storm increases. W. U. McDonald, Suzanne Marrs, and others have interpreted the storm as well. McDonald sees it as representing the "tumult of Ruby's emotions" (245), and Marrs sees it as reinforcing the "tremendous imaginative reaction Ruby has to the newspaper story (Marrs, *One Writer's Imagination* 32). The lightning and the imagined, leveled gun, taken together, suggest Ruby's sexual desire and dramatic expectation. Her realized question of whether her husband might really shoot her is now the crux of the story: "Ruby might have been dead at his hand" (28). That someone else named Ruby Fisher is indeed shot in Tennessee fulfills the abusive and violent apprehension of the story and is the doppelganger to the more fortunate tale of this Ruby from Mississippi.

The storm adversely affects Clyde, too, even before he returns home. Unlike his violent counterpart in Tennessee, Clyde is an almost silent man. His verbal expressions are monosyllabic. He is a passive, skittish man who stays at his whiskey still with its "thick brushwood roof" during the storm because he is "mortally afraid of lightning like this, and would never go out in it for anything" (24). Only in Ruby's imagination does Clyde become the man in the news story—the potent and violent male, wielder of deadly weapons and abuser of women. Pitched at a high crescendo now, the action of the story heightens even further as Clyde dramatically appears, like a mythical figure, swathed in mist and steam. The weather outside—and Ruby's emotional storm—reach their concomitant height as the lightning suggests the power of the male: "A whole tree of lightning stood in the sky. She kept looking out the window, suffused with the warmth from the fire and with the pity and beauty and power of her death. The thunder rolled. . . . Then Clyde was standing there, with dark streams flowing over the floor where he had walked. . . . From the long shadow of his steamy presence she spoke to him glibly and lighted the lamp" (26). For this and other Welty love stories, the simple lighting of a lamp is a profound indication of awakening sight. Clyde and Ruby will soon see each other more clearly.

The fury of the storm simultaneously evokes contrapuntal images of Clyde's passivity and his sexuality. Although he carries a gun, he is not deadly; he does not level this weapon at Ruby. As rain "drips down the barrel of his gun" and "streams began to flow" from him, however, the sexual metaphors for Clyde's diminished capability become clear: his gun points downward. He is unemotional but nonviolent: "[His] enormous hands seemed weighted with the rain that fell from him and dripped down the barrel of the gun. Presently he sat down with dignity in the chair at the table, making a little tumult of his rightful wetness and hunger. Small streams began to flow from him everywhere" (26). Welty's gun imagery is asexual here, but Clyde seems more interested in dinner. He is simply a big, hungry man.

The denouement must reconcile memory, fantasy, and the dramatic news story that has infiltrated the otherwise quiet and uneventful lives of this country couple. Ruby demands to know Clyde's position: would he ever shoot her? "They looked at each other. . . . It was as though Clyde might really have killed Ruby, and as though Ruby might really have been dead at his hand" (28). Ruby wonders "how it would be if Clyde shot her in the leg. . . . If he were truly angry, might he shoot her through the heart?" (25–26). The expected sound of a gunshot—which might have pierced the silence—occurs in the news but in another state and to another couple. That Mississippi Ruby is safe—but her wounded counterpart in Tennessee is unsafe—is the dark heart of "A Piece of News."

As Clyde protests his innocence, he reminds Ruby of his fundamentally mild-mannered personality. "It's a lie," Clyde says. "I'd just like to see the place I shot you!" (28). The psychological action increases the sexual implication. Sex is everywhere implied but never performed. Violence is also implied but not committed in this house. This Clyde will not shoot his Ruby. He will again see her as she wants to be seen: "beautiful and desirable"— but not "dead." They will reconcile; they may even love again, offstage.

As he hurls the offending, foreign "Tennessee" newspaper into the fire, Clyde exhibits passion but not of a sexual kind. He is emphatically committed to truthfulness. He distinguishes, even though Ruby cannot, between the factual news and the fiction that she has postulated from it. By flinging the newspaper into the fire, he extinguishes the factual news and the fictional construct that Ruby generated in her mind. His adamant refutation of the news story is thereby sufficient to reassure his wife of his gentle nature and integrity. She ultimately believes his honest appraisal, and they are finished, for now, with the coffee salesman, the bearer of the bad news.

Fire and water take on heightened symbolic connotations in Welty's stories. The paper that has so misled Ruby and Clyde disappears in a fireplace blaze: "It floated there a moment and then burst into flame. They stood still and watched it burn. The whole room was bright" (28). The intensifying of light—from the kindling of a dim lamp to the very bright firelight—indicates the fullness of understanding that Ruby and Clyde have now achieved. The weather, too, reemerges as symbol: the lovers' emotional crescendo diminishes simultaneously with the weather outside. The climax reached, the storm dissipates: "everything, outside and in, was quieted before she went to her supper. It was dark and vague outside." As the weather ameliorates, one final, aural image indicates the receding storm: it "rolled away to faintness like a wagon crossing a bridge" (29). Welty thereby deftly restores tranquillity to the Fisher marriage.

One of Welty's earliest portraits of marriage, "A Piece of News" relies on traditional comic devices: the characters' true identities must be reestablished for order to return. Who the real Ruby Fisher is must be reaffirmed, and that Clyde has not shot his Ruby—and that she is not "dead at his hand"—must be clarified before the couple may resume their peaceful country life. A long-standing, underlying marital trust resolves their conflict, and the potentially violent features of the story do not prevail. Once the conflict is resolved, the couple starts "all over" with each other, and they demonstrate the importance of restorative, regenerative, mature relationships.

The news has an important role in the story as Welty objectifies the marital conflict. News travels, crosses state lines, and threatens identity. Here the news carries the dark implication that the story could have turned out otherwise, and Welty implies that the violent can insidiously infiltrate the imagination of the innocent. Schmidt has argued that the story is "finally about the opposite of news—secrets and hidden meanings" (36). Welty couples, like the Fishers, live out in the country without economic means. For the most part they are not "pinched and bitter" but have each other—and they will weather the storm.

Water and War in "The Wide Net"

The protagonist of "The Wide Net," Hazel, feigns her drowning in the river to teach her husband certain lessons. As in "A Piece of News," this story has comic overtones, but potential tragedy moves through the story as a strong undercurrent. This story, too, has a rural, even pastoral, setting and a focus on marriage. Ruth M. Vande Kieft has argued that "The Wide Net" may be enjoyed as a "modern evocation of comedy in its most ancient ritualistic form" (58). The plot complication occurs when William Wallace,

Hazel's husband, irresponsibly stays out all night with his friends. Come morning, William is astonished to discover that his pregnant wife is missing. Desperate, he sounds the alarm, gathers his friends and neighbors, and searches everywhere. They even drag the river for the body of the wife he fears dead. The horror grows inside him that with her demise has come the death of their unborn child. The wife, of course, is, comically—and thankfully—at home hiding in the closet, but the poor husband cannot learn of it until he has internalized a few serious lessons about the value of life, wife, and prospective family.

Cloaked in the tradition of the comedic, then, but brooding nonetheless beneath, is a deeper, primal story of death and destruction—and the propensity for making war. The primal difference between men and women receives early focus, and the war theme emerges later on. First, Hazel's pregnancy and the husband's response to it cause marital complications: "William Wallace Jamieson's wife Hazel was going to have a baby. But this was October, and it was six months away, and she acted exactly as though it would be tomorrow. When he came in the room she would not speak to him, but would look as straight at nothing as she could, with *her eyes glowing*. If he only touched her she stuck out her tongue or ran around the table" (34; emph. added).

Because of her pregnancy, Hazel's behavior toward her husband has altered. In her special condition—"her eyes glowing" with the private satisfaction of her pregnancy—she becomes selfish and removed from her husband; worse, she refuses his touch. William Wallace's erratic reaction becomes a consequence of her changed behavior or of his own fears about becoming a father (Pollack 7). The river dragging and inherent journey have attracted critical attention. Harriett Pollack, Jim Owen, and Robert Phillips Jr. have seen mythical underpinnings to the story. Pollack views the story as "a vernacular tale about a back-country couples' marital squabble that slips into the mythic tradition of the heroic quest." She points to the allusions to Virgil's *Aeneid*, among other works, upon which Welty draws (9). For Owen the story follows the "conventions of the classical romance . . . [in which] a writer must present two true lovers who become separated by terrible obstacles; then one or both of them must wander for years, during which numerous events occur, including (though not limited to) imagined deaths, kidnappings, mistaken identities, and other sorts of trials and tribulations" (34). Phillips sees the setting as one "of romance," and for him the "landscape is mythical." When her husband retaliates by staying out all night, Hazel responds dramatically: she prepares a suicide note and vanishes. William Wallace's attention, then, is precipitously focused: he is deeply frightened and upset by the suicide note and is too scared "after one look" to "read the exact words," and he "crushes the whole thing in his hand instantly" (35). In a simile that reinforces the rurality of the story, his face is "red like the red of the picked cotton field," and he races for help to drag the river for Hazel's presumably dead body.

In early grief William Wallace elegizes his wife and their young marriage. Assuming that Hazel has drowned in the river, he recalls their love story as he yearns for her return. His rhapsodic remembrances are comic and bathetic. He reveals in his ungrammatical language their happy days in country life. The day he first "seen" her was at a chicken dinner with her family: "we was face to face with each other across [the table]" (37), and they've been face to face ever since.

William now vividly recalls Hazel's fear of water, and his terror of her presumed death by drowning becomes magnified. Even the shallow water of a creek terrifies her—"I used to have to pick her up and carry her over the oak-log bridge . . . she'd shut her eyes and make a dead-weight and hold me round the neck, just for a little creek" (39). Hazel's dread fear of water, even of "a little creek," and the idea of her "dead weight" render the possibility of finding Hazel's drowned body even more horrible to consider.

In the woods, too, the golden fall leaves also remind him of his pregnant wife and her now beatified condition: "William Wallace . . . thought of Hazel with the shining eyes, sitting at home and looking straight before her, like a piece of pure gold, *too precious to touch*" (49; emph. added). Although he cannot understand her feelings, in her present state she seems "untouchable." The loss of communication and understanding is the source of difficulty between them, but the story is not ready for resolution.

For Welty water often evokes mystery, emotion, dream, and death. The wayward husband ponders the river with an expression that is suggestive of his uncertainty in the face of Hazel's mysterious disappearance: "A deep frown was on his forehead, as if he were compelled to wonder what people had come to call this river, or to think there was a mystery in the name of a river they all knew so well, the same as if it were some great far torrent of waves that dashed through the mountains somewhere, and almost as if it were a river in some dream, for they could not give him the name of that" (49). He looks at the river "as if it were a mystery to him" (50); the smell of the river "spread over the woods, cool and secret" (48), and a "great far torrent of waves" suggests his emotional turmoil and also perhaps impending war (49). His proximity to the river indicates the nearness of mystery and his obscure awareness of life's incomprehensible currents. The river slows "nearly to stillness," and a veil of the shining willow trees encompasses it. He declares: "It's deep here. . . . Remember?" (50). The depth, stillness, and secret smell of the river herald William's approaching epiphany and new appreciation of his marriage.

Seasonal imagery reinforces the change that William faces. His friend Doc says, "We're walking along in the changing-time. . . . Any day now the change will come," as he anticipates the change of the season—the onset of winter. The forest will boast its magnificent colors: "Sweet-gum red, hickory yellow, dogwood red, sycamore yellow . . . and the nuts will be dropping like rain all through the woods here" (48). The serenity of the river envelops them, and for a moment the woods and the water suspend time and transport them to the primordial: "The sandbars were pink or violet drifts ahead. Where light fell on the river, in a wandering from shore to shore, it was leaf-shaped spangles that trembled softly, while the dark of the river was calm. The willow trees leaned overhead under muscadine vines, and their trailing leaves hung like waterfalls in the morning air. The thing that seemed like silence must have been the endless cry of all the crickets and locusts in the world, rising and falling" (51). The woodland settings are, as in most Welty stories, paradisiacal, and nature calms and restores the human world.

As William contemplates the grandeur of the river, he responds to its age, shifting appearances, and moods: "The winding river looked old sometimes, when it ran wrinkled and deep under high banks where the roots of trees hung down, and sometimes it seemed to be only a young creek, shining with the colors of wildflowers" (52). The alligator, which figures symbolically in several Welty stories, also carries in this story an important symbolism of age as well as mythological significance. It lies so still "they could hardly tell when it was he started to move." Even though the alligator in this story is a baby, it seems "like the oldest and worst lizard" (53). The seeming agelessness of this animal carries multiple meanings. On the one hand, the alligator, like the river, appears by turns old and young and symbolizes the ancient, mythological, mysterious, and yet lethal force in nature. Others have linked the alligator with the dragon. Pollack, for example, sees the snake and serpent imagery as linked to the king of snakes and dragon as part of the epic hero's journey (10). On the other hand, this alligator is a juvenile and thus represents the serious potential of the wife, as well as the river, to reproduce and also inflict pain and even, perhaps, death. This complex image of primordial infancy is instructional for the hero. The alligator is young but of the river; the child is now imagined to have met a watery death; the ageless reptile—both old and young—will carry the hero back through the river to the great and ageless earth, his place of origin. In doing so, William reconnects with origin in a symbolic way appropriate for a new father.

Another dark undercurrent of "The Wide Net" lies at midstory, in the drowning of Grady's father. The comedic melts away, and despair grips the narrative. If for William the river represents a journey toward understanding the origin of life, for his friend Grady its lesson has been death, for in its waters his father drowned. The spectral features of his drowned father ripple before him, and grief takes hold: "Grady's inflamed eyes rested on the brown water. Without warning he saw something . . . perhaps the image in the river seemed to be his father, the drowned man—with arms open, eyes, open, mouth open. . . . Grady stared and blinked, again something wrinkled up his face" (57). The haunting image of the drowned man, with open arms, eyes, and mouth, recurs in other Welty stories and novels, notably in *The Optimist's Daughter,* each time to haunt and agonize. Grady's tears of loss are dark and tragic counterpoints to William's own luckier story.

William Wallace's repeated diving to the low depths of the river in search of Hazel indicates his embrace of the darker potentialities and associates him with drowning as well. He stays underwater so long that others fear that he has drowned. "All day William Wallace kept diving to the bottom. Once he dived down and down into the dark water, where it was so still that nothing stirred, not even a fish, and so dark that it was no longer the muddy world of the upper river but the dark clear world of deepness, and he must have believed this was the deepest place in the whole Pearl River, and if she was not here she would not be anywhere. He was gone such a long time that the others stared hard at the surface of the water, through which the bubbles came from below." In his dive to the deepest part of the river, William enters a zone of troubling uncertainty. He recognizes that Hazel's and his worst fears could be realized: "So far down and all alone, had he found Hazel?" (56). This question begs the next: at the bottom of the river, will he see the drowned visage of his wife, who was afraid to wade across even a tiny creek, staring back at him from a watery grave? These questions invoke tragedy and edge the story toward a dark nihilism.

William's disturbing dive has captured the attention of numerous scholars. John Alexander Allen calls William's experience a "revelation" that draws him "into nature's most potent and ecstatic secret" (47). Michael Kreyling contends that "time itself, change, decay, eventual death" present themselves to William, but he "does not fully comprehend" them (*Achievement* 21). Albert Devlin has noted that "often Welty will endow objects and places with the pathos of diminished personal space" (105), and Peter Schmidt has remarked that Welty stories depict "violent activity packed into hidden, claustrophobic spaces" (4). Devlin and Schmidt cite other examples such as the cage in "Keela" and the rain barrel in "Clytie," respectively, and the depths of this river also surely qualify as both a hidden and potentially violent space in which Grady's father did drown and in which Hazel may have drowned. Harriet Pollack sees William's immersion in the river as a way of his intuiting "what Hazel must feel as she prepares to give birth" and his effort to "accommodate something female and puzzling" (10, 11).

William's plunge into "the deepest place" in the river indicates his movement toward psychological awareness and understanding. His river baptism initiates a new comprehension: now he can empathize with the growing child—in the womb of his wife. He can now perceive the changes taking place within his wife and her little control over them. Her pregnancy, he now sees, engenders hope and change, as a harvest does: "She had been filled to the brim with that elation that they all remembered, like their own secret, the elation that comes of great hopes and changes, sometimes simply of the harvest time, that comes with a little course of its own like a tune to run in the head, and there was nothing she could do about it" (56).

From his dive into the river, William emerges reborn as the hero. His sins are washed away, and he becomes sanctified, as Welty moves from the comic to the hero's quest. William's immersion in the river, which also links him to the drowning of Grady's father, the false drowning of Hazel, and the possibility of William's own drowning, eventually frees him from the emotional entanglements so far. He must break free of the nets but in a new and positive way. William, trapped by marriage, seeks the release of staying out all night, drinking too much, and shirking his marital responsibilities, if not philandering. The release he needs now is one from which he will emerge with fuller wisdom. The reward for this young husband who has mourned, reminisced, elegized, eulogized, cut his foot, and plunged with a full heart into his river baptism is to find his wife and know her anew.

The marital crisis in "The Wide Net," as in "A Piece of News," disrupts the ordinary lives of the couples, but the instructive complication ultimately results in renewed but chastened awareness and vitality. The denouement in both stories involves domestic reconciliation, which begins in "The Wide Net" when William reenters his house and hears Hazel call out his name. The tone is once again comedic. William feels the "wildest heart" of joy, relief, and renewed appreciation as "he went up on the porch and in at the door, and all exhausted he had walked through the front room and through the kitchen and heard his named called" (70–71). Hazel's vocal gesture reestablishes connection with her husband, and he finds relief.

Hazel's voice, most suggestively, comes from the bedroom: "After a moment, he smiled, as if no matter what he might have hoped for in his wildest heart, it was better than that to hear his named called out in the house. The voice came out of the bedroom" (70–71). Having come through his trial by water and endured the "agony of the blood and of the heart" (57), William is now fully prepared to appreciate his wife's changed condition. He feels joy and accepts his paternal responsibilities in a new way. That

Hazel's voice comes to him "out of the bedroom" is also a welcome call to renewed sexuality. The neighborhood boys nearby playfully toss the alligator in the air "like a father tossing a child" (66), in a simile that prefigures William's coming role as father.

As in "A Piece of News," the weather and the moon figure prominently in "The Wide Net." As a storm halts this river-dragging crew and forces them into reflective stillness, an image of ancient and mythic import appears: "The rain struck heavily. A huge tail seemed to lash through the air and the river broke in a wound of silver" (62). The lashing tail again calls to mind the alligator and dragon, which in mythology is the symbol of "that which must be conquered to achieve manhood, consciousness, the good," or "immortality" (Burrows, Lapides, and Shawcross 453). Now the forces of the earth take on more magical and mythic significance: the "wound of silver" suggests the emotional slash from which the lovers, and the heavens, must eventually heal and represents the clashing of earthly forces that all must contend with and respect.

In both "The Wide Net" and "A Piece of News" meteorological events mirror human actions, and vice versa. The weather restores its calm both in nature and in the lovers' understanding. The potential violence in the ancient alligator's tail has been calmed for now, and the river is quiet. One final and rare spectacle of the natural world replaces the disturbing mystery of the silver wound in the sky and heralds with a heavenly splendor the reunion of the lovers: a nocturnal rainbow welcomes William back to Hazel. Naoko Fuwa Thornton sees the lunar rainbow as a "token of the covenant of trust between Hazel and the celestial and William Wallace and the terrestrial, but ultimately it is between his family—William Wallace, Hazel, and their future posterity—and nature with its ever-repeating cycles" (68). A meteorological rarity, this rainbow appears, most romantically, at night: "When he got to his own house, William Wallace saw to his surprise that it had not rained at all. But there, curved over the roof, was something he had never seen before as long as he could remember, a rainbow at night. In the light of the moon, which had risen again, it looked small and of gauzy material, like a lady's summer dress, a faint veil through which the stars showed" (70). The heavens and the mortals below declare what each other is about. Moonlight swathes the house in gauze of natural light—the best kind—especially in a Welty love story. The overarching grandeur of the rainbow serves as an appropriate meteorological ending to the comic tale. In the grand traditions of Shakespeare and Jane Austen, Welty's lovers learn from their mistakes, and only then will their marital crises abate. The night sky celebrates with natural wonder the restoration of human calm on earth below.

True to comic form, then, William finds Hazel alive and well and not grotesquely drowned in the river, as she might have been. Coquettishly, she waits for her husband in the bedroom, and when he finds her there, he spanks her playfully in the shimmering moonlight (71). Peter Schmidt argues that in this scene William Wallace "tries to accommodate himself to [his wife's] point of view, not his," and as such he is "no longer fighting for the possession of the baby but willingly conceding her special power" (142). One final gesture makes clear that William Wallace has changed his marital stance: "out from the top step, out across their yard where the China tree was and beyond, into the dark fields where the lightning-bugs flickered away. He climbed to his feet too and stood beside her, with the frown on his face, *trying to look where she looked*" (72; emph. added). Finally, William can look in the direction in which his wife is looking.

The couple relinquishes their oppositional stance and achieves equal marital footing. The chase has now drawn to a happy conclusion: "It was the same as any other chase in the end" (72). William Wallace "climbed to his feet too and stood beside her." On equal ground he and Hazel now demonstrate a collaborative readiness for parenthood. Hazel looks away from him, and into the future. This time, however, instead of opposing her, as he has done before, or running away from her, William looks where she looks. Hazel, who received the spanking as a penalty for her precociousness, is also ready for improved behavior. Chastened, the couple gazes in the same direction—both fully expectant.

This essentially traditional view of "The Wide Net," however, does not fully consider the most mysterious and troubling images that make it a war story. This tale may have a double ending—either the hero and heroine are reconciled, in comic tradition, and will have children, and the generations will go on, or like Aeneas, William will return to destruction: "Carthago delenda est." Welty wrote "The Wide Net" just before the attack on Pearl

Harbor, and the context is the advent of war. A letter written by Eudora Welty to Diarmuid Russell, and included in Marrs's biography of Welty, describes the training flights in the skies over her home in Jackson, Mississippi, in September 1941: "Are big bombers flying all over New York and do they fly low, in under your desk? They do here, they fly under my bed at night, all those in the Louisiana Maneuvers go over Jackson when they make a curve, and really one went under the Vicksburg bridge over the Mississippi River the other day, too lazy to clear it. I feel as if my bones are being ground to pieces but I suppose I will get used to it if I stay here for Jackson is filled with air bases, air schools, air fields, and barracks and tents, a changed little place, loud and crazy" (*Eudora Welty* 80).[4] Welty was clearly aware of the war that was going on in Europe at the time and knew that the United States was preparing for it. With the war well under way in Europe, and the likelihood increasing that the United States would enter it, finding references to war in "The Wide Net" is not surprising.

The tension in the story escalates when William Wallace realizes that his wife is missing. He sees that "she had left him a little letter, in an envelope." After taking one look at the letter, he is too "scared to read the exact words, and he crushed the whole thing in his hand instantly" (*Wide Net* 35). The letter he crushes, reminiscent of so many war letters received, has bad new inside—news so bad he cannot bear to read it.

The protagonist's full name also carries the connotation of war. William Wallace Jamieson's name recalls the national hero of Scotland, Sir William Wallace (c. 1270–1305), who was known for courage and fearlessness in battle. Sir James Ferguson's 1938 *William Wallace, Guardian of Scotland* makes clear the heroic acts and violent death of a patriotic hero who sacrificed himself in war for liberty. What remains unanswered, however, is whether the seemingly mild-mannered, albeit-sometimes-inebriated, and out-all-night hero of Welty's story is the namesake of the Scottish folk hero.

Other names in the story carry rich connotation. Virgil Thomas is surely not an accidental naming either. For assistance William Wallace seeks out his friend Virgil Thomas, whom he sees going into Virgil's house. Welty's language moves the story toward the mythic and symbolic: William Wallace "could just see the edge of Virgil, he had almost got in, he had one foot inside the door" (35). The story will build not only upon mixing of the realistic and the mythic but also the allegorical. Harriett Pollack has noted the likeness of Welty's country Virgil to Virgil's Aeneas, "who wandered from his duty and his destiny in Queen Dido's Carthage. William Wallace has strayed from his husbandly devotion at a carnival in Mississippi's Carthage." Pollack sees Welty having drawn upon Virgil in that she transforms "a realistic story into one lightly laced with the heroic epic, and then transforms the epic form she has lightly evoked" (8). Virgil's Aeneid, she points out, "is not a single, privileged reference that readers must find evoked by the text in order to appreciate it. Nor is it a single key allusion that all studious readers must inevitably find (19). Michael Kreyling sees evidence of Dante's having taken Virgil as a companion in his search for Beatrice, and later of "the attitude of the Madonna in Hazel's final gesture." "Like Aeneas, who voyaged into the underworld," Pollack notes that "William Wallace dives to the deepest spot in the Pearl River" (9). "The Wide Net," she notes, "builds on generic mixing; it is a vernacular tale about a back-country couple's marital squabble that slips into the mythic tradition of the heroic quest" (7).

The perplexing description of William Wallace's neck merits interpretation. Virgil implies that at a carnival in Carthage, Mississippi, William became inebriated. Virgil says: "It was nice to be sitting on your neck in a ditch singing . . . in the moonlight" (38). On a realistic level the image describes William Wallace's drunkenness at the fair. He ends up sitting and singing in a ditch in a town called Carthage. A real town in Mississippi bears this name, but Welty never uses real place names such as this one without a reason, just as William's friend by the name of Virgil is no accident. "Sitting on your neck" also may have been a common phrase of colloquial speech. The pose, however, is not a usual position that a person takes, even when drunk. The expression may refer to a person who is inebriated and unbalanced but also may connote the world having turned upside down.

Another possible reading is that William Wallace is a soldier at war or even a casualty of war. "Sitting on your neck" may suggest a broken neck or describe someone who has been tossed on top of the head or whose head is sitting at a ninety-degree angle from the rest of the body. William's drinking buddies may represent soldiers, like so many who died with broken necks in trench warfare—the consequence of war. If William Wallace is a soldier on his neck in a ditch somewhere, then he is presumably injured or dying, and the images that follow for the rest of the story could be his final thoughts, hallucinations, or dreams. When his wife looks as if she were "looking down on him" at the end of the story, she could be looking down at her dying husband. In any case the presence of war in the story must be a reflection of Welty's awareness of war developing around her.

As Welty begins to build an allegorical tale, her sense of time in the story suspends, slows, and indicates the onset of a dream sequence and allegory that initially will confuse the hero but in time leads him to epiphany. When Virgil asks William Wallace, "Haven't you had enough of the night?" he implies that William Wallace has indeed not had enough of the dark (35). Allegory takes hold. For William Wallace signs and clues early in the stories indicate that the dark night of the soul is yet ahead of him. On the way to drag the river for his wife, for example, William Wallace, with Virgil by his side, stops his headlong plunge into the river to chase a rabbit—just to catch him—not for sustenance. Virgil must yank him back to his almost blunted purpose. William Wallace has entered an oneiric world of suspended time and confused purpose.

Language continues to suggest a dream sequence as a band of people enter the Natchez Trace and proceed "through the deep woods" and "in a place so dim and still." These descriptions of the Trace initially seem poetic but realistic. As the narrative progresses, the legendary Natchez Trace takes on a sense of the magical and mysterious, a place in which unrealistic action might occur. A freight train passes by, and Welty describes it as being "like a little festival procession, moving with the slowness of ignorance or a dream, from distance to distance" (47). William Wallace now views the world in suspended time and from a skewed perspective.

"Talk of war" occurs when the doctor speaks. Doc is a rural sage, a kind of doctor perhaps—although maybe not an M.D.— but he does minister to snakebite, gunshot, and psychic trauma. His proclamations may signal a clue to this puzzling tale when he declares: "We're hearing talk of war" (44). When William Wallace and Virgil approach "Old Doc" for use of his wide net, Doc predicts, "We're walking along in the changing time," and he warns that "any day now the change will come" (48). He literally may be referring to the change in season—the upcoming winter—when "It's going to turn from hot to cold" and "Old Mr. Winter will be standing at the door" (48), but if so, the story operates on a much more simplistic level. Pollack views Doc as a "seer" and "oracle" (9). Naoko Fuwa Thornton sees his "oration [as] irrefutable folk belief" (65). On the allegorical level Doc may prophesy the oncoming war, which is near at hand, with bombers that are already practicing and turning overhead in the hometown of the author and that seem close enough to be under her desk and bed.

Dreaming and memory continue to dislocate William Wallace and raise a question about the stability of his situation. He may not be where he thinks he is, or he may be unable, because of illness or impending death, to determine where he is. William Wallace's dislocation intensifies as he approaches the river. Unexpectedly, he cannot remember its name, even though he has always fished in it. He asks his friends, "What is the name of this river?" and they look at him "as if he were crazy not to know the name of the river he had fished in all of his life. But a deep frown was on his forehead, as if he were compelled to wonder what people had come to call this river, or to think there was a mystery in the name of the river they all knew so well, the same as if it were some great far torrent of waves that dashed through the mountains somewhere, and almost as if it were a river in some dream, for they could not give him the name of that." The question posed is why William Wallace would not at this moment recall the name of the river with which he has had the intimate acquaintance of a lifetime. The prophetic language recurs as Welty further dislocates her hero. The realistic story line recedes as William Wallace dives into uncharted waters. The river, formerly so well known to all, now carries symbolic association. The river has great mystery now, as if it were another river in another location—a distant location—where "some great far torrent of waves" roll and "dash on distant shores" (49). The protagonist's visions appear "as if in some dream." His friends cannot assist him in his new situation: "no one can give him the name" of his land of dreams, what or where he is, and what river may now be rushing past. The "far torrent of waves" may be an image of war and may refer especially to the distant shores on which World War II was unfolding.

In Welty's stories approaching large bodies of water often implies that the protagonist is about to cross the river Styx—the mythical river of death. The same is true in "The Wide Net." William Wallace no longer simply stands on the bank of the Pearl River, that familiar river in which he has fished all of his life. He now stands at the edge of the river "as if it were still a mystery to him." In this portentous dream, imagination, memory, or hallucination, he is standing on the bank of the proverbial river of death, and he is poised to cross. He is, like Hamlet, on the precipice of fate, at the boundary of "the undiscover'd country, from whose bourn / No traveller returns" (3.1.79–80). His counterparts, whose time to cross has not yet arrived, cannot know, understand, or name what his fate will be. Like Bowman in "Death of a Traveling Salesman," William cannot discern where he is or where he is going.

Indeed, the river of death is a great mystery, and the wide net of this story, in the allegorical sense, is the skein of death, which catches all. The net "won't let nothing through, she won't let nothing through," chant Sam and Robbie Bell, as if they are the Greek chorus on the sidelines (51). "Since the net was so wide, when it was all stretched out it reached from bank to bank of the Pearl River, and the weights would hold it all the way to the bottom" (50). That the net is golden suggests the mythical as well: "The net that was being drawn out, so old and so long-used, it too looked golden, strung and tied with golden threads" (49). The net sweeps up all the living, and those caught in the golden net of fate will see a world beyond, as they leave this one behind.

The devil, too, makes an appearance here. Satan traditionally represents "the force that opposes the hero and the achievement of his task. . . . It is symbolized by darkness, a cloak, a monster, a serpent. . . . It may involve destruction, descent death, irregular shapes, that which is considered evil or nonspiritual" (*Myth and Motifs* 461). "Rassle with him, son!" are words that surely invoke Satan's presence here (51, 54). In crossing the river, "they swam like fiends" (54). Virgil appeared to have swum across the river and engaged in a strange encounter with an "undersized man with a straw hat." The movements in this passage again appear dreamlike. Patting the stranger with a hand, "the way he would pat a child," Virgil's gestures at first seem soft and friendly, but the result is that the stranger falls to the ground. All is not as it seems: "Virgil had already swum across and was up on the other bank. He and the stranger could be seen exchanging a word apiece and then Virgil put out his hand the way he would pat a child and patted the stranger to the ground. The little man got up again just as quickly, lifted his shoulder, turned around, and walked away with his hat tilted over his eyes." The full meaning of this encounter is unclear, but it engenders further foreboding, both in the striking of the stranger to the ground and in that the hat "tilted over his eyes" has a sinister connotation. Later the man claims he is "harmless as a baby," but a question remains: "What did he look like up close?" (55). The presence of the devil seems likely.

Appearances belie darker actions taking place. William's dive to the bottom of the river also carries similar suggestions: "Had he found . . . down there, like some secret, the real, the true trouble that Hazel had fallen into about which words in a letter could not speak?" The darker implication is that the faked drowning is not the real trouble here. The suggestion is that William Wallace may be dying or dead or perhaps Hazel is the recipient of one of those letters that the government sends to the widows of deceased soldiers. The narrative continues with other forebodings: "It could be nothing but the old trouble that William Wallace was finding out, reaching and turning in the gloom of such depths" (56–57). Again, the implications are that the story may not have the happy ending that readers tend to expect. The depths are too enshrouded with gloom and the "true trouble" and the "old trouble" too looming. When William Wallace comes up, "it was in an agony from submersion, which seemed an *agony of the blood and the very heart, so woeful he looked.* He was staring and glaring around in astonishment, as if a long time had gone by, *away from the pale world* where the brown light of the sun and the river and the little party watching him trembled before his eyes" (57–58; emph. added). From "away from the pale world" and in "an agony of the blood and the very heart," William Wallace's activities surely indicate a nearness to the world of death. He performs a dance so wild "that he would die next" (59). Other images of death accrue. A buzzard is turning overhead; Virgil claims, "It's time we ate fish." Because the fish is a symbol for Christianity, perhaps he invokes Christian rite. At this moment an old white church is close by, and eventually, with Virgil standing nearby, "the door shut on him" (70). The nearness of death is unmistakable.

The white heron, though extraordinarily beautiful, is also a sign of doom. The presence of a white bird usually symbolizes death in Welty's stories, and here is no exception: "In a shadowy place something white flew up. It was a heron, and it went away over the dark tree-tops. William Wallace followed it with his eyes, and Brucie clapped his hands, but Virgil gave a sigh, as if he knew that *when you go looking for what is lost, everything is a sign*" (54; emph. added). Welty strategically places these clues to the deeper reaches of the story. Perhaps she depicts the image of the lost soldier. Perhaps her real story is of a man near the moment of his death or his psychologically darkest place. He does not recognize where he is. He does not recognize the river he has known all of his life. The strong suggestion is that the river he sees is not the river he thinks it is. Virgil is his guide to the river dragging, and surely Virgil's presence recalls Dante's guide through the underworld. The location, after all, is Carthage, the city the Romans won in a vicious war. They won the war by destroying the city so thoroughly that it would never rise again. The complete destruction is memorialized in the famous, ancient phrase attributed variously to Cato, Plutarch, and Pliny the Elder: "Carthago delenda est." William's hometown of Carthage, Mississippi, has resonances for this story that extend far beyond the local.

Welty is a writer of great depth who frequently employs allegory as well as subtle allusion and connotation. That the setting for this story is associated with Carthage further informs the war theme, as does the hero's name and his ferocious Scottish predecessor. William may potentially lose his wife in this story, but alternatively, the more submerged idea perhaps is that she comes perilously close to losing him. Her fear of losing him perhaps informs her initial actions. William appears resurrected after his near-death experiences, but one interpretation could be that he is not. The story could be a Greco-Roman, Dantesque vision of war, destruction, death, and loss, in which those who are left behind must endure. When Hazel is "looking down on him" at the end of the story, she may be holding her dead husband in her arms. In this story of unfathomable depths, "everything is a sign."

"Ancient Communication" in "Death of a Traveling Salesman"

The practical, contented, and fruitful marriage of the country couple in "Death of a Traveling Salesman" contrasts with the gathering loneliness of R. J. Bowman, the traveling salesman who wanders a metaphorical road spiraling from a lost and barren state of mind to death. Like the hero in Hemingway's story "The Short Happy Life of Francis Macomber," who dies shortly after his epiphany, in which he makes a crucial realization about his life but too late to live it, so too does Welty's rural, tragic hero—the salesman. Welty, the master of dualities, balances dark and light and the tragic and comic. Bowman finds his heart pierced by Cupid's arrow. He holds his hand to his chest; he will literally and figuratively die of a broken heart. Welty's juxtaposition of the sophisticated city salesman's misery with the contentedness of the country couple illustrates what it takes to achieve, sustain, and lose love, and the author presents themes to which she would return again in her early stories and late works—especially *The Optimist's Daughter*, a novel of love and loss.

Comfort and security, vulnerability and insecurity, in the story lead into a focus on love and lovelessness. Bowman always thought of himself as a man with a secure position. In fourteen years of his work as a traveling shoe salesman, he had "never been ill before and never had an accident." To show for his success, he could "put up at better hotels in bigger towns." Now, however, he must recognize his changing situation. He feels unwell, and he must admit to his illness. His previously high sales "record was broken, and he had even begun almost to question it" (232). His illness leads to his confusion and insecurity.

As the main character, Bowman, drives his car along a dirt road out in the country, Welty shifts the narrative to dream sequence, hallucination, and the premonitory. Bowman thinks that the "time did not seem to clear the noon hurdle" and clouds float "perilously close to the car." His car wheels stir "their weightless sides to make a silvery melancholy whistle" (234). Such language moves the story quickly away from the realistic and indicates that an allegorical level of meaning underlies the plot line. These early indicators suggest that the "salesman" hero is headed for heaven.

Slowly, the salesman realizes his whereabouts. He is lost on a road out in the country: "Why did he not admit he was simply lost and had been for miles?" Bowman exhibits a condescending attitude when he thinks of asking country folks for directions: "He was not in the habit of asking the way of strangers, and these people never knew where the very roads they lived on went to" (233). This arrogance toward the country people ultimately will not serve him well. Eventually, he will see that they indeed do know where the roads lead and instead, he is the one less sure of the way.

Insecurity and security accrue thematic importance as Welty reveals significant characteristics of the lives of Bowman and the couple he meets out in the country. The salesman initially thinks of himself as a man with a secure position. When his car runs off the road, Bowman self-assuredly believes he must turn to others out in the country for assistance. When he sees the country woman, he tacitly believes he can correctly estimate her age: "Bowman, who automatically judged a woman's age on sight, set her age at fifty" (236). He asks with "his old voice, chatty, confidential, inflected for selling shoes," whether she and Sonny live alone (238). He considers hugging this "old woman" out of sympathy for her, but he finally concludes it improper to "embrace" an old woman (241). His errors in judgment eventually prove fatal, but for now he is sure of his assessment of what and whom he has found in the country.

Bowman's sense of security resurfaces when he reaches the cabin of Sonny and his wife. There he once again feels "hopefully secure" (237), in spite of his illness and the "betraying of all his weakness" (238). Nonetheless, he talks in his chatty voice with its salesman-like inflections: "he was not strong enough to receive the impact of unfamiliar things without a little talk to break their fall" (239). His words prove premonitory: he will confront "unfamiliar things," and even "a little talk" will not break his ultimate fall. The beds and bedrooms Bowman encounters emphasize the developing love theme. In his infirmity he recalls his grandmother's bed— one of comfort and security: he wishes he could "fall into the big feather bed that had been in her room" (232), to "sink submissively into the pillows, to wait for his medicine" (237). He becomes more aware, however, that the security of his grandmother's bed is now lost, and he senses his perilous condition.

The beds that this salesman has frequented contrast with the warm, fruitful, marital bed he will find at Sonny's house. Bowman's restless traveling life has taken him to countless empty hotel rooms, where relationships are short and unfulfilling: "Weren't they all, eternally, stuffy in summer and drafty in winter? Women? He could only remember little rooms within little rooms, like a nest of Chinese paper boxes, and if he thought of one woman he saw the worn loneliness that the furniture of that room seemed built of." Nonetheless, Bowman seeks any hotel room at Beulah in which to "go to bed and sleep off his fatigue" (232–33).

Bowman's association with Beulah is symbolically crucial to the meaning of the story. Albert J. Devlin has pointed out that although "Bowman's destination is Beulah, a hamlet in Bolivar County in northwestern Mississippi," the word *Beulah* also refers to "a state of repose that evokes the journey of Bunyan's pilgrim and countless other legendary antecedents" (104). The hero is on his way to heaven.

Uncertain of his whereabouts and his health, Bowman slowly comprehends the love story that is unfolding before him. After his car stops, he meets the country couple who offer to help him. First, he notices that Sonny and his wife stand "side by side" (241). The look of satisfaction in the face of the wife bewilders him. He senses what he believes is a "conspiracy" of commitment between the two: "These people cherished something here that he could not see, they withheld some ancient promise of food and warmth and light. Between them they had a conspiracy. He thought of the way she had moved away from him and gone to Sonny, she had flowed toward him. He was shaking with cold, he was tired, and it was not fair." Lamplight and firelight for Welty again signify clarity of vision, and the truth slowly dawns on Bowman that his initial judgment about this woman's age is flawed. She is not old but young: "He set his cup back on the table in unbelieving protest. A pain pressed at his eyes. He saw that she was not an old woman. She was young, still young. He could think of no number of years for her. She was the same age as Sonny, and she belonged to him" (247). When Sonny proudly announces that his wife is pregnant, Bowman feels that this news is "unfair." Once he was good at determining a woman's age. His misjudgments now indicate his faltering abilities and portend his coming death, the approach of which he also misinterprets and fails to see.

Pregnancy profoundly unsettles the protagonist of this story. When Sonny proclaims his wife's pregnancy, he wields a significant blow to Bowman. In *One Writer's Beginnings* Welty described that in this story she "approached and went inside with [her] traveling salesman, and had him, pressed by imminent death, figure out what was there . . . 'He was shocked with knowing what was really in this house. A marriage, a fruitful marriage. That simple thing. Anyone could have had that.' Writing 'Death of a Traveling Salesman' opened my eyes. And I received the shock of having touched, for the first time, on my real subject: human relationships" (87). R. J. Bowman now senses that "some sort of joke had certainly been played upon him," yet he can clearly see that "there was nothing remote or mysterious here—only something private. The only secret was the ancient communication between two people" (251). Finally, he comprehends the truth of the situation: the country couple has "a fruitful marriage. That simple thing."

The education of R. J. Bowman in the satisfactions of love is not yet complete. He must observe even more closely the strength and success of this marital relationship, symbolized by the marital bed of Sonny and his wife. "He could see the other room, with the foot of an iron bed showing, across the passage. The bed had been made up with a red-and-yellow pieced quilt that looked like a map or a picture, a little like his grandmother's girlhood painting of Rome burning" (247). He expects that the couple will offer him what Ann Romines sees as "the comfort and the quilt-warmed bed" ("Powers of the Lamp" 5). For the last time Bowman's confidence betrays him. "But he had not known yet how slowly he understood. They had not meant to give him their bed" (249). Ruth Vande Kieft has observed that at this juncture Bowman is "beautifully ready for love" (*Eudora Welty* 39). He dissolves in emotion as he hears the "breathing, round and deep, of the man and his wife in the room across the passage. And that was all. But emotion swelled patiently within him, and he wished that the child were his" (249). Ann Romines adds, "As if he too is pregnant, 'emotion swelled patiently within him'" (*Home Plot* 197). Although Bowman feels that "some sort of joke had certainly been played upon him," his judgment and vision have cleared: "There was nothing remote or mysterious here—only something private. The only secret was the ancient communication between two people" (251). The sweet, contented, fruitful marriage of this country couple now is fully apparent.

Another bed in this story has dark, awful ramifications, however, and the dichotomy between the sweet and bitter, light and dark, image patterns is now fully established. Bowman's car is like a cradle to rock a grim child. This dreadful image emerges early in the story and prefigures the salesman's demise. Romines describes the car as sinking "into a crevice (which suggests the entry to a womb)" (*Home Plot* 195). Unlike a womb, however, the car takes on the mythic significance of conveyance into the realm of death. Early on, when the salesman realizes he is lost on the road, his car stops at the "road's end" (234). Welty's description turns macabre when the car becomes enmeshed in dense vines that "rocked it like a grotesque child in a dark cradle." The car is now a cradle from which the passenger will not safely emerge.

The image of the car as a rocking cradle is intentionally misleading. The narrative direction suggests otherwise: the traveler cannot see his imminent death in it. The salesman predictably proceeds to look for roadside help to extricate his car, but he fails to see the more immediate necessity of evaluating the range and limitations of his own life. He is thus blind to his own fate and—like a doomed Greek protagonist—misreads, misapprehends, and misinterprets the "signposts" (232). He remains oblivious to the fact that his end is imminent. The tragedy of this story is that when the traveling salesman finally gains insight and understanding, he will only have a brief moment to register his own failures before he dies. His is a life unfulfilled—like that of a child who too soon perishes. As the vines entwine this cradle, only to release it "gently to the ground," the metaphor shifts to that of the grave. Suspended for a time in the limbo of vines, the car emerges as a clear symbol of Bowman's fate. The final image of the car is as "a boat." Welty often refers to the mythical figure Charon, whose boat ferries the dead across the mythical river Styx. Bowman's car has brought him to that lonely point of no return.

The two children of this story, one imagistically figured as in the dark cradle, the other about to be born to Sonny and his wife, are fixed in juxtaposition to amplify the emptiness of the salesman's life—no love, no heir, and no one to cradle. The story builds to anguish as Bowman, the "bowed man," acknowledges that love is the crucial ingredient missing from his life. His greatest regret is the child he did not have. He is now fully aware that the country folk, whom he initially disparaged but who have generously helped him, are the ones enjoying "a fruitful marriage. That simple thing." Ruth Weston points out that what Bowman "senses between the couple is no Gothic plot but, ironically, the 'secret' of their coming child" (*Gothic Traditions* 29). His revelation is simple: the rootless traveling salesman deeply "wish[es] that the child were his" (249). Carol Ann Johnston and others have also discussed Bowman's increasing self-understanding. The traveler's excruciating moment of deepest self-understanding comes only seconds before his death. The persona of the traveler is suggestive of the grotesque child because he has grown old without love, hope, or progeny. His existence worsens with the blinders of his own ignorance and prejudice. The childless traveler cannot extricate himself in time from the thick vines of his emotional and psychological predicament, and he dies alone—without wife or child.

Considering Welty's family history, a reference to a cradle carries increasing significance when that image is dark and grotesque. To describe the salesman's car as a "dark cradle" may itself refer to the grave of a child. Perhaps the writer's imagination, in visualizing a child she would never have or the brother she had lost in his infancy, and whom she never had seen, could only perceive the loss of this innocent as manifestly twisted and grotesque. For Welty, for whom faces and names are essential human descriptors, a faceless and nameless child represents—at least—an inexpressible loss and a collapse of the promise of family, heredity, and identity. The "grotesque child in a dark cradle" of her first story may also be, consciously or not, a fictional representation of the brother she would later memorialize in her late memoir, *One Writer's Beginnings*. There she describes her brother, lost in infancy, whose eyes in death were grimly covered with the silver coins, in keeping with a residual superstitious family ritual.

Welty's personal life may appear in the story in other ways as well. Her personal relationship with John Robinson, the high school acquaintance with whom she fell in love, is an important—perhaps crucial—autobiographical background for this story. Biographer Suzanne Marrs has described Robinson as "tall, slender, and rather debonair" and as "a man so handsome that one of Eudora's New York friends would call him an 'Adonis.'" Marrs traces their relationship and convincingly asserts that Eudora Welty was "deeply in love with him," that these feelings may have developed "as early as 1937," and that perhaps Welty "felt ready for 'a marriage, a fruitful marriage, such as the one . . . in 'Death of a Traveling Salesman'" (*Eudora Welty* 56). Welty's relationship with Robinson may be an important factor in Welty's development of the lonely salesman who is stunned to discover the centered calmness and essential happiness of the rural couple who are expecting a baby. If they could have such a happy marriage, with such apparent ease and with so little else, surely that outcome would be possible for the author herself.

Written at the time in the writer's life when she was of childbearing age but unmarried and childless, the dark cradle metaphor in "Death of a Traveling Salesman" may also have been for the author a self-referential and bleak contemplation of her own empty cradle. The tragic, peripatetic protagonist, whom the gods will slay, sees only too late that "a fruitful marriage" —that is, one with love, sex, and childbearing—is for the parents in the story an essential celebration of life. The traveler may well be an autobiographical, male transference of the female writer, and as such, even as a young woman, Eudora Welty may have seen herself in the traveler, who is "bowed" by—or perhaps humbled by—longing or grief and the difficulty of finding the right partner. In her work for the WPA, not long before she wrote this story, she literally traveled alone and by car down many country roads across the state of Mississippi. She was not a salesperson, but her travels in her car may have come to symbolize for her the vehicle for traversing her own psychological roads as she came to terms with sex, love, loneliness, and death.

That no one hears the breaking heart of the bowed man in the last moments of the story is a sharp indication of the traveler's stark aloneness. Tragically, he sees and apprehends love and its ultimate value in life only to lose it all too soon. His heart bursts with longing at the end of the story. If the traveler is an autobiographical representation of the author, then she sought a fruitful, lasting love. For the author, however, a fulfilling marital union—"that simple thing"—would prove complicated and ultimately elusive.

"A Breaking of the Nets!": Prevention and Liberation in "Livvie"

Fertility in "Livvie" links thematically with other early rural stories in which childbearing occurs or is about to occur. Michael Kreyling, Peggy Prenshaw, Robert Kloss, and Garvin Davenport, among others, discuss the fertility and regeneration that pervade the story.[5] The heroine is clearly desirous of a child, yet she has none, and images of her monthly cycle and of the fruitfulness of the natural world around her and of babies and children occur frequently. "Livvie" exemplifies Eudora Welty's adept interweaving of subtle motifs and patterns as her stories unfold. Sexual imagery is certainly predominant here, but barriers, nets, traps, and symbols of exclusion are contrapuntal to them in this Natchez Trace story. Solomon, the older husband, begins confining and almost imprisoning Livvie from the world from the outset of the story. Julian Smith likens the story to the "Song of Solomon" and emphasizes the eroticism of the love songs in that work. Marriage is more like kidnapping, rather than joyful union: Solomon "carried Livvie twenty-one miles away from her home when he married her. . . . He was good to her, but he kept her in the house" (153). Kloss notes that the husband keeps his wife "secluded and guarded," cites Welty's description of the house as a "cage," and correlates this idea with contraception (72).

Livvie's marital life is one of confinement. Her aged husband wants to prevent her from interacting with other people or meeting someone new who might lure her away. She has not seen her mother since her wedding day (162), and the pictures over the living room mantel are of his people rather than both of theirs (154). He has forbidden her to "look at a field hand, or a field hand look at her. There was no house near, except for the cabins of the tenants that were forbidden to her, and there was no house as far as she had been, stealing away down the still, dark Trace" (157). Solomon's strictness inhibits Livvie's free expression—she wants to sing when she irons but holds back (158). When she walks the Trace, even the thistles on the path threaten her like the "prophets in the Bible in Solomon's house" (157). She fears waking her husband at mealtime "because even in his sleep he seemed to be such a strict man" (159). When she briefly allows herself to daydream about escaping to the fields, she admonishes herself and returns to her chores (162). Livvie even tries to stop the frogs from singing for fear that their croaking will disturb her sleeping husband (159). Perhaps she is kind and thoughtful in not waking him, but the image of his strictness, even while he is asleep, suggests that fear drives her motivations more than her essential kindness does.

Physical dividers and restraints reinforce the image of Livvie's stifled environment. One day Livvie climbs on a high bank to see the angel wings on a statue in the graveyard of an old church. The angel wings imply freedom, albeit in death, which Livvie has not yet known but may long for. She notices that the trees are encased. They have "great caterpillar nets which enclosed them" (157). These nets call to mind her imprisoned life and fruitless marriage. She imagines freedom, however: "Oh for a stirring of the leaves, and a breaking of the nets!" (158). The "deep road" surrounds Solomon's fields "like a moat to keep them in" (161), and he is the center: "while all this went around him that was his, Solomon was like a little still spot in the middle" (162). Solomon's moat successfully binds Livvie within his domestic compound. The bottle tree in the yard, which many have seen as symbolic, keeps birds away but also inhibits the tree from reaching its full flowering. The bottles cover the blossom ends of the tree branches in an image of contraception. As such, the bottle tree suggests Livvie's infertile situation, in which barriers prevail, but in the fullness of time, a young man, Cash, will ultimately break one of the bottles—a sign of her new life, one in which Livvie and Cash will be fruitful and multiply. The disparity in years may be partly responsible for Livvie's emotional distance from Solomon, but the impenetrability and ultimate mystery of the individual consciousness is also a crucial barrier. Welty explores these ideas through Livvie, who cannot see into and know her husband's thoughts and dreams.

Welty returns to this idea in *The Robber Bridegroom*, when Rosamund seeks to unmask her husband to know his identity. In *The Second Sex* Simon de Beauvoir discusses the essential impenetrability here: "There is mystery on both sides: as the other who is of masculine sex, every man, also, has within him a presence, an inner self impenetrable to woman; she in turn is ignorant of the male's erotic feeling" (256). In sleep Solomon seems to Livvie almost, but not quite, decipherable: "his face was like new, so smooth and clear that it was like a glass of jelly held to the window, and she could almost look through his forehead and see what he thought" (160). Later, as he sleeps and presumably dreams, Livvie ponders further the private, uncommunicated consciousness, which separates her from her husband like a "rail fence": "Now what did he dream about? For she saw him sigh gently as if not to disturb some whole thing he held round in his mind, like a fresh egg. So even an old man dreamed about something pretty. Did he dream of her, while his eyes were shut and sunken, and his small hand with the wedding ring curled close in sleep around the quilt? . . . but even while she scrutinized him, the rods of the foot of the bed seemed to rise up like a rail fence between them, and she could see that people never could be sure of anything as long as one of them was asleep and the other awake" (162–63). His consciousness is impenetrable to her, and even though she "scrutinizes" him, she cannot know his full identity or thoughts.

The bedroom of Solomon and Livvie, as is typical in a Welty love story, indicates the psychological status of the relationship. Welty describes the bedroom in detail: the "bright iron bed" has polished knobs "like a throne, in which Solomon slept all day"; the curtains are "snow-white," an additional winter image; the lace bedspread that belongs there has been replaced with Solomon's quilt. Welty usually gives the appropriate name of the quilts in her stories: this one is "Trip around the World" (154), chosen perhaps to indicate that Solomon has traveled and Livvie has not yet. Livvie's one possession, the picture of the "little white baby of the family she worked for," hangs symbolically in this room. Peter Schmidt has argued that "the picture of the white child that she has nursed" reduces Livvie's identity "to her role as servant" and suggests that she is little more than Solomon's nurse and servant (124–25). The baby picture may be the child she has cared for who belongs to someone else, but it also forecasts that she may now soon have a baby of her own.

The bedroom in this story foretells death rather than life. This bed is not shared: Solomon takes the middle of it, and Livvie never sleeps in it but stands beside it or holds onto it (159, 161, 163). The picture over his bed is also significant: "there was a picture of him when he was young. Then he had a fan of hair over his forehead like a king's crown. Now his hair lay down on his head" (159–60). That picture is a reminder of Solomon's lost youth. No progeny will come of this union, for this bed is primarily a deathbed rather than one of a fertile marriage. Solomon can only offer Livvie his final blessing.

When bed becomes coffin, as it also does in other Welty stories and her last novel, *The Optimist's Daughter*, love, death, and memory inextricably combine. The physical divisor of husband and wife is death, and Solomon must succumb. As her name indicates, however, Livvie will retain and develop her sexuality, fertility, and full life. After Solomon's passing, the nets holding her fast will fall away.

A divider also initially separates Livvie and her new suitor, Cash: she is "on one side of the Old Natchez Trace," and he is on the other (169). He quickly leaps this impediment, however, to take her from Solomon just before Solomon's death. Solomon and Livvie must still resolve their emotional dilemma before Livvie can be free. Solomon must untangle the nets and lower the barriers he has created. He clears away the restrictive web that has ensnared them both. He finally acknowledges that his attempts to prevent Livvie's departure were unwise. In his final wisdom he sees that age cannot constrain youth: "So here come the young man Livvie wait for. Was no prevention. No prevention" (175). In these words, says Ruth Vande Kieft, Solomon surrenders with "beautiful candor, grace, and dignity" (*Eudora Welty* 62). Peter Schmidt sees that Livvie's "liberation from her oppressive husband is accomplished more through the efforts of another man than through her own" (123–24). Solomon's realization of his mistakes in judgment ultimately frees his wife to move into her future.

Before relinquishing Livvie, however, Solomon tells their love story. Spoken with his dying breath, Solomon eulogizes their love as he recollects their early moments together. Although he is now too old to "lift" her, either physically or emotionally, he knows she is still young: "When Livvie married, her husband were already somebody. He had paid great cost for his land. He spread sycamore leaves over the ground from wagon to door, day he brought her home, so her foot would not have to touch ground. He carried her through his door. Then he growed old and could not lift her, and she were still young." He asks for God's forgiveness for his selfishness in marrying "too young girl for wife," and he relinquishes her to the world. Livvie mourns as his words flow: "Livvie's sobs followed his words like a soft melody repeating each thing as he stated it. His lips moved for a little without sound, or she cried too fervently, and unheard he might have been telling his whole life, and then he said, 'God forgive Solomon for sins great and small. God forgive Solomon for carrying away too young girl for wife and keeping her away from her people and for all the young people would clamor for her back'" (176). As his narrative draws to a close, the "obstruction" to death lifts (173). Solomon goes in peace, and Livvie will begin her life anew.

Images of unleashing replace those of constriction. The liberated imagination provides Livvie one kind of freedom. Sitting beside Solomon on the bed while he sleeps, Livvie "surrounded herself with a little reverie"; she imagines "that the quiet she kept was for a sleeping baby, and that she had a baby and was its mother" (159). Clearly, she is ready for a child of her own. Her second reverie, which is part memory and part imagination, occurs when the man Michael Kreyling calls the "itinerant cosmetics peddler" allows Livvie to try purple lipstick that smells like chinaberry flowers (*Eudora Welty's Achievement of Order* 24). The synesthesia of the purple scent reminds Livvie of her home and parents. Memory and imagination engage. She sees them at home gathering figs and fishing: "in an instant she was carried away in the air through the spring, and looking down with a half-drowsy smile from a purple cloud she saw from above a chinaberry tree, dark and smooth and neatly leaved, neat as a guinea hen in the dooryard, and there was her home that she had left" (165). She travels freely through dreamscape and memory.

The weather and season mirror the emotional condition of the characters in this story, as in other stories by Welty. Release from trapping nets and from the cold of winter and approaching death, which Solomon symbolizes, is now possible. He lies under a quilt, motionless, "as if it were winter still" (172); in sleep he seems to be "walking somewhere where she could imagine snow falling" (173). His hair has grown old too: the "spring had gone out" of it (160). The images of snow, the absence of spring, and the chill of winter indicate his age and impending death.

Livvie and Cash represent by contrast the green season of spring. When "the first day of spring" arrives, Solomon keeps his quilt high up around him (159), but Livvie feels "the stir of spring close to her." Welty personifies spring as a suitor: "It was as present in the house as a young man would be" (160). Plowing and planting in the fields outside emphasize the concomitant renewal of the earth: "In the air and all around, like a bright halo around the white lady's nodding head, it was a true spring day" (168). Like the "laid-open earth" (162), Livvie is fertile.

Stillness and winter dissolve with these images of bursting of spring and herald Livvie's liberation from marital repression. When she sits by Solomon's sickbed, she is "so still she could not hear herself breathe" (158, 164). At the moment of Solomon's death, Livvie is motionless; she is balanced precisely between her past and her future: "she did not move. As if something said 'Wait,' she stood waiting. Even while her eyes burned under motionless lids, her lips parted in a stiff grimace, and with her arms stiff at her sides she stood above the prone old man and the panting young one, erect and apart" (174). Livvie's posture of stillness indicates her paralytical emotional position. She is not yet ready to leave Solomon's prone body for the phallic Cash.

After Solomon is gone, eventually, Livvie returns to action with dynamism. The life force rushes through her like the "pulsing color" of her newly acquired lipstick (168). The verbs *pulsing, throbbing,* and *hoof pawing* suggest the sexual force taking hold in the story (173). Cash stands "throbbing in his Easter clothes" (175), and both lovers are "dazzled" when he kisses Livvie for the first time: "He kicked up his heels. . . . such an abandon and menace were in his laugh. Frowning, she went closer to him and his swinging arm drew her in at once and the fright was crushed from her body, as a little match-flame might be smothered out by what it lighted. . . . and she was dazzled by herself then, the way he had been dazzled at himself to begin with" (171).

Cash breaks the chains of impediment; he moves "as if he could break through everything in the way" (170). He seizes Livvie and "dragged her hanging by the waist round and round him, while he turned in a circle, his face bent down to hers." Returning to sexuality, Livvie clings to her past for one more moment as she holds Solomon's wristwatch. Her time for him has passed, however: "The first moment, she kept one arm and its hand stiff and still, the one that held Solomon's watch" (177). The two new lovers begin to move "around and around the room" together while the birds are flying, crisscrossing, and singing outside. Just as Dr. Courtland in *The Optimist's Daughter* holds a watch in his hand at the moment of the Judge's death, similarly Livvie holds her husband's watch, but her feet take the next step forward, and she moves into the future, with its promise of fulfillment.

Ultimately, "Livvie" is two love stories in one. Now a widow, Livvie must relinquish love to death, but subsequently she turns to the living world—an important life lesson. This bittersweet story depicts sadness and hope, death and love, and dark loss giving rise to the light of renewed love.

The Original Smile in "At the Landing"

If "Livvie" focuses on young love, burnished by knowledge and death, "At the Landing" considers its darker complexities. Like Snowdie MacLain, Mattie Will Sojourner, and others, Jenny Lockhart, the initiate of "At the Landing," believes in love, even though it is elusive and for her proves ultimately abusive and harmful. Jenny's eventual rape at the end of the story, unlike Rosalind's in *The Robber Bridegroom*, is not mutually agreeable. This one has a mysterious cast, however, because of Jenny's "Mona Lisa" smile at the end of the story.

An old order must clear away before Jenny may know love. Her grandfather, who has forbidden her to speak to Billy Floyd (who eventually will become her lover), falls ill and dies. Before his death, he has a premonitory dream of a disastrous flood, heralded—or perhaps generated, at least symbolically—by the mythical powers of Billy Floyd, who seems to roil the waters. The old man predicts Jenny's fall into love and sexuality, but her later rape seems as unprepared for as the Fall of Eve and the flooding of the Mississippi River.

This story takes place against the backdrop of the flooding river, chaos, and wildness, just as "The Wide Net" does. If water in Welty stories suggests deep emotion, then roiling water portends the chaotic psychological state of the protagonist. The flooding river anticipates Jenny's violent fate, even as her hometown called "The Landing" is disappearing in floodwaters. The ungovernable force and shifting movement of the river imagistically parallel Billy Floyd's inconstancy. Even before she knows him well, she senses his unsettled nature. She learns quickly by watching Billy Floyd running free in the fields that she can know love but perhaps not for long. She senses that her time with him is as a "staving moment by the river" that would "reach its limit" (197).

Billy Floyd is love incarnate. When Jenny is in the presence of him, she knows that "clear love is in the world" (198), and she feels the "wound" of love after she has been near him and he departs. Then she laments that "Floyd was in the world" and wonders "what more love would be like" (205, 208). She thirsts for knowledge: "If she could find him now, or even find the place where he had last passed through, she would gain the next wisdom" (211). She is like Eve, the first female, in the Judeo-Christian tradition, who knew love.

Edenic references abound, and the story focuses on surrendering and resisting, or as Welty puts it, "unsurrendering" (185). Initially an innocent, Jenny is "too shy of the world" and remains securely within the bounds of her family home (180). As such, she may be another autobiographical creation. Welty describes herself in *One Writer's Beginnings* as a shy person who eventually plunges into life and love. So, too, does Jenny. The biographical details of Welty's life support this interpretation. She carefully guards the glass prisms, which hang "everywhere" in Jenny's house (181). They signify her initial, guarded state and portend her surrendering and unsurrendering.

Jenny's grandfather rules his household with a stern hand and forbids certain behaviors. He detests raving "as a force of Nature," and he insists that his daughter and granddaughter resist outbursts of temper. The grandfather's rules affect her. Jenny sees Billy Floyd in the post office but turns away because she recalls this rule: "when the postmaster had pointed his finger at her, she remembered that she was never to speak to Billy Floyd, by the order of her grandfather" (196). Upon meeting Floyd, she is "stiff and stern" and takes the "posture of a child who is appalled at the stillness and unsurrender of the still and unsurrendering world" (185). The rigidity of Jenny's body recalls a similar stance that Livvie takes at the moment before her surrender into motion, sexuality, and knowledge. The strictness and "glass prisms" of the household may be a reflection of Welty's childhood rearing under the watchful eye of a mother known for her firm opinions.

Jenny's fall occurs, and she knows "that her innocence had left her" (186). Her departure from her home includes her journey through the Mississippi swamp. As she leaves the town, it seems to acquire "a languor and a kind of beauty from the treatment of time and place." Welty's southern Eden is verdant and lush. In obvious symbolism Jenny walks with "passion flowers" all around her: "Pears lying on the ground warmed and soured, bees gathered at the figs, birds put their little holes of possession in each single fruit in the world that they could fly to. The scent of lilies rolled sweetly from their heavy cornucopias and trickled down by shady paths to fill the golden air of the valley. . . . Then green branches closed it over, and with her next step trumpet and muscadine vines and the great big-leaved vines made pillars about the trunks of the trees and arches and buttresses all among them. Passion flowers bloomed with their white and purple rays about her shoulders and under her feet. She walked on into the streaming hot shade of the wilderness, and put out her hands between the hanging vines. She feared the snakes in the sudden cool" (210, 212). The image of the snake is predictable in this Edenic scene. Even the grand mimosa tree tempts her in its fragrant "allurement": "There was an old mimosa closing the ravine—the ancient fern, as old as life, the tree shrank from the touch, grotesque in its tenderness. All nearness and darkness affected it, even clouds going by, but for Jenny that left it no tree ever gave such allurement of fragrance anywhere." Like the Tree of Knowledge from which Eve partakes, the mimosa and fern, "as old as life," beckon her to move forward through "time and place" in search of "the next wisdom" (211). When at the end of the story she smiles the "original smile," she reveals her experience with earthly love, in both its pleasure and pain.

Relinquishing her innocence, Jenny experiences love in a primal way. Twice Billy Floyd is described as "used and worldly" or "handled and used" (194). Welty also emphasizes his bestial nature. Following their love scene,

Jenny and Billy Floyd eat wild meat and partake of sheer primal existence: "She knew from him nevertheless that what people ate in the world was earth, river, wildness and litheness, fire and ashes. People took the fresh death and the hot fire into their mouths and got their own life" (201). The images here are carnal and elemental.

Fire, water, and air are typical motifs in Welty's love stories. The elements take on symbolic and abstract meanings. Jenny mimics Billy's wild, almost savage ways as she eats: "She ate greedily as long as he ate, and took what he took. She ate eagerly, looking up at him while her teeth bit, to show him herself, her proud hunger, as if to please and flatter him with her original and now lost starvation" (201–2). Billy has dark skin, is mistaken for a gypsy, and is known in town as "the wild man." He is Welty's Adam, but Billy has the blood of a Natchez Indian. Few people know his exact ancestry: "they had never been told quite who he was or where he had come from." The ladies of the town speculate about his origins (as often, it seems, as he walks by their houses), and like the Furies, they talk "as if they could take his life up into their fingers with their sewing and sew it or snip it on their laps" (207). His mask seems impenetrable, as does Jamie Lockhart's in *The Robber Bridegroom*. The ladies weave his heritage with their stories, and what captivates them most is his unfathomable identity.

Jenny's path, like that of her original ancestor, becomes increasingly hazardous the more she learns of love. Michael Kreyling observes, "Sorrow, distance, mystery, and separation" can be the "fate of each heart impelled toward love" (*Eudora Welty's Achievement of Order* 28), and he notes the "vital paradox" of love in this story. Garvin Davenport adds that "Jenny more than Livvie and certainly more than Josie, comes to understand the pain and the dangers of love as well as its limitations" (199). She becomes aware, Kreyling adds, of "the price exacted for following her lover's summons" (30). Jenny discovers what Livvie also understood about the sleeping Solomon: that "as she was living and inviolate, so of course was he" (188). Like Livvie, Jenny knows she cannot violate this ultimate distance between two individuals. She respects love and honors it, and she does not despair. She believes that "love might always be coming": "a great radiant energy spread intent upon her whole body and fastened her heart beneath its breath, and she would wonder almost aloud, 'ought I to sleep?' For it was love that might always be coming, and she must watch for it this time and clasp it back while it clasped, and while it held her never let it go" (205). Her anticipation that love "might always be coming" sustains her.

Jenny personifies love but disassociates herself from it, and from herself, in an effort to understand it: "But it was when love was of the one for the one that it seemed to hold all that was multitudinous and nothing was single any more. She had one love and that was all, but she dreamed that she lined up on both sides of the road to see her love come by in a procession. She herself was more people than there were people in The Landing, and her love was enough to pass through the whole night, never lifting the same face" (209–10). Perhaps allusive of Hawthorne and Joyce, Jenny's dream sees her "love come by in a procession" and her love as abundant enough to light all the faces there. In the moon, a common symbol of love in a Welty story, Jenny sees "its own changing and its mysteries of days and nights" (198). The moon continues to cast her into a thoughtful mood: "When she saw the moon come up that night and grow bright as it went above the flood and the boats in it, she was not as sorrowful as she might have been. . . . There was a need in all dreams for something to stay far, far away, never to torment with the rest, and the bright moon now was that" (202). Welty's editor once said to her, "You should always get your moon in the right part of the sky" (*One Writer's Beginnings* 11). Here the moon brings on the contemplative in Jenny and a sense of growing distance between the world of loving—and her.

At the end of the story Jenny endures what many have seen as multiple, or gang, rape. Ann Romines even suggests that Jenny "may or may not survive a gang rape" and sees the story as "ambitious and troubling as anything Welty ever wrote" (*Home Plot* 209–10). The rape that apparently occurs in the final scene of the story is somewhat unexpected. Some early images suggest breaking and pain, and possibly they foreshadow the final, troubling actions of this story. The last image that closes the story, however, describes Jenny with an "original smile." This point is most ambiguous and bears further analysis. That smile links Jenny with Eve and the "original sin" and suggests that she has participated in it. She seems to be emerging from it, although to what future is unclear. If she has participated in sex—the original sin—against her will, then the meaning of

Jenny's smile is even more unclear. If Jenny smiles because she somehow feels satisfaction, then perhaps she is thinking or imagining some positive outcome, despite what seems to be a chilling experience. A dark and violent event concludes the story, but her original smile connects Jenny with Eve, for whom sex led to pleasure and reproduction but with the loss of innocence and the addition of violence and drastic change. Jenny's smile may reconnect her with her earlier hopes and dreams and shield her against remorse and regret. Love "might always be coming."

As stories about poverty and love, "Death of a Traveling Salesman," "A Piece of News," and "The Wide Net" depict domestic, country settings in which, despite less than ideal economical conditions, marriages of hard work, pride, and attraction flourish. The couples in these stories are not sentimental or overly romantic. They find sustenance in rural life, even though they have few material possessions. They work together to make a home and family, and they take pride in the coming of a child. The characters have a sense of security, contentment, and deep satisfaction. With little need to verbalize their feelings, they are good caretakers of a home and of each other. Although the seemingly sophisticated, arrogant, Prufrockian city protagonist, the salesman, initially assesses country lives as unimportant, he eventually respects and longs for their simplicity. These country relationships offer more of value than he has found in his drafty hotel rooms.

Dark undercurrents of pain, violence, and tragedy lurk and swirl through the pages of the early stories too, however, and sometimes claim victims, as do the waters that claim Grady's father's life and the roiling flood that upsets Jenny's hopes for the future. While set primarily in rural areas or out of doors, "Livvie," "At the Landing," and "The Whistle" reveal anguish and loss that counterposes hopes, dreams, and wishes. Welty's country characters are survivors who cope with adversity and work through confrontations to reconciliation. The ancient communication can seem like a deep "conspiracy" to those who watch from afar, are alone, and cannot participate. The simple contentedness of country couples contrasts with a bitter aloneness, and Welty sets clear dualities: love can flourish, even in impoverished circumstances, but the power of "that simple thing"—a fruitful marriage—can remain elusive.

CHAPTER 2

"The Quiet Arcade of Identity"

Grief and Aloneness

In her essay on Katherine Anne Porter, Eudora Welty states emphatically that "we need to give and receive in loving kindness all the human warmth we can make" (*Eye* 40). For some of Welty's characters, however, this goal proves difficult to accomplish. She considers grief and heartbreak or lives in which sufficient human warmth is neither given nor received. For Welty the "dark side" can be grim, indeed. She depicts psychological pain, loss, longing for meaningful contact; some stories focus on pain, loss, death, grief, rape, and even murder. Danielle Pitavy-Souques has pointed out that the "truth of what it means to be an individual . . . involves suffering *and* language," and that language is often of pain (142). Welty's stories include those of sadness, solipsism, unwanted aloneness, despair, and suicide.

Not all of these stories have a tragic tone, however. Humorous accounts of dissatisfied lives, such as of Leota in "Petrified Man," focus on the desire for a more fulfilling existence and envy of others. Sister, in "Why I Live at the P.O.," is a funny, eccentric woman but one who finally must be counted among the lonely. Combining the tragic and comic for a profound effect is a signature of Welty's fiction; she is a master at incorporating both. In her more comic portraits, tragedy lurks perilously close at hand; in some stories, as the comedic recedes, tragedy comes to the fore. Pain or grief becomes palpable, as it does in Emily Dickinson's poems about the visceral experience of pain. The central characters in "Flowers for Marjorie" and "Clytie" have a sadness and instability that lead to murder in one case and suicide in the other. The need for human warmth may be an implied but unreachable ideal in Welty's stories of the dark side.

Clytie's fate is among the most profoundly disturbing of the portraits Welty created. This character loses the will to live and drowns herself. Others who show desolation or despair include the couple in "The Whistle," who endure the effects of deep poverty, and Mrs. Larkin in "A Curtain of Green," who finds little relief from her strenuous grieving—some relief eventually comes but only in losing consciousness as the rain shower touches her face in her garden. In the painful balance between loving and losing, Welty asks the most probing questions about life without love.

Love and death take full dramatic sympathy in "Clytie," "A Curtain of Green," and "Flowers for Marjorie," stories that pointedly explore the dark side of love and anticipate Welty's deep consideration of this topic in *The Optimist's Daughter*. Like Laurel Hand, who grapples with death and widowhood in that novel, Mrs. Larkin confronts desolation and isolation following the death of her spouse. Laurel's movement into the inner sanctum of her mother's sewing room parallels the spiritual journey begun by Mrs. Larkin's movement in the garden. Separation, stillness, and grief accompany her shift from marriage to widowhood. St. George Tucker Arnold sees this shift as one from "the union of fully mature lovers to the despair of personal meaninglessness" (58). Ruth Vande Kieft stresses that "these are the darkest mysteries that Miss Welty ever explores, for in no other stories does she confront her characters with all the terrors of chance and oblivion. . . . The stories tell us something about her philosophical vision . . . as pessimistic and existential" (*Eudora Welty* 32).

Mrs. Larkin's grief mirrors her alienation from the community. Her garden is a highly symbolic place with multiple layers of meaning that resonate within the story and beyond to other works and to Welty's life. The garden, "large" and "densely grown," with a border "high like a wall" (208), metaphorically represents Mrs. Larkin's psychic landscape and is a self-made, protective shield she creates to avoid intrusion into her physical and psychic space. Only memory can draw her through these barriers to the point of reliving the pain of her husband's death. In memory she can recall the moment almost as if it were in a theatrical scene. As the curtain draws back, she sees the accident in her mind's eye: "But memory tightened about her easily, without any prelude of warning or even despair. She would see promptly, as if a curtain had been jerked quite unceremoniously away from a little scene . . . the blue automobile in which her husband approached. . . . In the freedom of gaily turning her head, a motion she was now forced by memory to repeat as she hoed the ground, she could see again the tree that was going to fall" (210–11). The "little scene" before her, with the curtain "jerked" away, by fate, is tragedy and accident, and her memory forces her to turn her head repeatedly back to this dread moment in time. The scene lends an unrealistic quality to the moment. She finds it hard to believe that death could occur by accident. Work in the garden both shields her from her own thoughts and plunges her more deeply into memory of them. Garden work has a therapeutic function, however turbulent the soul may be. Gardening is a "preoccupation and a challenge" to her, and only in this "ceaseless activity" can she "cope" both with the overgrowth of plants and with her own emotions (209).

The story is in large part a biographical portrait of Eudora Welty's mother, Chestina Andrews Welty, whose garden work was often therapeutic for her and for Eudora. Biographer Suzanne Marrs has noted that this story "found its starting point in the depth of Mrs. Welty's love for her husband, in her abiding grief at his loss (a grief that loomed over a concerned daughter), in her intellectual and creative toughness, and in her inability to retreat into a mindlessly conventional consolation." Marrs adds: "After the death of her husband, Chestina Welty found solace in the creative work of gardening, not in the social display of the garden. With Eudora as her interested and committed 'yard man,' she worked long hours among her plant and flowers. . . . She found a creative activity. . . . Her work in the garden was not unlike Eudora Welty's work in fiction" (*One Writer's Imagination* 5–6).

Mrs. Larkin and the community are isolated from each other, as was Welty's mother as she became more reclusive. Marrs here, too, sees oblique references to Chestina Welty (*Eudora Welty* 60). The story has a biographical cast to it, including the prominence of Mrs. Larkin in town and the community respect accorded her. Larkin's Hill is named for Mrs. Larkin's husband's father (210, 211), but she is less active in the community, and she has become an object of curiosity. The neighbors spy on her and claim she never speaks at all anymore. In spite of her gardening skill, she never sends them flowers: "They might get sick and die, and she would never send a flower" (209). Her lack of participation in the time-honored tradition of the giving of flowers marks her as someone who has, in her grief, withdrawn from society and friendship. Society, in its fickle manner, withdraws from her in return.

Townsfolk know her "place in her garden," but they lose interest in her griefs and woes. They see where she is but then let her go: "At first . . . they had called upon the widow with decent frequency. But she had not appreciated it, they said to one another. Now, occasionally they looked down from their bedroom windows as they brushed studiously at their hair in the morning; they found her place in the garden, as they might have run their fingers toward a city on a map of a foreign country, located her from their distance almost in curiosity, and then forgot her" (210). Welty's comment is social criticism of those who abandon, forget, and lose patience with and interest in those who grieve too long, become withdrawn, and can no longer find the heart to socialize. Welty's mother may well have experienced some of these unforgiving societal pressures.

As Mrs. Larkin's world narrows, she becomes self-contained and is a fixture among her flowers. Several times the narrator describes her as immovable either because she cannot or will not extricate herself from memory and emotion: "this slanting, tangled garden, more and more over-abundant and confusing, must have become so familiar to Mrs. Larkin that quite possibly by now she was unable to conceive of any other place" (208). Like her flowers and plants, she resides with her memories. Welty would later describe memories of the dead in *The Optimist's Daughter* as "undisturbed and undisturbing." Memory will continue to be with her as she resides in her "quiet arcade of identity" (214). Her personality, much like that of Welty's mother, is strong, silent, stoic, and even in grief, uncompromising.

Welty's description of identity as an "arcade" deserves further note. Mrs. Larkin's grief is nonverbal and personal: it cannot be shared. The intense light of the sun fixes her image against the backdrop of the garden, like a scene in a fading photograph: "Now the intense light like a tweezers picked out her clumsy, small figure in its old pair of men's overalls rolled up at the sleeves and trousers, separated it from the thick leaves, and made it look strange and yellow as she worked with a hoe" (207). In her memory she replays the scene of her husband's accidental death, but each time she is powerless to save his life: "From her place on the front porch she had spoken in a soft voice to him, never so intimate as at that moment, 'You can't be hurt'" (211). Love, as Michael Kreyling has written, "is powerless to protect against death," which "threatens the very life of love" (*Eudora Welty's Achievement of Order* 13). Although she may wish to alter fate and "bring out from obliteration her protective words . . . so as to change the whole happening" (211), she knows she cannot. In fact, for a time she stops moving at all, not even to cultivate and thin her flowerbeds: "Mrs. Larkin rarely cut, separated, tied back. . . . To a certain extent, she seemed not to seek for order, but to allow an over-flowering" (209). Her gait, too, reflects her sense of helplessness; she has a "drooping, submissive walk" (213). Her burden weights on her "heavily."

Mrs. Larkin's psychic pain becomes more evident as the story proceeds. Repetition of the word *beat* indicates her building frustration, which almost impels her to strike her yard helper. The sun and rain alternately "beat down so heavily" upon her each day that her struggle is akin to the "inexhaustible" specter of oblivion. Like the rain that continues to "beat and fall" (215), her incessant hoeing continues to "beat down the juicy weeds" in an effort that Kreyling has called "retaliation" (*Eudora Welty's Achievement of Order* 13). When one day she faints in the garden, her hair is "beaten away from her forehead." These images reinforce Mrs. Larkin's resignation: "The day's work would be over in the garden. She would lie in bed, her arms tired at her sides and in motionless peace." She succumbs psychically "against that which was inexhaustible, there was no defense" (215).

Mrs. Larkin's physical activity—hoeing in her garden—is like the alternation and fluctuation of her thoughts and emotions. The motion of the hoe, swinging back and forth, focuses her, philosophically, on two poles—life and death—but even more pointedly on mortality, accident, and oblivion, on the one hand, and the unaccountability of fate, on the other: "so deeply did she know, from the effect of a man's danger and death, its cause in oblivion; and so helpless was she, too helpless to defy the workings of accident, of life and death, of unaccountability. . . . Life and death, she thought, gripping the heavy hoe, life and death, which now meant nothing to her but which she was compelled continually to wield with both her hands, ceaselessly asking, Was it not possible to compensate? to punish? to protest?" (213). Her philosophical reverie shows a nihilistic and irreligious vision that may link to Welty's own view or that of her mother. If oblivion is all that humankind may expect in the ultimate future, then danger and death have a finality from which it is impossible to recover. The passage may align Mrs. Larkin with Faulkner's Addie Bundren, whose "getting ready to stay dead a long time" suggests a dark resignation to fate without heaven. That Mrs. Larkin's physical and psychological activities occur in the garden reinforces Welty's focus on the natural world as an index of human emotion. Larkin comes to her conclusions there: life and death are ultimately inseparable; life, while it exists, is precious. Her deep emotions lead her to spare the innocent yard helper, Jamie, after she momentarily thought of killing him. Michael Kreyling summarizes effectively that "this is the world, accident and love, life and death; and although these are antithetical, their coexistence is not unnatural" (*Eudora Welty's Achievement of Order* 14).

Emotional movement commences for Mrs. Larkin only when she comes out of her psychological self-absorption and feels tenderness toward another human being (214). She finds some relief but only in a loss of consciousness when she faints and also by the natural action of rain. As is so characteristic of a Welty love story—albeit in this case a sad one—the natural world responds empathetically, and the widow who cerebrates too much but cannot cry feels the shower of the warm rain on her face. The earth weeps on her behalf. Arnold sees her as joining with "the Great Mother of all life" (58). Vande Kieft posits: "No rational answer comes to Mrs. Larkin. There is only release, touched off by the sudden fall of a retarded rain," which triggers in her "a blissful surrender to the mystery of nature, to the inevitable" (*Eudora Welty* 30). Abandoned in the conclusion of the story even by Jamie, who runs away from her, Mrs. Larkin can only arise to continue her solitary life. The garden has offered some relief and consolation. Mrs. Chestina Welty's garden, in which she spent much time, must have been a similar place for the working of hands, thoughts, and feelings after the death of her husband, Eudora Welty's father.

A Dark Rose for "Marjorie"

"Flowers for Marjorie" is one of Welty's most grim and disturbing stories, in which murder occurs where love should flourish and death is a consequence of the ending of love. The story in some ways resembles Faulkner's "A Rose for Emily" in its focus on murder and roses that should have been a gift. Both stories feature a murder and a rose motif, but in this story the victim is a woman. In Faulkner's the reverse is true.

This story concerns pregnancy and the male reaction. Similar to "Where Is the Voice Coming From," Welty explores the psychological portrait of the murderer. She centers the consciousness of the story in the mind of one who takes the life of another, and she shows the emotional turmoil that builds toward an act of violence. Structurally, this story shares some similarities with "The Wide Net" in its portrayal of a young marriage and forthcoming pregnancy. Both stories consider what Daniel Curley sees as the "quiet security of [the] pregnant wife," in which the woman is "concerned with the inner world of her pregnancy" (221). One story ends happily, however, and the other tragically.

The inwardness of the pregnant woman alienates the male and precipitates his sense of rejection in "Flowers for Marjorie": "Her fullness seemed never to have touched his body. Away at his distance, backed against the wall, he regarded her world of sureness and fruitfulness and comfort, grown forever apart, safe and hopeful in pregnancy, as if he thought it strange that this world, too, should not suffer" (195). "Backed against the wall," by joblessness and hunger, Howard becomes desperate; he is unable to find work and is saddled with the increasing responsibilities of supporting his growing family. He battles despondency in the face of failure. He loses the battle with his own emotions and lashes out at the person closest to him: he stabs his uncomprehending wife below the breast. She dies quietly, without speaking a word, and retains a serene pose, seated near the windowsill. The red blood first spills into her "open hand" and then pools in her "lap" which is "like a bowl." In "The Wide Net" the expectant couple seems to reconcile at the end of the story, but here the reverse is true. The finale is desperation and murder.

"Flowers for Marjorie" is a tragic counterpart to Welty's lighter, comic stories, antithetical to the love story and illustrative of what Welty calls the dark side of love. The images that usually suggest love—a spray of roses, a love song, pictures of embracing couples—here are grim reminders of the obverse. After he kills his wife, Howard walks through the city. Reminders of love are everywhere. He spies a contraption made of a bulb and long tube entitled "Palpitator—the Imitation Heart. Show her you Love her" in a store window (197). Ironically, the gadget mocks the fate of this marriage as well as Howard's anger and frustration that have centered on his wife. On the subway train Howard sees advertisements picturing "many couples embracing and smiling," and a beggar sings "Let Me Call You Sweetheart" in return for a handout (198).

The rose carries symbolic meaning for this story. The "flowers" of the title are the first suggestion of traditional love, and the rose might predictably have been the flower that the loving husband would give to his expectant wife. Howard wins roses by chance for becoming "the ten millionth person to enter Radio City" (200), but he is in no position to consider traditional ideas of romance. He is an unemployed and starving person and even crazed perhaps by hunger. He can think of his wife only as a burden that cannot be borne much longer, and indeed, he has murdered her before the story reaches midpoint. The roses are a haunting reminder of the marriage that might have been. The ads he has seen of lovers embracing only taunt this husband, whose emotions have turned violent and for whom romantic love is now gone. The beggar's song, "Let Me Call You Sweetheart," is the final sardonic note in the story. The beggar must leave empty-handed.

Roses take on more prominence and deeper significance at the end of the story. Howard returns home after the murder and his subsequent lengthy walk through town: "Then the roses gave out deep waves of fragrance" (184). The senses again predominate. The roses are now deeply linked with Marjorie—with her person and with a dream of happiness that might have been. Her death has occurred, yet she is still present; her body is still stationed in the windowsill. Before Howard alerts the policeman to the dead woman upstairs, implicating himself, he first buries his "eyes, nose, and mouth" in the rose bouquet. His gesture of sense, smell, touch, and perhaps even taste of the roses recognizes the physicality of his wife, her body, the body of their unborn child, and their life's blood. His act is a farewell and perhaps an unconscious acknowledgment of lost romanticism as he pays a last homage to the emotional wants and needs that have been unfulfilled and relinquished. He is "embarrassed to be asking anything of a policeman and to be holding such beautiful flowers" (185). The roses are his last physical link to Marjorie. He grasps them now but must soon release them—permanently.

The red rose petals, reminders of Marjorie's spilled blood, pooled on her lap, now splatter on Howard's clothing. The policeman notices Howard's stained clothing and draws the conclusion: "And I don't suppose the red drops on your pants are rose petals, are they?" Howard will drop the bouquet, mindlessly, on the sidewalk: "When the roses slid from Howard's fingers and fell on their heads all along the sidewalk, the little girls ran stealthily up and put them in their hair" (185). As the story draws to a close, the rose image retains prominence. The roses that "fell on their heads" are turned upside down, like the difficult mental state of Howard and the ruined life of Marjorie and their child. That the little neighborhood girls run "stealthily" up and put roses in their hair is a sad reminder of what other children are doing, amid the griefs of the adult world. Welty has other stories and one novel that end with a focus on children. The freshness and innocence with which they approach imagination, play, and pretending is contrapuntal to the dire circumstances going on in the apartment above their heads. As the policeman leads Howard upstairs to confront the adult truth of his wife's death, the girls outside decorate their hair with the carelessness of innocence, if not their hope for the future, that rose petals can bring.

"As Pink and Crowded as an Old-Fashioned Rose": Hope in "The Key"

Other stories in the early volumes also depict characters for whom love is elusive and sad. By the persistence and intensity of their search, they underscore Welty's sense that love is valuable in human life. By virtue of its absence or of deep complications of finding it, love for these characters is deeply valuable indeed. "The Key" depicts a strained marriage between two people who are also handicapped by deafness. At once the deafness links and victimizes the couple. Unlike the others around them in the train station (and elsewhere), Ellie and Albert Morgan have shielded one another from isolation and loneliness. While they may not have married for love and were drawn together by their common disability, each still hopes to fall in love: "Maybe when we reach Niagara Falls we will even fall in love, the way other people have done. Maybe our marriage was really for love, after all, not for the other reason—both of us being afflicted in the same way, unable to speak, lonely because of that. . . . You can take hope" (60).

Daniel Curley has pointed to Niagara Falls in this story as "the great marriage symbol" (210): "They had told her when she was a little girl how people who have just been married have the custom of going to Niagara Falls on a wedding trip, to start their happiness; and that came to be where she put her hope, all of it. So she saved money. She worked harder than he did, you could observe, comparing their hands, good and bad years, more than was good for a woman. Year after year she had put her hope ahead of her" (68). Niagara Falls symbolizes all the "hope ahead of her."

Ellie and Albert have contrasting ideals. Ellie, as Curley says, is eager "to capture happiness" (210), but she conceives of it, much as Jamie Lockhart does early in *The Robber Bridegroom*, as something "for later and for further away" (87). Albert's hopes are simpler. He wants a peaceful marriage in which Ellie does not talk as much or worry, and the sky, in a bed image characteristic of Welty's love stories, is "like a coverlet." His vision of happiness involves placid, rural domesticity: "an uneventful day on the farm—chores attended to by a woman working in the house, you in the field, crop growing, as well as can be expected, the cow giving, and the sky like a coverlet over it all—so that you're as full of yourself as a colt, in need of nothing, and nothing you" (65–66). For Albert happiness is vital: "But happiness, Albert knew, is something that appears to you suddenly, that is meant for you, a thing which you reach for and pick up and hide at your breast, a shiny thing that reminds you of something alive and leaping" (66). His focus on the vitality of happiness—as "alive and leaping"— suggests his desire for an emotional charge that will leave him vibrant "as a colt" and "in need of nothing" (66).

The rose image here indicates the physical differences between the two of them: Ellie is "a large woman with a face as pink and crowded as an old-fashioned rose." Albert is small and "effaced" by comparison (56). Images of fullness and emptiness, noise and silence, and solidity and the ephemeral, illustrate the emotional poles of the characters and the irresolvable tension between their satisfaction and dissatisfaction. Ellie's purse, repository of all she has saved, also leads to further description of her size and shape: "One of those black satchel purses hung over her straight, strong wrist. It must have been her savings which were making possible this trip. And to what place? you wondered, for she sat there as tense and solid as a cube" (56). Ellie's tension, no doubt, is a result of her desire for romantic love—and her worry that it will not develop after all.

The key represents Albert's potential for realizing his dream but complicates rather than resolves the conflict between the couple. A red-haired man who drops a key adds to the dichotomous portrait: "his intensity . . . seemed to have impressed the imagination with a shadow of itself, a blackness together with the light, the negative beside the positive." His life has both "his joy and his despair," a "fullness and the emptiness" (62). Later this mysterious man's wildness, restlessness, weariness, and searching further mirror the vague discontent of Ellie and Albert. Louise Gossett argues: "By means of the key . . . Welty sensitively indicates that he wishes to be set apart from his wife, to enjoy 'the secret and proper separation that lies between a man and a woman'" (*Violence* 105). Alfred Appel observes: "Even if a shared isolation forces or draws them together, people must still be able to keep their secret key—in whatever form it may take" (19).

Noise and silence further suggest the incompatibility of the couple, the fine distinctions the hearing people can make and the silence that the deaf endure, even as they may increase their senses in feeling and seeing. The story opens with aural imagery and a focus on the raw night sounds of insects, which will later appear imagistically depicted as paralyzed in "amber": "It was quiet in the waiting room of the remote little station, except for the night sounds of insects. You could hear their embroidering movements in the weeds outside, which somehow gave the effect of some tenuous voice in the night, telling a story. Or you could listen to the fat thudding of the light bugs and the hoarse rushing of their big wings against the wooden ceiling" (55). The room is so quiet that the key makes a sound when it falls. The sound irritates the hearing people in the train station and simultaneously calls attention to the deafness of the couple; they do not hear the key drop to the floor, even though it makes a "fierce metallic sound": "Everyone, except Albert and Ellie Morgan, looked up for a moment. On the floor the key had made a fierce metallic sound like a challenge, a sound of seriousness. It almost made people jump. It was regarded as an insult, a very personal question, in the quiet peaceful room where the insects were tapping at the ceiling and each person was allowed to sit among his possessions and wait for an unquestioned departure. Little walls of reproach went up about them all" (58).

The couple also does not hear the call for the train departure. If the train to Niagara Falls represents the potential for love between Ellie and Albert, the chance is lost, for the train "noiselessly" leaves without them. The "moment of hope" is "killed" and preserved "like an insect in amber" (61). The silence and the "hoarse rushing" of the insects reflect the two married partners: one worships the peacefulness of silence; the other needs talk and desires a reply. Even though the key may signify momentary distraction, if not hope for their separate dreams, the red-haired man who watches them compassionately from across the room realizes the "uselessness" of giving them the key. The story amplifies earlier themes in Welty's work on the separateness of individual identity and the elusiveness of knowing the consciousness of another. Hope though they may for a romantic life, these individuals cannot understand each other's dreams.

"Rosy like These Flames": Imagination and Madness in "Clytie"

Although some of Welty's characters survive a life of physical and emotional drifting, one of Welty's loneliest characters—Clytie—does not. Welty described her own impetus in writing the story in a 1978 interview with Jan Gretlund: "I have seen here and there a family going to seed right in the public eye. These things exist in life; of course, Faulkner saw the same kind of thing in Oxford" (quoted in *Conversations* 221). "Clytie" and "A Curtain of Green"—and Faulkner's "A Rose for Emily"—share some important features. The town name in the two Welty stories honors their old and respected families: "Larkin's Hill" and "Farr's Gin." The citizens of these towns formerly admired but now pity the protagonists. A symbolic remainder of Clytie's once grand and wealthy lifestyle, the diamond cornucopia pin that she wears on her black dress, like her house itself, suggests the disparity and incongruity of the former Farr wealth and present poverty (151). No one speaks to Clytie anymore, and in a similar manner the community has once observed but now forgotten Mrs. Larkin. The women resemble each other in appearance, though not in age. Welty, who chooses words with extraordinary precision and deliberation, selects the same adjective to describe their outward appearance: *disreputable* (170, 210).

Others also have seen this story as a somber one. Louise Gossett sees it as "an elegy for love," and the story does end in suicide, so *elegy* seems appropriate (*Violence* 107). Alun Jones writes of "Clytie" that "Welty reserves her deepest compassion for those who recognize their need for love but are refused—as in the pathetic story of Clytie in *A Curtain of Green,* trapped in a house of lonely and demanding selfishness, who finds release from the sufferings of her absurd, unlovely and unloved life in the companionship of death. . . . Only Clytie goes out, pathetically wandering in the rain and searching for a world of love which she associates faintly with her youth" ("World of Love" 178).

Like Mrs. Larkin, Clytie finds her resolution in the natural world. One woman faints in the garden; the other, although she unfortunately drowns in the rain barrel, describes it as her "friend," and the images are of the natural—the rain barrel is "fragrant" with the scent of "ice and flowers and the dew of night" (170). The rain drenches Clytie's hat so that it looks "absurd and done for" (160), and it also "beats" Mrs. Larkin's hair and face. Both women are "done for" in various ways. They sense the presence of the natural world even as they are suffering. Clytie dies of loneliness; Mrs. Larkin endures a metaphorical death of grief.

Judgment, a frequent Welty theme, appears again as Clytie's psychological condition veers toward madness. As her perspective warps, she loses her bearings. Her myopia is tantamount to her failing ability to judge herself or others accurately. She cannot "see who it was" now when she goes out walking and people pass by. Her sister Octavia tends toward paranoia, and she also cannot distinguish between friends and traitors. Clytie dreams of trust and peacefulness, but she does not locate either in the world around her. Like Faulkner and his suicidal Quentin Compson in *The Sound and the Fury,* Welty's Clytie descends into mental distraction: "[Some] dream was resumed. In the street she had been thinking about the face of a child she had just seen. The child . . . had looked at her with such an open, serene, trusting expression as she passed by! With this small, peaceful face still in her mind, rosy like these flames, like an inspiration which drives all other thoughts away, Clytie had forgotten herself and had been obliged to stand where she was in the middle of the road. But the rain had come down, and someone had shouted to her, and she had not been able to reach the end of her meditations" (170). The "rosy flames" of her imagination lead Clytie to intense reverie, but all too soon a sharper reality intrudes. She cannot accept what Ruth Vande Kieft calls "the ghastly disparity between what she once was and ought to have been (the loving, laughing creature of her youth) and what she has become (ugly, warped, inverted)" (*Eudora Welty* 40). Her imagination leads her to an ultimate reverie—that of her own reflection in the rain barrel.

Clytie's brother Gerald has retained memories of lost love. Although Clytie is an "old maid" (157), Gerald once was married, and his memories and thinking about what went wrong paralyzes him spiritually, just as a severe stroke physically immobilizes their father. Clearly deranged, Gerald recounts the circumstances that forced his wife to leave him: "Rosemary— she had given up a job in the next town, just to marry him. How had it happened that she had left him so soon? It meant nothing that he had threatened time and again to shoot her, it was nothing at all that he had pointed the gun against her breast. She had not understood. It was only that he had relished his contentment. He had only wanted to play with her. In a way he had wanted to show her that he loved her above life and death" (162).

In his crazed rationale Gerald sees his love for Rosemary as a spiritual one that transcends the boundaries of life and death. His version of love, however, cannot support or sustain a realistic relationship or preserve it. Incapable of accurately judging the world around him, Gerald believes, when he hears the barber running out past his door, that the footsteps belong to Clytie's lovers: "Where do you keep your men?" he taunts. "Do you have to bring them home?" (170). Gerald's suggestion that Clytie is promiscuous insults her partly because it is the ironic inverse of her social status: she is completely isolated from everyone.

The only man Clytie does approach, besides those in her family, proves so repulsive to her that she recoils violently. Mr. Bobo, the barber who shaves her father's face, stands so close to Clytie in the hallway that she touches him once: "The terrible scent of bay rum, of hair tonic, the horrible moist scratch of an invisible beard, the dense, popping green eyes—what had she got hold of with her hand! She could hardly bear it—the thought of that face" (170). This face, along with the others, in a story about the unreachable and inscrutable face of humanity, becomes threatening rather than trusting for Clytie.

Ultimately, Clytie trusts only one face—her own—but seeks comfort in the "featureless" version she sees when she looks into the rain barrel. She saw a child in the street whose face seemed to encourage peace, and in her own visage she finds it now. In some ways like Mrs. Larkin, whose troubles ease with pelting raindrops, Clytie finds relief from her psychic burdens in water: "She bent her angular body further, and thrust her head into the barrel, under the water, through its glittering surface into the kind, featureless depth, and held it there" (171). Welty would later return to this haunting image of a face held beneath water, with almost verbatim language, but metaphorically, in *The Optimist's Daughter*, in the description of Judge McKelva's face at the moment of his death: "as if he had laid it under the surface of dark pouring water and held it there" (33).

Clytie's featurelessness in water, in a story of people and their faces that could have offered her a modicum of solace, kindness, or hope but did not, beckons her toward the oblivion to which she silently delivers herself. The calm and beckoning rain barrel waters extinguish the "rosy flames" of her imagination.

Here are the stories of the other side—the bitter end of a relationship, the dashed hopes for a relationship that cannot come to be, the loss of a cherished loved one to death, the jealous murder of a pregnant wife, the crushing aloneness that only suicide seems to alleviate. For one who championed receiving "in loving kindness all the human warmth we can make," Eudora Welty nonetheless realized, intellectually and personally, that this goal is sometimes impossible to achieve. Unafraid to grapple with tragedy and the raw psychological pain it invokes, sometimes along with bloodshed and often with tears, Welty depicted grief, death, and psychological tension with the same and powerful and perceptive clarity that is characteristic of her approach to fiction. With sympathy and close, intense scrutiny, she considered the dark side of love.

CHAPTER 3

"Like a Rose Forced into Premature Bloom"

Dreaming and Telling in "A Memory"

Welty stories usually consider love in dramatic terms. Loneliness emerges early as a theme, and characters come into the reaches of society and interact with it. Welty's early forays into the subjects of lovelessness, loneliness, and the solitary life include stories that depict the emotional cost of losing, the search for caring, and a keen anticipation of love. Mrs. Larkin and Clytie feel the effects of a community that is distant in their hour of need, and in "Asphodel," "Lily Daw and the Three Ladies," "Petrified Man," and "Why I Live at the P.O." Welty approaches the obverse—in which a community can intrude in ways that are less beneficial to an individual. Families, large and small, close or extended; packs of bandits; or a small circle of good friends can support, denounce, ignore, harm, or rescue the individuals or those who are in relationships. Welty's long-ranging dialectic between the value of privacy and the importance of communal life continue over time and reemerge in her later works as well. The conclusions she draws are complicated.

"A Memory" and "The Winds" depict young women seeking to know or understand love. The protagonist's first feeling of love is the topic in "A Memory," but like the adult male narrator who reflects on his youth in James Joyce's "Araby," Welty's presents an older, wiser narrator female reflecting on her past. Nonetheless, both stories reflect on the theme of the "foolish blood" of adolescence and the misjudgments of a young ego "driven and derided by vanity" (Joyce 35).

Judgment and misjudgment resurface as key themes to emphasize the narrator's youthful experience in "A Memory." The perspective she gains in her painting lessons make more accurate her delineating and reflecting on her other experiences: "Ever since I had begun taking painting lessons, I had made small frames with my fingers, to look out at everything." The narrator's judgment is the central focus. She sees people and landscapes with the painter's eye, or with Welty's autobiographical sense, the photographer's frame: "From my position I was looking at a rectangle brightly lit, actually glaring at me, with sun, sand, water, a little pavilion, a few solitary people in fixed attitudes, and around it all a border of dark rounded oak trees, like the engraved thunderclouds surrounding illustrations in the Bible" (143).

This perspective has not affected the narrator's "austere," judgmental stance about the world, however: "I was at an age when I formed a judgment upon every person and every event which came under my eye," she recalls, naively insisting upon the absolute conformity of others with her own opinions and judgments: "When a person, or a happening, seemed to me not in keeping with my opinion, or even my hope or expectation, I was terrified by a vision of abandonment and wildness which tore my heart with a kind of sorrow." In such a state of "heightened" fear and wildness —panic—the girl's judgments are faulty: "from the smallest gesture of a stranger I would wrest what was to me a communication or a presentiment" (143). Encountering love for the first time falls prey to the problem of her erroneous judgment. She recognizes love immediately but continues to require "absolute conformity to my ideas in any happening I witnessed" (144).

Only experience, Alun Jones concludes, will finally "disorder her dream" ("World of Love" 102). Barbara Fialkowski sees "A Memory" as a story "of adolescence, for the young girl is in love from a distance with a young boy in her class" (68). Gary Carson adds: "The accidental touching of a schoolboy's hand" causes the young girl to transform the moment into one of "an ideal romantic love. . . . This transcendental union, limited to her own imagination, is a means of escaping her loneliness and attaining a personal sense of protection and inviolate purity in the face of a threatening natural and social world outside the self" (423). Chester Eisinger, on the other hand, views the story as an "exercise in aesthetics in which Welty is engaged in nothing more or less than framing contrasting pictures" (10). Ruth Vande Kieft notes that the young protagonist has a "premonition" that "there is for human beings no dignity nor identity, that beyond the chaos of matter lies oblivion, total meaningless" (*Eudora Welty* 28).

The narrator's parents realize that self-centeredness characterizes her perceptions of the world around her, but they are astonished at her imaginings and prescience. This passage, too, is almost certainly autobiographical, especially in the depiction of the concerned and observant parents and in the garden trellis, a notable feature of the Welty garden at home in Jackson, Mississippi: "My father and mother, who believed that I saw nothing in the world which was not strictly coaxed into place like a vine on our garden trellis to be presented to my eyes, would have been badly concerned if they had guessed how frequently the weak and inferior and strangely turned examples of what was to come showed themselves to me" (144). Welty may be describing her own parents' attempts to "coax" into place the contents of their daughter's fertile imagination, without much success on their part.

The narrator's presuppositions about love meet a challenge at the beach. In her typical way the female narrator judges them by her own standards, which are highly idealized and askew. Unlike her vision of love, which "would swell with a sudden and overwhelming beauty, like a rose forced into premature bloom for a great occasion" (145), the sight she encounters on the beach is not one of beauty.

The rose image is evocative because it is "forced into premature bloom." The technique of "forcing" roses is one that rose gardeners know well. In employing this strategy, these gardeners give roses the exact environment they need to bloom indoors, or early, even though the season or certain outside conditions would not otherwise permit it. Forcing roses might take place to have blooms for a specific occasion. The blooms do not last, however. They will wither shortly.

Welty metaphorically compares the narrator's immaturity and skewed perspectives on love and other matters to the "overwhelming beauty" of a rose but one that is "forced," or pushed, to grow sooner than anticipated. The sights of the bathers at the beach come into diametrical opposition to the narrator's established views and aesthetics of perfection, symbolized by the "sudden and overwhelming beauty" of the forced rose. The narrator's view of love swells magnificently, like the rose, but will fade in compromise once she begins to understand and accept a more reasonable and normal approach to life.

Scholars have variously commented on the beach scene. Vande Kieft says "the family group of bathers" is "vulgar" (*Eudora Welty* 28). Fialkowski describes them as the "sensual and the sensual is ugly" (68). Ruth Ann Lief adds: "In the dual role of dreamer and observer, she juxtaposes the memory of her only physical contact with the boy she loves to the vulgar sex-play of the people she sees on the beach. . . . they reveal to her in its commonest version . . . a dimension of love which is still mysterious to her" (346).

Love does not conform to the narrator's naive conceptions, which are too abstract and platonic. She must force herself into greater understanding, like the altered rose in bloom. She must shift her view to accept the impurities she has dreaded discovering. When the boy of her early affections has a nosebleed in class, she empathizes with him but nonetheless faints from the shock. This action is the first vulgarization of her ideal. Her love is a boy with a bleeding nose. The second is the accommodation she must make in viewing the bathers. They initially disgust her in their abhorrent physicality. One of the little boys on the beach is "greatly overgrown," with cheeks that "ballooned outward and hid his eyes"; the others lie on the beach in "leglike confusion" (147); fat hangs upon the arms of the woman "like an arrested earthslide on a hill," and her breasts are "heavy and widening like pears" (148). The narrator feels repulsion at these irregular forms of humanity. She likens the smile of the man to a panting dog. From her angle the bathers seem "resigned to each other's daring and ugliness" (149). Even when she closes her eyes in condescension and avoidance, she still can hear their bodies: "I could hear also the thud and the fat impact of all their ugly bodies upon one another"; she feels "victimized" by their very presence on the beach as by "the ravages of a storm" (151).

The bathers further shatter the young girl's idealized views. After she sees them, she has trouble recalling her earlier idealizations, and by the conclusion of the story the mental images of bathers are in the forefront of her mind. Like the metaphorical rose, she is now forced to incorporate their images into her former, naive conceptions: "I could imagine the boy I loved walking into a classroom, where I would watch him with this hour on the beach accompanying my recovered dream and added to my love" (151). Experience, however, now alters her judgment. She now "adds" an "accompanying" version of love to her original one. This alteration is subtle but crucial in tempering her initial impression of love, which is inevitably "solitary and unprotected" from time and maturation but which lives like a framed photograph in the memory. Welty's story shows that overly idealistic love is the kind Shakespeare warned against in his sonnet, the kind that "alters when it alteration finds."[1] Realistic attitudes prevail, and judgment, perception, and increased knowledge become more accurate and mature. The young protagonist—like "a rose forced into premature bloom"—has had an unexpected flowering.

"Its Own Secret Pleasure": Longing in "The Winds"

> *Elaine Wolff to Eudora Welty:* "You should write a story about a tornado."
> *Eudora Welty to Elaine Wolff:* "I did."[2]

Expectant youth seeking love is a prominent theme in "The Winds." Although Josie has some premonitions of future love, for much of the story she naively avoids the topic. Sheltered in the house of her parents and protected by her father's embrace, Josie imagines for a moment what the "big girls" are doing on their hayride. Swiftly, however, her thoughts return to her childish games.

Games and fairy tales suggest that Josie has not yet achieved a "metamorphosis" from child to mature woman, to use Michael Kreyling's term (*Eudora Welty's Achievement of Order* 27). Against the background voices of "the pitch of their delight" of the hayriders, the young protagonist yearns for summertime with its "monkey-man" and his organ, accompanied by the "circle of following children," of which she is one (114, 120). She looks for "signs of the fairies," and she and her brother build an elaborate sand castle in which their imagined queen resides. The rite they perform for imagined entry into the castle presents love in storybook rhetoric: "I am thine eternally, my Queen, and will serve thee always and I will be enchanted with thy love forever" (121). Other activities and games the brother and sister play include digging a hole to China (139); crafting a boat out of a shoe box and pretending that it sails the nights, candlelit through tissue paper windows (133); eating a banana rapidly in a race without breathing (126); singing children's rhymes such as "London Bridge" (132); and playing a "stately game" by the flowering hedge called "Here comes the duke a-riding, riding, riding" (131). Josie speaks to Cornella, a maturer girl who lives across the way, in a chant that recalls the fairy tale of Rapunzel: "Cornella, Cornella, let down thy hair, and the King's son will come climbing up" (124). Josie's imaginative childhood and fairy tale draw to a close when summer ends but linger in her dreams and memory. She wishes for the richness of this time of year to be extended: "It kept her from eating her dinner to think of all that she had caught or meant to catch before the time was gone" (125). She did not have sufficient time to enjoy the summer and all that it implies.

The moon again carries romantic implications. In what seems a precursor to her autobiographical account in *One Writer's Beginnings* of first becoming aware of the roundness of the moon, Josie's fascination with the moon suggests her desire to know and experience love: "Above everything in the misty blue dome of the sky was the full white moon. So it is, for a true thing, round, she thought . . . words in her thoughts came shaped like grapes in her throat. She felt lonely . . . 'Did you know the moon was round?' 'I did. Annie told me last summer.' . . . But I must find out everything about the moon, Josie thought in the solemnity of evening." The rising and falling of the ocean tides, governed by the moon, become metaphors for the rising and falling of her emotions and the condition of her heart and mind: "The moon and tides. O moon! O tides! I ask thee. I ask thee. Where dost thou rise and fall? As if it were this knowledge which she would allow to enter her heart, for which she had been keeping room, and as if it were the moon, known to be round, that would go floating through her dreams forever and never leave her, she looked steadily up at the moon. The moon looked down at her, full with all the lonely time to go" (133). This passage and the song "Beautiful Ohio," which crosses Josie's mind while she rests in her father's arms, prefigure the focus on Ohio, the place of Welty's father's birth, in *The Optimist's Daughter* and *One Writer's Beginnings* and link the story to Welty's autobiographical writing.

The moment that draws Josie the closest to passion occurs when her family goes to the Chautauqua to hear a trio playing chamber music. The performance moves her, and phallic imagery suggests that the time of "waiting" may be diminishing: "If morning-glories had come out of the horn instead of those sounds, Josie would not have felt a more astonished delight. She was pierced with pleasure. . . . Between herself and the lifted cornet there was no barrier, there was only the stale, expectant air of the old shelter of the tent. The cornetist was beautiful. . . . Josie listened in mounting care and suspense, as if the performance led in some direction away—as if a destination were being shown her. . . . and it seemed to her that a proclamation had been made in the last high note of the lady trumpeteer when her face had become set in its passion, and that after that there would be no more waiting and no more time left for the one who did not take heed and follow" (136–38).

Even though she feels "panic" at the "thought of the future" (134), Josie seeks through her friend Cornella to know vicariously "the secret and the punishment of the world" (125), and she fully intends to experience someday "all that was wild and beloved and estranged" (139). She is like the author of the love note Josie finds in the street, impatient to know the "When? When? When?" of love (140). Her predicament is impatience in waiting for love to arrive. Welty offers her own account of similar childhood curiosity:

> From the first I was clamorous to learn—I wanted to know and begged to be told not so much what, or how, or why, or where, as when. How soon?
>
> *Pear tree by the garden gate,*
> *How much longer must I wait?*
>
> This rhyme from one of my nursery books was the one that spoke for me. But I lived not at all unhappily in this craving, for my wild curiosity was in large part suspense, which carries its own secret pleasure. (*One Writer's Beginnings* 22)

Welty asks "how much longer must I wait?" and her character Josie also longs for a time when "there would be no more waiting" (138).

"Lily Daw and the Three Ladies"

Few of Welty's characters exist in a social vacuum. Those who know love generally operate in a community that can be supportive, indifferent, or intrusive. Shelley Fairchild points to the need for privacy in *Delta Wedding* when she says, "We live most privately just when things are most crowded, like in the Delta, like for a wedding" (85). Edna Earle calls outsiders "the wrong element" in *The Ponder Heart* and takes pride in her family's exclusiveness (13). The potentially destructive actions of those outside the immediate sphere of the family unit can occur. In *Losing Battles,* for example, Julia Mortimer's accusations that the newlyweds Jack and Gloria are illegally married becomes a threatening problem that the young couple has to face. Welty's characters dodge, embrace, or balance their public and private needs and responsibilities to achieve an acceptable distance from and interaction with the society around them.

Centers of communality such as the general store, the beauty parlor, perhaps even the train depot, and especially the post office figure centrally in Welty's stories of love in relation to society. Members of the community exchange information in the form of news sharing, or gossip, which can compensate on some level for other social vacuums. Occasions that draw together large crowds, such as weddings, funerals, or unusual town events, such as the dragging of a river or a homecoming, provide opportunities for characters to focus upon the love they see around them and to talk about it. Busybodies and gossips are usually Welty's opportunity for comic portraiture. By talking about love and sex, they live vicariously or harmlessly ventilate their emotions.

Love in relation to society is a central focus in "Lily Daw and the Three Ladies." Reputation and respectability as forged by societal intrusion affect the private affairs of love. Michael Kreyling has seen "Lily Daw" as a story about "strife between self, which desires its own freedom and an unobstructed path towards it, and society, which demands conformity and surrender of the self for the common good, the single straight and narrow path" (*Eudora Welty's Achievement of Order* 7). Societal issues come to the fore almost immediately. Even before they know of her plans to get married, the three ladies of the town of Victory plot the fate of Lily Daw without her knowledge or consent. Ruth Weston theorizes that "through the motion of three figures around Lily, we are drawn into the scene, to Lily, as by the line of perspective in a painting. The description of Lily as small, as compared with the larger figures who loom threateningly over her, contributes to our heightened sense throughout the story of her oblique perspective below the level of and from the midst of the circling ladies" ("American Folk Art" 8–9). These ladies take on a communal responsibility for Lily because she "wasn't bright" and because her father tried to abuse and even kill her (4).

With settings of community socializing—the post office, beauty shop, and train station—this story contrasts the community vision of Lily's happiness with that of her own. Concern for Lily's reputation, and fear that she will become pregnant, compel the three ladies to hasten Lily's departure to the Ellisville Institute for the Feeble-Minded. Lily's freedom is indeed compromised and subsumed as the social mores carry the day. Compared with the advantages a marriage, even with a traveling musician, might bring to Lily's life, the choice of life at Ellisville is grim indeed.

Lily has met a man who proposed marriage. One lady duly reports that Lily stared at this man, a xylophone player in the traveling tent show, during the entire performance: Lily "didn't turn her head to the right or to the left the whole time" (4). The ladies in Lily's community still find the idea of a lover—and the possibility of a happy life with him—incomprehensible:

> Lily bit her lip and began to smile. She reached into the trunk and held up both cakes of soap and wagged them.
>
> "Tell us," challenged Mrs. Watts. "Who you're going to marry, now."
>
> "A man last night."
>
> There was a gasp from each lady. The possible reality of a lover descended suddenly like a summer hail over their heads. Mrs. Watts stood up and balanced herself.
>
> "One of those show fellows! A musician!" she cried. Lily looked up in admiration.
>
> "Did he—did he do anything to you?"
>
> "Oh, yes'm," said Lily. (9)

Lily understands the rhetoric of love. The respectability that the community of ladies desires for Lily is not important to her "feeble" mind. Horrified that the xylophone player "did something" to Lily and, even worse, that she is pleased by it, the community recoils.

Welty wryly contrasts the clash between the strict societal values expressed by the prim ladies and Lily's free spirit. Lily proudly retorts, "Going to get married, and I bet you wish you was me now" (8). The irony is clear. If the ladies were happily married, they might not be as intent on intervening in Lily's life. Meanwhile, Lily is not too feebleminded to recognize envy. Still, the ladies assume this man is "after Lily's body alone and he wouldn't ever in this world make the poor girl happy, even if we went out and forced him to marry her like he ought—at the point of a gun" (10).

This protective community of women, intent on protecting Lily's reputation, acts, as Chester Eisinger characterizes them, as the "custodians of moral principles and norms of respectable behavior" (8). Peter Schmidt argues that "as the story develops, the women's tyrranization over Lily becomes more obvious" and that "a reader cannot help but notice ironic parallels between the ideas of marriage and confinement" (14). Weston writes that the story "portrays a community tangle of women who close in around a little innocent wild life to see it safely entrusted to one institution or another—to the asylum or to marriage ("American Folk Art" 12).

The ladies around Lily refuse to accept her lover, and simultaneously they are terrified by a possible pregnancy out of wedlock. Their convincing descriptions of Ellisville lure the skeptical girl, and for a while she prefers Ellisville to marriage. The gifts the ladies offer as a trade parody the wedding gifts Lily should be receiving: "a pair of hemstitched pillowcases," a big cake, a "pretty little Bible with your name on it in real gold," and a "pink crêpe de Chine brassière with adjustable shoulder straps." Lily's prospective bridegroom does arrive, however, and although in one of a series of misconnections her hope chest goes off on the train to Ellisville by mistake, as the story closes, the lover and his "little Lily" are about to marry.

The community intrudes further to decide whether the marriage will take place, and Mrs. Carson must then bribe Lily with ice cream to stay home from Ellisville. The ladies next encircle the xylophone player, as if to entrap him, so that they can ensure his captivity in Victory and marriage to Lily. In a community celebration the band plays, the people cheer, and the three ladies usher Lily into marriage, whether or not she now desires to go. Although the story is comic and ends with a celebration, the intrusiveness of the townsfolk is the focus. The dark implications of this story lie in the clash of values and attitudes, the unsettling levels of social intrusiveness and lack of individual privacy. In Welty's story the potentially disastrous consequences of these factors do not take hold, but that they easily might have makes for a comic, if uncomfortable, ending.

The post office in Welty stories functions much as the general store or porch does for Faulkner—a place where folks go to hear the news, especially if the postmistress is gregarious and (also like Faulkner) has no qualms about opening mail that belongs to other people. Welty's P.O. functions as the inscription engraved on the United States Post Office in Washington, D.C., prescribes—as a "messenger of sympathy and love, servant of parted friends, consoler of the lonely, bond of the scattered family, enlarger of the common life" as well as the "carrier of news and knowledge." The post office compensates for lack of fulfillment in romance. Henry David Thoreau says in one of his later essays, "Life without Principle," that people go "desperately" to the post office. "Just so hollow and ineffectual, for the most part, is our ordinary conversation. Surface meets surface. When our life ceases to be inward and private, conversation degenerates into mere gossip. . . . In proportion as our inward life fails, we go more constantly and desperately to the post-office. You may depend on it, that the poor fellow who walks away with the greatest number of letters, proud of his extensive correspondence, has not heard from himself this long while" (109–10). Thoreau describes the dilemma of characters like Sister in "Why I Live at the P.O.," the women in "Lily Daw and the Three Ladies," and Sabina in "Asphodel," for whom the post office serves as the reminder of love and its absence.

Letters usually carry personal, confidential, or secretive information that excludes, especially if written between lovers, the outside world. As such, in Welty's tales letters aptly represent the tension between social and private life. Homer Brown notes that traditionally letters in literature are "bearers of gossip" or of a "private communication rather than public one." Letters signify a "pact between individuals in isolation," and as "privileged communication," they both require and presuppose an "I and a Thou, an I-or-a-Thou, and a Thou-for-an-I" (Brown 574, 578). The tension between private affairs and communal ties frame the stories "Why I Live at the P.O." and "Asphodel."

Welty's inspiration for "Why I Live at the P.O." stems from a visual image: "I once did see a little post office with an ironing board in the back through the window. This was in some little town—less than a town—some hamlet in Mississippi. And I suppose that's what made me think of it. Suppose somebody just decided to move down there" (*Conversations* 161). This example illustrates how Welty often began her stories—from an aural or visual cue. In "Why I Live at the P.O." those cues led Welty to imagine a fascinating character and a theme of tension between the domestic and private sphere of life and communal activity that Welty explores again and again in various works. The image of the ironing board at the back door of the post office led Welty to "Why I Live at the P.O." She began to consider who would move into the P.O. as a domestic space—and why. The result is the funny and sad portrait of Sister, a woman who has taken up residence in the post office. Narrated from the point of view of the postmistress, the story traces the history of the decision to move to the P.O. Welty says she depicted the way "people who live away off from nowhere have to amuse themselves by dramatizing every situation that comes along by exaggerating it—'telling it.' . . . It's just the way they keep life interesting— they make an experience out of the ordinary" (19–20). In *One Writer's Beginnings* Welty adds further that for this story she chose "the form of a monologue that takes possession of the speaker. How much more gets told besides!" (12).

What "gets told besides" Sister's decision to move to the P.O. is the story of her emotional life. The marriage and fully expressed sexuality of her sister, Stella-Rondo, Sister's own failures in love, and her alienation from her family are the narratives that unfold. That Sister lives in the post office, has immediate access to the mail, takes full advantage by reading the mail that belongs to others, and talks constantly point to her loneliness and need for vicarious fulfillment. Sister is a solitaire who nonetheless must interact with others and chooses one of the most public of arenas to call home. Her combining the domestic and the social into one living space indicates her deep need for both.

Sister's spinsterhood and jealousy of Stella-Rondo's marriage to Mr. Whitaker preoccupy her and outrage her younger sister. To make matters worse, Sister believes that Stella-Rondo has stolen Mr. Whitaker from her with supposed lies about her breasts: "Of course I went with Mr. Whitaker first, when he first appeared here in China Grove, . . . and Stella-Rondo broke us up. Told him I was one-sided. Bigger on one side than the other, which is a deliberate, calculated falsehood: I'm the same" (87). Stella's other lies make the accuracy of Sister's claims believable, although Sister is hardly as "helpless" as she would like to pretend (98). Sister complains several times about Stella's "unfair" winning of Mr. Whitaker, but their mother reminds Sister of the distinctions between marriage and childbirth in Stella-Rondo's life. "'But you must remember, Sister, that you were never married to Mr. Whitaker in the first place and didn't go up to Illinois to live,' says Mama, shaking a spoon in my face. 'If you had I would of been just as overjoyed to see you and your little adopted girl as I was to see Stella-Rondo, when you wound up with your separation and came on back home'" (94). Sister has not, however, led the life her sibling has, complete with sex, marriage, and a child. Mama's implication is that Sister has not yet fully lived. If she were to do so, Mama would be "overjoyed."

Stella taunts Sister and underscores her spinsterhood by emphasizing Stella's marriage and sexual life with Mr. Whitaker. The gaudy, "flesh-colored kimono" that Stella brings home symbolizes her marital activity: "it happens to be part of my trousseau," Stella explains, "and Mr. Whitaker took several dozen photographs of me in it." Even Stella's account of her separation from her husband includes the word *negligee* and flaunts to her spinster sister Stella's own sexually active status: "I only got home this morning after my separation and hung my negligee up on the bathroom door, just as nervous as I could be" (93). By the time Sister decides to leave for the P.O., the entire family has joined in a game of "Old Maid" to emphasize even further Sister's husbandlessness (99).

As she moves out of her family home and leaves for the P.O., Sister's parting words are "I've always got the P.O." These words belie her need for love and communication. The P.O. substitutes for a partner in the game of love and is her home away from home. Gossip, news, reading letters, meddling in the pharmaceutical orders Uncle Rondo receives in the mail, and "telling everybody in China Grove what you think is the matter with them" now are the primary activities of the postmistress because love has not come her way (102).

Pregnancy, sex, and illegitimacy fascinate Sister, much as they do Leota in "Petrified Man," partly because neither has a satisfactory personal life. Stella's "child of two" from her brief marriage is a subject Sister constantly mentions and thereby insinuates that Stella's child is illegitimate. She refers to the child as a "completely unexpected child" who came "without one moment's notice" (88). Although Sister insists that she "wouldn't be caught dead" in Stella's flesh-colored kimono, she protests too much. That Sister knows very little about Stella's pregnancy and separation frustrates Sister enormously. Finally, she announces in her proud lie that "if Stella-Rondo should come to me this minute, on bended knees, and attempt to explain the incidents of her life with Mr. Whitaker, I'd simply put my fingers in both my ears and refuse to listen" (104). The secrets that "get told besides" indicate her own unacknowledged need to live life as fully as possible— and perhaps with the same man that Stella had.

Ironically, the social connection that Sister desires becomes even more remote when she isolates herself from family and moves to the P.O.: Mama, Stella-Rondo, and Papa-Daddy all threaten to refuse to go there to receive their mail. Despite Sister's claims that her new life is "ideal," she laments later that "there's not much mail. My family are naturally the main people in China Grove," and some people have stopped "buying stamps just to get on the right side of Papa-Daddy" and have therefore turned against Sister (104). The feud becomes communal by the end of the tale. Sister maintains a certain amount of power, as do all the other postmistresses in Welty's stories (quite a few they are in number, and they are all women). As governess of correspondence, Sister can intercept and read the mail: "think of this: What will Stella-Rondo do now, if she wants to tell Mr. Whitaker to come after her? . . . It will be interesting to see how long she holds out." Sister has connived a way to intervene between Stella-Rondo and her husband, and now Sister can read their most intimate communications via the mail. When Stella-Rondo realizes Sister's potential for intrusion, she has "a conniption fit right there in the kitchen." Sister's meddlesome behavior shows no signs of diminishment by the end of the story. She vows to "draw my own conclusions and will continue in the future to draw them. . . . If people want to write their inmost secrets on penny postcards, there's nothing in the wide world you can do about it" (102). Welty's depiction of Sister is primarily a humorous one, but the story raises serious issues of that era: society labeled women who never married as "spinsters" and outcasts; compensation for loneliness takes place via vicarious participation in the lives of others; and balancing privacy and communal life is difficult. Although by today's standards, Eudora Welty was still fairly young when she wrote this story, by the standards of the day she was already older and not yet married, and as such Welty may have portrayed in Sister some autobiographical feelings about not having married.

For Welty characters like Sister, participation in love happens but only vicariously. Curiosity about love and active fantasy lives compensate for an absence of more satisfying emotional outlets. Individuals whose principal activity is gossip or fantasy about love typify Welty's isolated characters who find no relief for "the heart's overflow." They tip the balance toward communal rather than personal experience. Gossip, talk, and speculation about lovers ensure the lonely characters' participation in social activity, if not in love, and their imaginative lives offer them a kind of substitution for a physical participation in love.

Gossip can help form communal ties. As Homer Brown suggests, gossip or the "chorus of opinions" frequently found in novels is the "major community activity" in many works and affirms "one's membership in a community" (574, 578). "If letters are usually private communications," he concludes, "gossip is communal and, in fact, according to some anthropologists, both constitutes and regulates a community." The activity of gossiping itself can be "pleasurable" because it provides the illusion of company and community in which gossipers may tell and hear of "the private goings of people." By prompting communication, as Brown notes in quoting Dryden, gossip may even "preserve communial unity" (575).

The telling and hearing about love provides for some of Welty's characters a mode of inclusion in the world of romance, love, sex, and childbearing, especially for those who have little or no contact with love. As a literary device, gossip in its inventive, speculative nature forwards and complicates plot, introduces information and ambiguity, and calls into question the reliability of narrative sources. Without this imaginative component in narrative—which may, as Hawthorne observes in *The Scarlet Letter,* piece together important fragments—"there remains an unsightly gap, and a lack of continuousness and dependence in our narrative" (238–59). The Fairchilds in *Delta Wedding* illustrate the impulse both to hear and tell of passionate tales of the lives and loves of those around them. They tell stories often and with enthusiasm: "'Here's the way it was—' For all of them told happenings like narrations, chronological and careful, as if the ear of the world listened and wished to know surely" (19).

Later, in *One Writer's Beginnings,* Welty explains how she as a child connected gossip, listening, and narrating, or the telling of a story. She recalls Fannie, the "old black sewing woman," who brought to the Welty home, "along with her speed and dexterity, . . . a great provision of up-to-the-minute news." Welty's mother tried to stop the gossip: "'Fannie, I'd rather Eudora didn't hear that . . . I don't want her exposed to gossip,'—as if gossip were measles and I could catch it." The taboo gossip fascinated the young Welty. She found snippets of Fannie's tales "tantalizing": "I did catch some of them but not enough. 'Mrs. O'Neil's oldest daughter she had her wedding dress tried on, and all her fine underclothes feather stitched and ribbon run in and then—' 'I think that will do, Fannie,' said my mother. It was tantalizing never to be exposed long enough to hear the end" (14). As a storyteller, Fannie "just liked the telling. She was like an author. In fact, for a good deal of what she said, I daresay she was the author."

Telling and listening are both important ingredients in Welty's craft: "Long before I wrote stories, I listened for stories. Listening *for* them is something more acute than listening *to* them. I suppose it's an early form of participation in what goes on. Listening children know stories are *there.* When their elders sit and begin, children are just waiting and hoping for one to come out, like a mouse from a hole. . . . My instinct—the dramatic instinct—was to lead me, eventually, on the right track for a storyteller: the scene was full of hints, pointers, suggestion, and promises of things to find out and know about human beings. . . . I had to grow up and learn to listen for the unspoken as well as the spoken—and to know a truth, I also had to recognize a lie" (14–15).

Community talk in Welty's stories focuses on love, and gossip indicates a need for compelling human connection that might be achieved if not through love, then in the telling of it. Welty treats such characters comically when the effect of their activity is relatively harmless. No matter how private some of Welty's characters intend to be, "the big public tree" always listens for what Welty refers to in "The Wanderers" as the "magical percussion" of love in the community. Lovers often come to know the experience of "the world beating in their ears" (244). Virgie Rainey, Ran MacLain, Mrs. Fletcher, and Jack and Gloria Renfro, among others, learn that tales will be told, and secrets will eventually "come evident, show forth from the person, become part of the public domain" (237).

"The Wildness We All Worshipped" in "Asphodel"

Narrating, gossiping, storytelling, and listening provide an avenue for "old maids"—Cora, Irene, and Phoebe—by which to participate in the telling (and vicariously in the loving) of the ill-fated but highly charged marriage of Sabina and Don McInnis in "Asphodel." For the site of the ritualistic storytelling, the ladies choose Asphodel, the supposed place of Don's adulterous trysts. Welty carefully contrasts the wildness of the place with the virginal narrators to dramatize their need for love or at least fantasy.

The setting intoxicates the ladies as they wade in the creek and picnic and reminisce about Sabina's story. The indulgence of their actions at Asphodel suggests their desire to participate in some way in Sabina's love story, but they must resort to hanging "their narrow maiden feet . . . trembling in the rippling water" (96), eating the lush array of peaches, figs, pomegranates, and grapes" that they brought, and drinking from their "thin dark bottle of blackberry cordial" (97). Symbolically, the "frieze of maidens" on the columns of Asphodel fill with color as the ladies indulge their senses and their fantasies (96). Suggestive of the elusive Don, whom the ladies will conjure up with their storytelling, the horse that brought them to this place "flaunts" his tail at them from the nearby hill (97).

Like the story they tell, the baskets of food the ladies bring overflow with bacchanalian excess: "the baskets were opened, the cloth was spread with the aromatic ham and chicken, spices and jellies, fresh breads and a cake, peaches, bananas, figs, pomegranates, grapes, and a thin dark bottle of blackberry cordial." Their lavish eating and drinking substitute for the sexual intoxication and satiety that they imagine and desire. Welty describes the summer day with images of dreamlike timelessness: "The women reclined before the food, beside the warm and weighty pedestal. Above them the six columns seemed to be filled with the inhalations of summer and to be suspended in the resting of noon" (97). Phallic imagery sets the mood for the retelling of Sabina's love story.

With pomegranate-stained mouths the ladies "begin to tell over Miss Sabina's story" of her tempestuous marriage to the passionate Don McInnis. A "great, profane man" who usually "swayed with drink," Don wins the hand in marriage of Sabina because she has grown too old "for suitors; she was instructed to submit" (99). This marriage hardly begins as a love story. The lips of the ladies move together—they know this story so well: "It was like an old song they carried in their memory" (98).

Phallic and Edenic imagery produce an ominous tone: "Not one blade of grass grew in the hard green ground, but in some places a root stuck up like a serpent." The allusion to Eden implies that the lovers will satiate themselves but eventually fall. The house in which Sabina marries is "dark," with long hallways, ebony beds, and "one completely dark inside room." This house is a "labyrinth": the men inside it are drunk, and even the flowers in the baskets "wilted in the heat and showed their blue veins" (98–99). The foreboding images presage the dark fate of the McInnis marriage.

The marital ceremony itself is grand, and the ladies recall their excitement and intrigue as they remember the wedding of Sabina and Don McInnis: "On the marriage night the house was ablaze, and lighted the town and the wedding guests climbing the hill. We were there. . . . And the bride . . . the stiff white gown she wore! It never made a rustle when she gave him her hand." Charming though this wedding may have been, the bridegroom turns out to be vulgar, animal-like, and profane: "Mr. Don McInnis, with his head turning quickly from side to side, like an animal's, opened his mouth and laughed. . . . He had a sudden way of laughter, like a rage, that pointed his eyebrows that were yellow, and changed his face" (99). The ladies' talk recalls their embroidering with threads and with words the way young girls gossip about sex, and his sexuality intrigues them, even in their old age, as they reimagine McInnis's "dangerous," animalistic behavior on the wedding night. He is like a wild beast charging through the woods and "trampling" the flowers: "We remembered that, that roar, that 'What, Miss Sabina?' and we whispered it among ourselves later when we embroidered together, as though it were a riddle that young ladies could not answer. . . . He was dangerous that first night, swaying with drink, trampling the scattered flowers, led up to a ceremony there before all our eyes, Miss Sabina so rigid by his side. He was a McInnis, a man that would be like a torch carried into a house" (100). The ladies conclude that "he had the wildness we all worshipped that first night, since he was not to be ours to love" (101). Apart from the world of love and passion, like "faded garlands" in their abstinence (100), these ladies continually must weave and reweave their tale of romantic passion to keep and retell for a lifetime.

Storytelling provides these ladies with a vicarious participation; they seem sated upon the conclusion of their narration. First, they imagine that "something wild" might carry them off, and Don McInnis seems to appear to them naked and looking "rude and golden as a lion" (109–10). They run in fear of confronting this naked man (or spirit). As they conclude their feast of eating, drinking, and storytelling, their vision of sexuality disappears. Garvin Davenport summarizes that Phoebe "experiences at least a momentary taste of renewal, of involvement in the world of adult sexuality" (196). The "thriving herd" of goats near the ladies suggests that McInnis's wanton spirit abides in the ruins of Asphodel. Once the story is "closed and complete," the ladies are sated, as if they had indulged in the physical act of love: "In some intoxication of the time and the place, they recited it and came to the end. Now they lay stretched on their sides on the ground, their summer dresses spread out, little smiles forming on their mouths, their eyes half-closed, Phoebe with a juicy green leaf between her teeth. Above them like a dream rested the bright columns of Asphodel, a dream like the other side of their lamentations" (109). Telling Sabina's story offers to them a ripened love but one that they may share only through the imagination.

The same ladies who commemorate Sabina's story are also the gossipers who report to her the infidelities of her husband. Sabina places "great blame on the whole town" after she evicts Don from the house and the marriage. She eventually turns "all her will . . . upon the population" (104). Predictably, the place that most clearly represents the collective population of the town, onto which Sabina can focus all of her hate, is the post office. During her initial outrage Sabina vows to avoid the post office for the rest of her life: "'But at the end of the street there was one door where Miss Sabina had never entered,' said Phoebe. 'The door of the post office. She acted as if the post office had no existence in the world, or else she called it a dirty little room with the door standing wide open to the flies. All the hate she had left in her when she was old went out to a little four-posted whitewashed building, the post office. It was beyond her domain. For there we might still be apart in a dream, and she did not know what it was" (106).

The post office is the "little common green" that represents the townspeople as a community and also a place that facilitates communication and caring. Sabina beats upon "the little communication door" of the post office when she finally goes there to die. Sabina's response is a rejection of community. She associates gossip in the town with Don's philandering, and she withdraws from her friends because their gossip implies to her their participation in her betrayal. The "dream" she cannot share is the hope of love, happiness, or anticipation of love, symbolized by the love letters there. Her separation from her husband severs her forever from the world of love, and the love letters (and even the regular correspondence) represent a "privileged communication" that she can no longer tolerate. In withdrawing from love, Sabina refuses to acknowledge the post office because it represents the continuity of love in the community.

Sabina's dying day testifies to her denial of love and community relations. In a scene reminiscent of "Lily Daw and the Three Ladies," in which members of the community stand inside the post office with their mail while Lily's fate balances precariously, the death scene in "Asphodel" depicts Sabina's alienation from communal life: "'But in the end, she came in,' said Irene. . . . 'We were there,' she said, 'It was mail time, and we each had a letter in our hands. We heard her come to the end of the street, the heavy staggering figure coming to the beat of the cane. We were silent all at once. . . . We held on to our letters as on to all far-away or ephemeral things at that moment, to our secret hope or joy. . . . It was as if the place of the smallest and the longest-permitted indulgence, the little common green, were to be invaded when the time came for the tyrant to die" (106).

The post office as the scene of Sabina's death is ironic commentary on her loneliness and final humiliation in love. Bursting with a "fury and a pleasure" at the thought of the secret hopes of the townspeople, Sabina shreds the letters of the community, crying out, "Your lovers" (107). "In a frenzy she tore all the letters to pieces, and even put bits in her mouth and appeared to eat them" (108). Sabina embraces but destroys symbols of love. In eating the love letters of other people, she expresses her need to envelop, connect with, and communicate. As Sabina injests the letters, she also destroys them, rejects the loves of those whom she envies, and she reveals her anger and disappointment. Knowing that she "never got a letter in her life," Sabina exiles herself from human connection. Her condemnation of all communication, especially words of affection, is the raving of a woman bred in grandeur but bereft of love and communal relationships.

"'Petrified' Man"

The beauty parlor—like the post office and the barbershop that Katie Rainey recalls in *The Golden Apples*, with its "vulgar man talk"—provides another locale in which women can gossip about love in a communal setting. "Petrified Man" is a darkly comic story about the unromantic characteristics of love, marriage, and childbearing told from the point of view of women with experience and narrated in language nearly equivalent to that of the disinhibited men in a locker room. A female gathering place, the beauty parlor allows a free discourse among them in which men are far from irrelevant but into which they only venture in the flesh in the form of a young boy who concludes the story. Although Alun Jones calls the story "a world ruthlessly dominated by women," in which the "men are all impotent before this monstrous regiment of women" ("World of Love" 181), another view is of a "den" where women convene regularly and familiarly to primp, gossip, boast, brag, and voice their prides and fears about sex, childbearing, and love. Here, in their "den of curling fluid and henna packs," the women can be "gratified" in their search for ways to "give curiosity its freedom" (33–34).

Scholars have analyzed the story in detail. Jeffrey Helterman argues that the tale is a "symbolic dissection of three loveless women," which depends upon the "mythic substructure of the tale of Perseus' confrontation with the three sisters of Graiae" (12). Robert Cochran sees the women as having "a sense of being violated virgins in pointedly repressed ways" (25); Chester Eisinger maintains that "justice and compassion are overwhelmed by a perverse absorption in the abnormal or freakish" (9); and Seymour Gross states that "these women . . . actually hate and emasculate their men—petrify them—because they hate nature" and "look upon pregnancy as something dirty and shameful done to them by men who should be making money not babies" (324). Ruth Vande Kieft sees the theme of the story as "woman's inhumanity to man" (*Eudora Welty* 72).

Like "Why I Live at the P.O.," this story is one that Welty calls "by ear" stories (*Conversations* 258), in which she draws on the "fund in your head, having heard people talk and noted in your mind all your life the way people say things" (162). "Just like hearing a song," she adds, "once heard—you could sing it again" (258). "Petrified Man" is a tale of talking—the "way people say things"—yet simultaneously it has a plot that centers on gossip. Like Sister and Stella-Rondo in "Why I Live at the P.O.," Leota and Mrs. Fletcher in this story reveal their essential characters and conflicts as the dialogue unfolds.

Preoccupation with sex and sexual secrets distinguishes Leota from the other women in the story. She focuses on sex, lust, marriage, pregnancy, and childbearing. A lower-class Molly Bloom of the South, Leota is a marvelous character whose narrative weaves a tale that encompasses pregnancy, birth, and delivery but then turns to the deformed, "full-time" Siamese twins pickled in formaldehyde, pygmies, petrified men, and finally her own pathetic marriage to the sluggish, stonelike Fred: "All Fred does is lay around the house like a rug. I wouldn't be surprised if he woke up some day and couldn't move. The petrified man just sat there moving his quarter of an inch though" (41). Marriage, however, is the general topic, and stone imagery represents the dissatisfactions of the women more than it represents what Alun Jones calls their "ruthless domination" ("World of Love" 181). For Leota one petrified man calls to mind another—her lazy husband.

Marriage for Leota means lust and infatuation, quickly cooled to boredom. She clearly recalls passionate days in her relationship with Fred. "'Honey, me an' Fred, we met in a rumble seat eight months ago and we was practically on what you might call the way to the altar inside of half an hour,' said Leota in a guttural voice, and bit a bobby pin open." Sustainable love is, however, an unattainable ideal for her: "Course it don't last. Mrs. Pike says nothin' like that ever lasts" (44). Leota reads *Startling G-Man Tales* and *Screen Secrets*, which feed her fantasies, and the book *Life Is like That*, which Mrs. Fletcher reads under the hair dryer, emphasizes the resignation of the beautician to her lackluster love life. These magazine titles resonate with the lackluster marriages the women in the story have.

Dissatisfactions, jealousies, and longings for a sustaining, rejuvenating relationship cause Leota to attack Mrs. Fletcher and also to visit Lady Evangeline, the fortune-teller. Still curious about the degree of happiness achieved by her former boyfriend, Leota asks the fortune-teller for an evaluation of his marriage. Protesting that she is "not in love with him anymore, anyway, besides being married to Fred," Leota nonetheless eagerly listens to and takes comfort in the mind reader's conclusions: "'Honey,' she says, 'naw, he idn't. You write down this day, March 8, 1941,' she says . . . 'three years from today him and her won't be occupyin' the same bed.' There it is, up on the wall with them other dates—see, Mrs. Fletcher?" (43). The three-year wait and her current unhappiness are causes enough for Leota's deflated expectation of love and marriage.

Mrs. Fletcher's marriage also receives much attention in the story. Although she brags proudly that she and Mr. Fletcher met in a respectable place—in comparison to Leota's rumble seat romance—Mrs. Fletcher reveals her marital problems before the story ends. She considers having an abortion without telling her husband, and she uses wiles to win him over: "I ask Mr. Fletcher's advice now and then, and he appreciates it, especially on something important, like is it time for a permanent—not that I've told him about the baby. He says, 'Why, dear, go ahead!' Just ask their *advice*" (41). She claims that "Mr. Fletcher and myself are as much in love as the day we married" (45), but she fears catching dandruff from him, as if he had a sexually transmitted disease. She makes him do bending exercises nightly. In neither example does she show a romantic posture. True, Leota has humiliated her by guessing the fact of her pregnancy, but Mrs. Fletcher's bragging belies her happiness.

The dramatic center of the story involves Leota's revelation of two points of intrigue: Mrs. Fletcher's pregnancy and the capture of the rapist/petrified man. Leota combs "as if to hold Mrs. Fletcher down by the hair" as she asks her prisoner directly: "'Well,' Leota answered at last, 'you know what I heard in here yestiddy, one of Thelma's ladies was settin' over yonder in Thelma's booth gittin' a machineless, and I don't mean to insist or insinuate or anything, Mrs. Fletcher, but Thelma's lady just happ'med to throw out—I forgotten what she was talkin' about at the time—that you was p-r-e-g., and lots of times that'll make your hair do awful funny, fall out and God knows what all. It just ain't our fault, is the way I look at it.' . . . There was a pause. The women stared at each other in the mirror." Leota elicits more information about Mrs. Fletcher's "condition" in a series of leading questions and statements: "Now honey, I wouldn't go and git mad over a thing like that . . . I'm sure it was somebody didn't mean no harm in the world" (35); "I doubt if she e'vm knows you're on the way" (36); "How far gone are you?"; "Not that you look it" (35); "You just get you one of those Stork-a-Lure dresses and stop worryin'" (37).

An outward, public, sign of sexuality, pregnancy is a piece of news that Leota can now make available for the community to digest. Soon Mrs. Fletcher will be the object of as much talk and attention as Mrs. Montjoy, who recently delivered: "'Listen, honey, you're just a virgin compared to Mrs. Montjoy. . . . You know Mrs. Montjoy—her husband's that premature-gray-headed fella?' . . . 'She's in the Trojan Garden Club, is all I know,' said Mrs. Fletcher." The focus of Leota's story shifts not to the joy—but to the high degree of pain—that Leota imagines Mrs. Montjoy to have had during the delivery of her baby: "'Well, honey,' said Leota, but in a weary voice, 'she come in here not the week before and not the day before she had her baby—she come in here the very selfsame day, I mean to tell you. Child, we was all plumb scared to death. There she was! Come for her shampoo an' set. Why, Mrs. Fletcher, in an hour an' twenty minutes she was layin' up there in the Babtist Hospital with a seb'm-pound son. It was that close a shave. . . . Just wanted to look pretty while she was havin' her baby, is all,' said Leota airily . . . 'but I bet a hour later she wasn't payin' no mind to them little end curls. I bet she wasn't thinkin' about she ought to have on a net. It wouldn't of done her no good if she had. . . . Yeah man! She was a-yellin'. Just like when I give her perm'nent'" (45–46).

The dark side of "Petrified Man" emerges as Leota's narrative turns to the two dead, deformed, "pickled twins" in a bottle. Her talk of birth and gossip leads her to describe the preserved fetuses she has recently seen at the circus. This description of the grotesque, pickled twins takes her voice up to a "soft lyrical hum." Her insatiable interest in sex, birth, and deformity as well as her jealousy and childlessness suggest her unfulfilled status in the world of love: "'Aw. Well, honey, talkin' about bein' pregnant an' all, you ought to see those twins in a bottle, you really owe it to yourself.' . . . 'What twins?' asked Mrs. Fletcher out of the side of her mouth. . . . 'Well, honey, they got these two twins in a bottle, see? Born joined plumb together—dead a course.' Leota dropped her voice into a soft lyrical hum. 'They was about this long—pardon—must of been full time, all right, wouldn't you say?—an' they had these two heads an' two faces an' four arms an' four legs, all kind of joined here. See, this face looked this-a-way, and the other face looked that-a-way, over their shoulder, see. Kinda pathetic'" (40). The fate of the twins shifts Leota's focus: sex and childbearing also can lead to deformity and death.

The communal setting of the beauty shop in "Petrified Man" provides a good backdrop for the comic portrayal of women giving curiosity and gossip "its freedom" (33), but the dark side of the story, including horror, disease, deformity, and death—and to a lesser degree of severity, rivalry, jealousy, longing, and unfulfilled desire—weaves a more complex thematic fabric for the story, just as idiomatic expression adds narrative texture. These haunting realities shadow the more cheerful surface narrative of marriage, sex, and pregnancy. That the Petrified Man, who in the circus appears almost immobile, eventually turns out to be a flagrant rapist adds another layer of the sinister to the story. The word "petrified" in the title has a double meaning, however. Most of the men in this story initially at least seem stonelike, but they may also be "petrified," in the sense of fearful. Perhaps they are scared of the loud, tongue-wagging, gossip bearing women around them. Only the young boy at the close of the story seems fearless in tossing a bold comment to the ladies. The implication may be that like the other men around him, he too will become petrified of women, in this sense, by the time he reaches manhood.

What initially seems a funny story about a crude hairdresser needling her prim and proper client gives way to the grim and painful realities and consequences of sexuality, childbearing, deformity, and rape, and "Petrified Man" eventually reveals these gruesome secrets. The morbid interest Leota has in preserved fetuses is at first the occasion for exaggeration in storytelling but then becomes a sad reminder of the tragic fate of the "full-term" but deformed babies who did not survive to live birth. The same dark reality that may seem unlikely for most pregnancies potentially could recur in the lives of the characters such as Mrs. Montjoy or the prim Mrs. Fletcher, whose main concern seems to be whether dandruff is transmissible from her husband to her. These women may not expect that their children will end up on display at the circus, but someone's babies did end up as pickled atrocities to be gaped at and gossiped about by circus goers like Leota. Gossip in this story locates the tellers and the listeners within a community and provides the "illusion of participation" into what Brown calls the "private goings of people" (575). Love in "Petrified Man," as in "Asphodel," may best be understood through talk and the imagination rather than through personal knowledge.

As Welty depicts love and lovelessness in her early stories, those characters who marry can find love to be mysterious and enriching. Some know love but acknowledge its changeable nature. Welty's happiest stories depict couples sharing an "ancient communication." These early volumes also strike somber notes, however. Numerous characters search for happiness that they have lost or have never known. Lovelessness and sorrow temper the happy portraits in the first two collections. Welty recognizes the deep-seated human desire for love and caring, and yet some characters suffer in their search for meaningful relationships. In the worst cases murder and suicide result from the effects of isolation, as some face oblivion. Lovelessness in the early works also includes young characters who search, just as their older counterparts do, for a love they dream about or hope for. In some cases idealization gives way to more realistic attitudes about love, so that perception and judgment may mature. Waiting for love, or enduring the time of maturation, is a time of frustration in Welty's fiction.

The tension between privacy and communal life is an important theme in the early works that carries over to later novels. Welty's loneliest individuals often appear against the backdrop of an intrusive community or within group relationships. She contrasts the solitary life with the need for social context and shows a vicarious participation in love that occurs in gossip, talk, and speculation about the lovers of others. Gossip affirms membership and participation in a community, and telling or listening to stories about the love lives of others can be satisfying even when love itself is hard to find. Love is powerful and significant even when characters fail to find it or when it wanes or has not arrived. The insistent hunger for love in some form, imaginative or real, is present almost always. Welty's stories of loss and search show that sometimes efforts can fail but love is possible.

Taken as a whole, the first two volumes of Welty's short stories introduce the central themes about love upon which Welty further elaborates in her later career. Although her ideas in the later works deepen philosophically, Welty concerns herself for over forty-five years with the auspicious and unpropitious fates occasioned by the changing countenance of love.

CHAPTER 4

"Gossamer and Roses"

Fantasy and Responsibility in The Robber Bridegroom

Eudora Welty's first three novels—*The Robber Bridegroom, Delta Wedding,* and *The Ponder Heart*—emerge from the themes and crafting of her early short fiction and further her exploration of human relationships. These works focus on marriages and carry the hallmarks of romantic comedy, with strong historical content and a predominantly light tone, but each work alternates to the serious and sometimes devastating. This alternation complicates and authenticates Welty's writings about love. After a dramatic complication, for example, maturity develops in *The Robber Bridegroom;* problems of allegiance and familial obligation, as well as an uncertain future, temper pleasure in *Delta Wedding;* and loss, death, divorce, and missed opportunity lend a meditative tone to the essentially comedic in *The Ponder Heart.* Considered together, the three novels foster conclusions that Welty establishes in her early works—that love enhances life and imagination and unites families and communities, but bitterness, isolation, and loneliness remain painfully present.

The Robber Bridegroom weaves enchanting fantasy and a fairy tale into a love story set in the forest, complete with a rogue, planter's daughter, evil stepmother, magical woods, seduction, ravishment, and mistaken identity. Violence intrudes: rape and murder occur—but alongside marriage, a wedding, and the birth of twins. These components invoke Shakespeare's *A Midsummer Night's Dream* and *As You Like It* as well as the tales of the Brothers Grimm. Michael Kreyling observes: "While Welty plays variations on the plots of Shakespearean forest comedy, modern romantic comedy, backwoods farce, and the historical record, she dapples the sunny with the dark. The presence of the Natchez Trace Indians gives the novella a somber shadow" (*Understanding* 43). Although these classics texts inform the background of Welty's works, she focuses on a southern location—her homeplace—as the setting for her "Fairy Tale of the Natchez Trace." Jamie Lockhart, the woodland bandit, and Rosamund, the planter's fair daughter, begin their once-upon-a-lifetime saga with stylized romance but little maturity. Welty first takes up in "A Memory" the dichotomy of an idealized perfection versus the realities of the practical, domestic, and everyday life, and she strengthens that theme in *The Robber Bridegroom*.

Although she is given to flights of fancy, Rosamund's more mature attitudes about love do not spring full blown from her imagination. She has derived them in part from the model of her parents' love story. Her father, Clement Musgrove, narrates the history of his marriage to his first wife, Amalie—Rosamund's mother—in the "peaceful hills." The young daughter is an eager listener as the family story unfolds in which Amalie bore her husband "two blissful twins, a son and a daughter" (20). Rosamund will recreate this genetic lineage with fidelity when she repeats the familial pattern and gives birth to twins at the end of the novel.

Both Clement and Rosamund see marriage as a lost ideal, for one has lost his true love to death, and the other has found none yet. Alone at night, Clement dreams of his past great love and anguishes as he surrenders to memory: "In the dream, whenever I lie down, then it is the past. When I climb to my feet, then it is the present. And I keep up a struggle not to fall" (29). In his efforts to give due homage to his deceased wife but also make an effort to maintain his balance in the present world, in remarkable ways he prefigures Judge McKelva in Welty's last novel, *The Optimist's Daughter*. Like bookends, the two novels frame Eudora Welty's early and late work with a focus on love and loss, happiness and grief, in four bittersweet portraits of marriage. On the one hand, *The Robber Bridegroom* at first appears to be a rollicking tale of wild times on the Natchez Trace, but as in *The Optimist's Daughter*, a serious, prominent theme takes hold: the solid marriage of the parental generation will have a positive and lasting impact on the next. As such, the novels are highly autobiographical in nature and reflect the confidence engendered in Eudora Welty by the solid, lifelong marriage of her parents and the bond between them that death could not render asunder.

Clement's problematic second marriage contrasts profoundly with his blissful first union with Amalie. His new wife, Salome, is a bitter opposite;

she is masculine, and her manner and temperament are like iron—even "in her times of love." Clement describes her as "immeasurably calculating and just so, almost clock-like, in the way of the great Spanish automaton in the iron skirt in the New Orleans bazaar, which could play and beat a man at chess" (26–27). She is not a loving wife or a romantic one, and her name links her to the ruthless predecessor who in overbearing lust beheads her lover. As such, she represents a threat to her husband, Clement.

This second marriage as a poor substitute for the remarkable first one is a topic that Welty depicts again in *The Optimist's Daughter*, written thirty years later, in which the biographical comes increasingly to the fore. Laurel, in that later novel, and her father cope with his undesirable new wife, in contrast with the deceased wife, who seems a model of perfection. Laurel, like Rosamund, grieves for her dead mother and struggles to accept her father's new life; Judge McKelva, like Clement Musgrove, looks back with hindsight and regret. These relationships bear a close resemblance to the relationship of Welty and her parents. In an interview Eudora Welty said, however, that the second marriages of Clement and Salome and the Judge and the new wife, Fay, in *The Optimist's Daughter*, were modeled on someone real. "No one could make that up," she added (interview with Wolff). Even though no clear biographical source exists in Eudora Welty's immediate family for these difficult second marriages, they do serve to emphasize what is valuable about the primary marriage, and they show the dangers of triangular and quadrangular relationships, some of which Eudora Welty did see and experience in her own life.

Rosamund, too, longs for her mother and a return to the time of her parents' true love. She cries out to her father, "It is my own mother you love, swear it is so" (29). Amalie, however, is dead, and Rosamund, "so beautiful," whose name originates in early English love ballads and echoes Shakespeare's *As You Like It*, must nurture her memory and keep it "alive and evergreen" in Clement Musgrove's heart (30).

Clement's future is with his new wife, Salome, and their marriage begins in the romantic woodland setting that will later charm his daughter and her lover-to-be: "He rode south on the Old Natchez Trace and then took another trail branching off to the deepest woods, a part he had never searched before . . . on he rode . . . till he came all at once to the bluff where deep down, under the stars, the dark brown wave of the Mississippi was rolling by. That was the place where he had found the river and married Salome. And if he had but known it, that was the place where Jamie Lockhart had carried his daughter, there under the meeting trees at the edge" (104–5). In the lost love of her parents, and her father's abiding memories of it, Rosamund's future, including her paradisiacal life with Jamie Lockhart in the woods and under the Natchez Trace bluff, along the Mississippi River, finds a justifiable precedent.

Jamie, too, manifests romantic yearnings: "in his heart Jamie carried nothing less than a dream of true love—something of gossamer and roses, though on this topic he never held conversation with himself, or let the information pass to a soul." In hopes of "finding this dream on earth," even as he pillages the countryside, he saves a hope chest for this yet "unknown" love: "He had collected, whenever it happened to be convenient, a number of clothes and jewels for this very unknown, that would deck a queen and be missed if a queen left them off. But as for finding this dream on earth, that Jamie was saving until the last" (74). Jamie's dreams, however, are unrealistic. He expects love to align with his timetable and be appropriate to his plans. He believes that love can be "all divisioned off into time and place, and that many things were for later and for further away, and that now the world had just begun" (87). In time his idealizations will prove to need some adjustments, and the story provides them.

His misconceptions are part of the rising complication of the narrative and must be corrected before the lovers' problems can resolve satisfactorily. In this sense the plot has the traditional structure of comedy, especially that of Shakespearean comedy, in which the lovers' lives are crossed until certain hurdles are met. A wedding customarily follows. For now, however, Jamie is a lone man on horseback searching for love. The moon, traditionally associated in literature with the mutability of love, here symbolizes his confusion about love and his misconceptions: "Then Jamie waved his hand and rode away alone and still empty-handed, in the confusion of the moonlight, under the twining branches of the trees, bent on no one knew what" (75). He does not know what he wants or how to find it. His misunderstandings take the foreground, as he wanders aimlessly through the woods.

In their first formal meeting Jamie and Rosamund establish a second complication. He is too bright with "cleanliness, youth, wisdom" for Rosamund to recognize him, so she does not "see the first sign of her dark lover." Concomitantly, he does not recognize his Rose, for she is "so ragged and dirty." Their blindness to each other's true identity delays their establishing a mutual awareness and admiration. These mistakes and idealizations prove to be significant hindrances, and the comedy can resolve only after false illusions dissolve, mistaken identities clarify, and true identities are revealed. The ideal and realistic understanding must converge and rebalance before Jamie and Rosamund may marry: "Then he took his foot off the gangplank and came down and brought her home, not failing to take her by the priest's and marrying her on the way. And indeed it was in time's nick"—for she will soon bear twins, as did her mother before her (181).

Clement has much instruction for his daughter in the art of love. Although initially he could see only the past, as father he now has found clarity of vision in his daughter's future. Jamie wears the mask of a bandit, and as such he camouflages who he is, but Clement looks beyond the mask for Jamie's true character: "'If being a bandit were his breadth and scope, I should but find him and kill him for sure,' said he. 'But since in addition he loves my daughter, he must be not the one man, but two, and I should be afraid of killing the second'" (126–27). Jamie has two natures: the beastly and the gentlemanly. The former "beastly skin" of his wild side will molt, as will his naïveté about love. As is the case for her predecessor, Shakespeare's Rosalind, Welty's Rosamund is the catalyst in the maturation of her lover. Under her guidance her mate will learn to embrace situations maturely. As his tolerance and acceptance increase, as Gordon Slethaug argues, the lovers must "lose their simplistic visions of reality or be destroyed by them" (77). This battle, however, is one they do not lose.

Jamie and Rosamund learn about love painstakingly, however. Rosamund bemoans Jamie's penchant for disguise. She says, "He brought me his love under a mask, and kept all the truth hidden from me, and never called anything by its true name" (146). True to comedic love formula, the complications must rise even higher: Rosamund saddens even more once she discovers her lover's face: "'Now that I know his name is Jamie Lockhart,' she cries out, 'what has the news brought me?'" (150). At first she does not see the power of his name to "lock" his "heart" to hers, but slowly she learns that love, in its purest form, needs no masquerade. Rosamund eventually reaches this more complicated, less idealistic view. As the two characters work their way to the sedate and familial, *The Robber Bridegroom* draws to a quiet, mature close; just as the earlier Welty stories do—after great striving, masked identity, and mistaken notions, a calm rumbles "like a wagon crossing a bridge."

The forest is for Jamie and Rosamund the kingdom of love, their life there idyllic. Their verdant, woodland home carries the natural sounds and scenes of the wooded riverbank. These woodland settings are among Welty's most enchanting—a southern Eden: "How beautiful it was in the wild woods! Black willow, green willow, cypress, pecan, katalpa, magnolia, persimmon, peach, dogwood, wild plum, wild cherry, pomegranate, palmetto, mimosa, and tulip trees were growing on every side, golden-green in the deep last days of the Summer. Up overhead the cuckoo sang. A quail with her young walked fat as the queen across the tangled path. A flock of cardinals flew up like a fan opening out from the holly bush. The fox looked out from his hole" (77). The day she and Jamie spend wandering the woods together recalls Milton's *Paradise Lost,* in which Adam and Eve, tasting the "enticing fruit," retire to their bower of love in the woods:

> Her hand he seized, and to a shady bank,
> Thick overhead with verdant roof imbowered,
> He led her, nothing loth; flowers were the couch,
> Pansies, and violets, and asphodel,
> And hyacinth—Earth's freshest, softest lap.
> There they their fill of love and love's disport
> Took largely, of their mutual gilt the seal,
> The solace of their skin, till dewy sleep
> Oppressed them, wearied with their amorous play. (*Paradise Lost* 402)

Welty's lovers' feast "tasted as wild as a wild pear" (87), and "spice-dreams" envelop them in the fertile woods (86). Albert Devlin observes that "the day and the night derive their character from the disposition of Jamie and Rosamund, who both dominate time and claim the vast forest as a personal domain" (170). In this circadian rhythm day becomes a night canopy. Their bed, however, is not the elaborate, floral, Miltonic one. The lovers enjoy the simplicity of their southern pallet, pinewoods scented with muscadine: "One day Jamie did not ride away with the others, and then the day was night and the woods were the roof over their heads. The tender flames of the myrtle trees and the green smoke of the cedars were the fires of their hearth. In the radiant noon they found the shade, and ate the grapes from the muscadine vines. The spice-dreams rising from the fallen brown pine needles floated through their heads when they stretched their limbs and slept in the woods" (86). As day and night merge, the lovers suspend time while they are abed in the pine needles.

The wild wood begins to evoke domesticity, however, with a "roof" and the semblance of a hearth: "the green smoke of the cedars were the fires of their hearth" (86). The wooded home, private and apart, nestles "so deep and dark in the woods," Rosamund says, "that no one knows the way out except my husband, who brought me" (118). The woods signify the ungoverned, unbounded character of Rosamund's private relationship with her husband thus far. No one knows the way in or out of their hidden home. The community cannot impinge upon them yet: "So Rosamund stayed and kept house for the robbers. And at first the life was like fairyland. Jamie was only with her in the hours of night, and rode away before the dawn, but he spoke as kind and sweet words as anyone ever could between the house of sunset and sunrise. . . . She washed the robbers' shirts till she wore them out with her washing. . . . And she wove a mat of canes and rushes and made them wipe their feet when they came in at the door" (82–83).

Rosamund takes pleasure in knowing that she and her husband have a home away from family and outsiders. Rigid rules do not apply in their Edenic landscape away from society. The time apart, and the idyllic characteristic of life in the woods, embodies what Gloria Renfro and Robbie Fairchild long for in *Losing Battles* and *Delta Wedding*—a place away from others in which they may share time alone with their spouses. The life apart from others, however, is finally not sustainable. Reality eventually intrudes. Clement, at home, regrets never having seen his daughter's house. When Jamie and Rosamund move to New Orleans, Clement may visit them. He can now see who his son-in-law is, and his wise prediction for Rosamund's husband has come true: Jamie's "wild ways had been shed like a skin, and he could not be kinder to her than he was." Rosamund now proudly shows Clement her house "of marble and cypress wood on the shores of Lake Pontchartrain" (183). Welty first implies here what she reiterates in later words: loyalty, allegiance, and responsibility to family are necessary components of love and commitment that a couple should observe. The couple must join the family and community with expanded roles and familial obligations. A carefree life in the woods, however pleasurable and fanciful, cannot last forever.

Although the wild, natural setting of the woods in *The Robber Bridegroom* necessarily must shift to the everyday domesticity of life on Lake Ponchartrain in New Orleans, the love between Rosamund and Jamie does not wane. The physical move from their private, woodland setting, "so dark and deep," to the more social and public setting of their new, bustling, communal, city life parallels the psychological maturity of the characters as they take on conventional family roles, with all of the attendant responsibilities: parenthood, livelihood, and respectful caring for the elder generation. Nonetheless, the marriage does not darken or lose its magic. Life in the forest may be a "spice-dream" that must give way to more complex relationships, but as Welty takes leave of her characters, and as their responsible selves take hold, they cope with their developed circumstances of having conceived and borne twins. Clement sees during his visit that Jamie and Rosamund's relationship mirrors his own love story. Their cycle of love and marriage now offers them its own rewards, as the wilder days of love on the riverbank, under the wild plum trees, recede into the magic of memory. At the close of the novel the marital lessons Jamie and Rosamund have learned lead them to understand and perpetuate the relationship of Clement and Amalie: love matures, continues, regenerates, and moves through cycles.

CHAPTER 5

"Got Thorns"

The Complex Loves of Delta Wedding

Welty infuses *Delta Wedding* with all the "noise" and "commotion" of a Jane Austen novel (*Eye* 3). Within a framework of family and community Welty closely examines several marriages, including those of Ellen and Battle Fairchild and George and Robbie, as well as the upcoming marriage of Dabney and Troy. These unions resemble the characters in Welty's other works who have sustaining marriages, including Sonny and his wife in "Death of a Traveling Salesman," Hazel and William Wallace in "The Wide Net," Clyde and Ruby Fisher in "A Piece of News," Clement and Amalie as well as Jamie and Rosamund, in *The Robber Bridegroom*, and Gloria and Jack Renfro in *Losing Battles*. On the whole the relationships they have are unabashed and parade, rather than mask, evidence of the exuberant feelings of the couples.

The dark side of these seemingly affable relationships emerges, however, as is now evident as a pattern in Welty's work. War, death, and violence ravage the seemingly quiet life of the Delta people. Although these relationships, on the whole, depict accord between men and women, complications always occur. Ruth Vande Kieft writes of *Delta Wedding* that here "Miss Welty's vision of both the enormous qualities and limitations of love, the theme of 'love and separateness,' have also been fully explored . . . the novel, as John Crowe Ransom has named it, is a 'comedy of novel'" (*Eudora Welty* 103). Susan V. Donaldson points to currents and undercurrents: "anomalies like sudden violence, black religion, conjure, personal animosities, insanity, and unbridled sexuality." She adds that "nothing could appear more staunchly rooted in traditional gender definitions than the seemingly timeless world of the Fairchilds, who mourn the loss of one of their favorite sons, Denis, killed in the war, and anxiously minister to the needs of another favorite, George, who was wounded" ("Gender and History" 10). Barbara Ladd's essay on Pinchy's "coming through" elucidates African American characters such as Pinchy, who perhaps cannot claim central attention in the novel but establish the racial commentary of the novel ("'Coming Through'"). David McWhirter also argues generally that Welty's work "typically locates African Americans as significant but largely inscrutable presences at the margins of her narratives," but he also points to her "characteristic reticence in her representations of African Americans" (114). The marriage of Ellen and Battle Fairchild may be an autobiographical rendering of Welty's parents' marriage. Perhaps more than any other in Welty's work, this marriage, like Welty's own parental example, has a quality of love that extends through trial and time. Ellen and Battle continue to bear children during the course of *Delta Wedding*, a novel concerned on many levels with love and marriage. Ellen is expecting her tenth child, even though her ninth child, Bluet, is still a baby (167). Mrs. Welty did not bear as many children, but she did become pregnant when Eudora Welty was a young girl. As Ellen contemplates her new pregnancy, she marvels at the surprise of family resemblances and the mystery of heredity. She "had never had a child to take after herself and would be as astonished as Battle now to see her own ways or looks dominant, a blue-eyed, dark-haired, small-boned baby lying in her arms. All the mystery of looks moved her, for she was with child once more" (22). Welty's experience of watching her mother go through a pregnancy may be reflected in this statement.

In a manner consistent with Welty's mother, Ellen is also devoted to her children and husband. She instinctively responds to her baby's cry above all the commotion in the house: "But the baby had dreams and soon she would cry out on the upper floor, and Aunt Ellen listening would run straight to her, calling to her on the way, and forgetting everything in this room" (21). Ellen's baking of a cake for Dabney's wedding also may reflect Mrs. Welty's culinary prowess, which her daughter, Eudora, inherited or learned. In what Peggy Prenshaw calls "a ritual of love," Ellen follows Aunt Mashula's old family recipe ("Cultural Patterns" 59). Suzan Harrison observes: "Preparing food and providing meals for the family become synonymous with sustaining family connections and creating hope and love within the family." She adds that "Ellen Fairchild's cake baking merges with her concerns over her daughter's approaching marriage and her consideration of George and Robbie Fairchild's marriage, until the success of the cake and the success of the marriage become one and the same." Ellen carries out the familiar motions of preparing the cake, and in doing so, the old family recipe metaphorically suggests the secrets of a good relationship: "As Ellen put in the nutmeg and the grated lemon rind she diligently assumed George's happiness, seeing it in the Fairchild aspects of exuberance and satiety; if it was unabashed, it was the best part true. But—adding the milk, the egg whites, the flour, carefully and alternately as Mashula's recipe said" (*Delta Wedding* 26).[1] Ellen knows that love, like the cake she creates, comes of a watchful combining and alternating of ingredients; the yield is exuberance and then satiety. If unabashed, a love is true—but the alternation of ingredients makes a smoother whole. Ellen and Battle have the ingredients in their marriage that the old recipe calls for. Their daughter Shelley describes their open, trusting relationship: "I cannot think of any way of loving that would not fight the world, just speak to the world. Papa and Mama do not fight the world. They have let it in. Did they ever even lock a door" (85). These descriptors also apply to Welty's parents' loving ways.

The beds of *Delta Wedding*, as in other works by Welty, characterize and illuminate the quality of the relationships of those who lie on them. Welty describes the Delta land itself in terms of a big bed. She suggests the warm embrace that the land seems to offer its inhabitants. Her description continues with the luminousness of a Delta night and an image of the whiteness that a field of cotton reflects in the moonlight. In her metaphor Welty compares the softness and comfort of a cotton bed to the contentment of Ellen and Battle Fairchild and the fullness of the cotton fields to their fertility: "Cotton was everywhere, as far as the sky—the soft and level fields. . . . By night the Delta looked just like a big bed, the whiteness in the luminous dark. . . . Ellen at Battle's side rode looking ahead, they were comfortable and silent, both, with their great weight, breathing a little heavily in a rhythm that brought them sometimes together. The repeating fields, the repeating cycles of season and her own life—there was something in the monotony itself that was beautiful, rewarding—perhaps to what was womanly within her" (239–40). Patricia Yaeger notes the cottoned world in *Delta Wedding* "covered with lint from the cotton gin—a terror to clean, sticking to ceilings and lampshades," and she sees the whiteness of the cotton as a powerful signifier (*Dirt and Desire* 107).

Ellen and Battle exemplify the sustaining and regenerative nature of long marriage. They typify the loyalty and fidelity present in the marriage of Welty's parents, and in this sense, too, they may be a biographical representation of them. They have gone the distance of years together as a matched pair, and even in their silences together, they know contentment. Their marriage builds on the legacy of endurance in love that is present in their family.

Mashula has had her own love story, set against the backdrop of the Civil War. The night-light that Dabney breaks before her wedding originally belonged to Aunt Mashula, and the story it tells is of her enduring love. When her husband leaves for the war, Mashula burns the light in anticipation of his return. She "waited for Uncle George, waited for him to come home from the Civil War till the lightning one early morning stamped her picture on the window pane. . . . Only this little night light comforted her, she said. We little children would be envious to see her burn it every dark night" (45). In the same way that Rosamund's romantic ideals find their origin in the relationship of her parents in *The Robber Bridegroom*, so Ellen and Battle resurrect, reinvigorate, and continue the tradition of love that Mashula's light reflected a generation earlier. Dabney's early breaking of the night-light, however, seems to suggest, along with other pointers in the novel, her youthful disregard for the traditions set by her family or that her relationship may not be as luminous as that of her forebears.

The younger George Fairchild similarly fulfills his great-uncle's love story. Louise Westling sees George as exemplifying a typical male Welty character: "beloved . . . observed and indulged by a whole family, especially by its women" (*Women Writers* 32). He may be accustomed to women doting on him, but in his married life George takes his role as husband seriously, and at the same time he must meet the demands of a large family.

The marriage of George Fairchild and his young bride, Robbie, give the novel a romantic focus. The family remembers and tells of George's displays of "unabashed" feelings of passion for his wife. George, who is "turbulent and dark, almost Spanish" (51), passionately catches his wife in the river, strips her except for her undergarments, and carries her "thrashing and laughing on a bed of their darling sweet peas, pulling vines and all down on her" (25). Aunts Jim Allen and Primrose respond to this scene with appropriately staunch embarrassment, but Ellen, the truth-teller in this novel, clearly sees that George and Robbie are "so boldly happy." She thinks to herself, "no one can stare back more languorously and alluringly than a rescued woman," and she remembers Robbie's "slumbrous eyes and surfeited little smile as she lay on George's wet arm" (126).

Welty usually locates out in the open, in nature, such paradisiacal moments. On their bed of "darling sweet peas," George and Robbie strike the same pose that Hazel and William Wallace and others do at the end of a romantic chase, and the moon is always appropriately placed to set the tone: "Robbie had tantalizingly let herself be chased and had jumped in the river with George in after her, everybody screaming from where they lay. Dalliance, pure play, George was after that night—he was enchanted with his wife, he made it plain then. They were in moonlight. With great splashing he took her dress and petticoat off in the water, flung them out on the willow bushes, and carried her up screaming in her very teddies, her lost ribbon in his teeth, and the shining water running down her kicking legs and flying off her heels as she screamed and buried her face in his chest, laughing too, proud too" (25). His conquest is sexual and heroic.

George and Robbie resemble their woodland forerunners in *The Robber Bridegroom* as they lay "smiling and worn out, but twined together—appealing, shining in moonlight" with handfuls of India's "pomegranate flowers" strewn over them, with the moonlight brightly complementing the scene. Battle refers to the event as the night George and Robbie "put on the Rape of the Sabines down at the Grove" (58). Danielle Fuller writes that "Ellen reads this scene as a flirtatious and seductive demonstration of Robbie's physical attraction for and to George" but argues that theirs is a "game of pleasure and power" (7). Although serious rapes occur in Welty's stories and novels, and must be recognized as such, this scene, so characterized by Battle, is playful and calls to mind the ravishing of Rosamund by her bandit Jamie, in which the lady allows herself to be found and even returns the next day for another chance to find her rapist, better known as her lover, whom she will then allow to "rob her of that which he had left her the day before."

The relationship of George and Robbie is ultimately more complex than that of Jamie and Rosamund in Welty's first novel, even though both sets of couples do reflect one another in the similar instances of willing rapes and seducer-victims. Shelley reveals her inability to comprehend the intricacies of their relationship, especially later, after Robbie and George temporarily separate, but Shelley is willing to guess: "But Shelley felt that George and Robbie had hurt each other in a way so deep, so unyielding, that she was unequal to understanding it yet. She hoped to grasp it all, the worst, but fiercely feeling herself a young, unmarried, unengaged girl, she held the more triumphantly to her secret guess—that this confrontation on the trestle was itself the reason for Robbie's leaving George and for his not going after her" (88). Given her youth and inexperience as an "unmarried, unengaged girl," Shelley instinctively senses that the conflict that causes George and Robbie to separate, albeit temporarily, is a serious one—a problem now familiar in Welty's work: that the private sphere is in counterpoint to the honoring of familial ties and allegiances. The tension between privacy and communal responsibility becomes increasingly important in Welty's fiction. In this case Shelley's guess is accurate: George and Robbie are in opposition with each other, having taken "unyielding" stances with one another in their argument about the train trestle incident.

This near-accident, which Michael Kreyling says "gradually accumulates meaning as the novel moves through its stanzas" (*Eudora Welty's Achievement of Order* 74), occurs when George's feebleminded cousin Maureen catches her foot on the train tracks. Robbie begs George not to risk his life for his cousin, and George refuses her pleading and saves Maureen. The feud over divided loyalties thus begins: Robbie leaves her husband, and George goes home to Shellmound. Suzan Harrison writes of the incident: "Bringing tragedy so close to the charmed world of Shellmound, the episode of the mysterious girl stresses how precarious that charmed, protected quality is and qualifies the pastoral affirmation of love and marriage, suggesting the danger that lies beneath the idyllic surface—dangers that are far more serious for women than men" (*Eudora Welty and Virginia Woolf* 31).

The intensity of the emotions Robbie feels becomes clear to Shelley, who takes on more and more the characteristics of Eudora Welty as she observes others. Shelley discovers Robbie crying in the Fairchild's store:

"Robbie's tears shocked her for being unhesitant—for being plain, assertive weeping for a man—weeping out loud in the heart of Fairchilds, in the wide-open store that was more public than the middle of the road. Nothing covered up the sound" (138). Even in view of her disagreement with her husband, for Robbie the effect of the temporary separation is clear, and Shelley, like Welty, observes and notes the intensity that utter devotion can bring.

The intense relationship of George and Robbie remains in clear focus as the novel progresses. Welty devotes time and attention in describing their private life—in their bedroom—at home in Memphis. Their place and the details of their life, although in the city, call to mind the one-room cabin of Ruby and Clyde Fisher in "A Piece of News." Welty again takes an intimate look at George and Robbie's private life away from the clannish Fairchilds: "Just yet they had an old iron bed with a lot of tin rods head and foot, and she had painted it. There were unnoticeable places where the paint had run down those hard rods, that had never quite got dry, and when George went away on a case or was late coming home she would lie there indenting these little rivers of paint with her thumbnail very gently, to kill time. . . . They lived on the second floor of a nice, two-story flat, and nobody bothered them . . . they could lie there listening to the busy river life. . . . Then they would dance barefooted and drink champagne, and sometimes in the middle of the day they would meet by appointment in the New Peabody by the indoor fountain" (139). Their life together has charm: they dance barefoot, drink champagne, and meet at midday at the Peabody Hotel. Even without further dramatic seductions by the riverbank, they are at ease with one another, comfortable, romantic, and happy.

The compatibility of George and Robbie extends to their physical relationship. Welty is not shy in her description, centered in the point of view of Robbie, who recalls her intimate moments with George. In her aubade she remembers his "pure animal way of love": "Where he lay naked and unconscious she knew the heat of his heavy arm, the drag of his night beard over her. She knew what he cried out in his sleep, she was outside herself as a cup those three drops fell in. She breathed the night in beside him, away off from dreams and time and her own thoughts awake—the companion of his weight and warmth. Then she was glad there was nothing at all, no existence in the world, beyond George asleep, this real and forgetful exacting body. She slept by him as if in the shadow of a mountain of being. Any moon and stars there were could rise and set over his enfolding, unemanating length. The sun could lean over his backside and wake her" (148). George and Robbie provoke philosophical questions about love and marriage as the novel goes on. Robbie, for example, assesses her original expectations of marriage in terms of her current situation. As she walks back through the fields to find George at Shellmound, she ruminates: "Caught in marriage you were supposed to fling about, to cry out and ask for something—to expect something—what was the look in all unmarried girls' eyes but the challenging look of knowing what? But Robbie—who was greatly in love . . . did not know what. . . . In the depths of her soul she had first looked for one of two blows, or magic touches, to fall . . . she had been practical enough to expect alternate eventualities. But even now—unless the old bugaboo of pregnancy counted—there was no eventuality" (144). Like Mashula's old recipe, marriage to Robbie now seems to require a balance of alternating mixtures; she expects "alternate eventualities" of either "unnerving change" or "beautiful transformation" to happen in marriage (144).

Robbie, however, has now come to the realization that "there was no eventuality"—that marriage does not necessarily fulfill expectation or change fate, except perhaps in pregnancy. This change in her attitude compromises her pride and paves the way for her decision to go back to George. No chase ensues; George does not come after Robbie this time. She must examine her position without him and weigh her options. The separation is a trial of the marriage; the result is Robbie's dawning comprehension of the advantages and possibilities open to her. Although she now sees few "magic touches," she nonetheless convinces herself to reunite with her husband, and in doing so, she has been like a "stray fawn," lost but finding its way back home (155).

The boundaries that separate the couple from the outer circle of family and community become an overarching concern in the novel. Michael Kreyling has assessed "Robbie's insistence upon the flesh and blood of George—his pure animal presence" and says that it "collides with the desire of the Fairchild clan to have him at their liberty as paragon, hero, and scapegoat. In loving George, Robbie encounters an almost overwhelming force, the family's adoration of him. Her love, like Gloria's for Jack in *Losing Battles,* seeks the intimate, exclusive relationship. She can thus only clash with the Fairchilds, whose family love "ties individual members to the home ground" (65–66). Louis Rubin writes that the communality of the novel, "the constant coming and going in company with each other, protects the private loneliness of each participant" (6). John Alexander Allen describes Shellmound as a place that is a "changeless demi-paradise," in which Troy and the entire outside world are intruders (38).

Shelley, the outsider in the family circle, feels the collective way her family loves. She wishes her father would not "cherish" his children "all together in a bunch—separately, but not one to go unloved for the other loved." The Fairchilds are private people, however, even though they form their own large group; they appear to the outside as "a wall, we are self-sufficient against people that come up knocking, we are solid to the outside" (84), but Ellen notices that the psychological actions of the family also tend to happen collectively: "Ellen could see in a mental tableau the family one and all fasten an unflinching look upon George. . . . It was a look near to reproach" (161). The group makes an impression that the lone individual cannot.

In this atmosphere of strong opinion within a large, collective family, couples must try to find the privacy they need. George and Robbie "had had no time alone; here nobody had. So she spoke as though no one else but George were in the room. It was something not one of them had ever thought of" (186). Although they need privacy and are "Passionate, sensitive to the point of strain and secrecy" (222), George and Robbie kiss openly, and "the whole family watched them 'make up'" (189). Privacy issues within a larger family are in open tension.

The intersection between privacy and the place of family and community impacts Robbie perhaps more than anyone in *Delta Wedding.* Her insistence that George maintain absolute allegiance to her, over and above his obligations to this "bunch" of relatives and their various demands, threatens her relationship with him and his family. Robbie initially holds the marriage as leverage in pleading that George not risk his life on the train tracks for a cousin. Her bewilderment is apparent when he insists on doing so. She cannot envision a world without him: "'But you're every-thing on earth to me,' Robbie said plainly. . . . With an extremely con-scious, an almost brazen, power of explicitness that seemed to match George's, Robbie was leaving out every other thing in the world with the thing she said. The *vulgar* thing she said!" (187). Robbie does not compre-hend the strength of George's attachment to others, and she views mar-riage as including only two.

The family begs Robbie not to force a polarization. "It's not right to make him be pulled to pieces, and over something he did, and very honor-ably did," Ellen tells her. In her insistence that "when he loves me he re-ally hates you—hates the Fairchilds that he's one of!" Robbie "fights the Fairchilds" and positions herself against, rather than as part of, the broader scope of her husband's familial and social world (163, 162). Like Solomon in "Livvie," Robbie makes a mistake of exclusivity, and like Solomon, she must see her mistake and correct it. She cannot take George too far away from his family.

For George, however, the polarization is serious enough for him to leave Robbie, and this time he forces her to come back to him rather than chase her and concede himself. Indeed, the problem deeply threatens the security of their marriage. Both parties have good points to make: George maintains his devotion to his family, and Robbie is right to fear the deadli-ness of the train tracks—indeed, a strange, vagrant girl dies on the same tracks later in the novel. George's (and Maureen's) escape thus seems much less inevitable. Joyce Carol Oates sees the girl's death on the tracks as an-other indication of the Fairchild indifference to the larger world: "She is on the outside; she is excluded from society. Her existence is of no par-ticular concern to anyone. So, a member of this claustrophobic and settled world may well venture into hers, make love to her, leave her, and her death is a kind of natural consequence of her being excluded from the 'delta wedding' and all its bustling excitement." The quotation seems orig-inally to have appeared in: *Shenandoah* (vol. 20, Spring, 1969) and is on page (55). The fate of the vagrant girl is in juxtaposition to the activities of the Fairchilds, who have plentiful protection and support.

In *Delta Wedding* other relationships also are under scrutiny, such as that of Dabney and Troy, whose wedding provides the occasion for the novel and begins Dabney's initiation into love. Like the painter in "A Memory" and the budding Josie in "The Winds," Dabney fears sexuality almost as much as she feels its pull. On the night before her marriage, Dabney is metaphorically still only "looking in where it is dark" but entreats the night to illuminate its secrets for her. The cotton fields again metaphorically indicate experience and knowing. She would now enter marital, sexual experience, or walk "out into it": "She wondered if she would ever know. . . . What could she know now? . . . The cotton like the rolling breath of sleep overflowed the fields. Out into it, if she were married, she would walk now—her bare foot touch at the night's hour, firmly too, a woman's serious foot. She would walk on the clear night—angels, though, did that—tread it with love not this lonely, never this lonely, for under her foot would offer the roof, the chimney, the window of her husband, the solid house. Draw me in, she whispered, draw me in—open the window like my window, I am still only looking in where it is dark" (90).

Dabney's sexuality takes center stage. Michael Kreyling says that "Dabney rushes into the conflicts of life with a headlong earnestness that her older sister cannot match" (*Understanding* 100). Her aunts avoid asking her about her relationship with Troy, and the night-light again suggests sexuality: "They were afraid to ask her, little old aunts. She thought of how they drew back to see her holding their night light" (48). Later Dabney proudly announces that she hopes "to have a baby right away," and although this comment sends waves of "delight and terror" in the younger sister, India, her aunts only respond with shyness and embarrassment by "looking at nothing." Sexual awareness is a topic they ignore. "Little girls don't talk about honeymoons," Aunt Jim Allen cautions her niece. "They don't ask their sisters questions, it's not a bit nice" (46). When Dabney first announces her upcoming marriage, Jim Allen retreats from her niece's sexual maturity: "Things aren't going to be any different, are they?" (48).

The bed quilt that Troy's mother sends as a wedding gift also symbolizes the changes that marriage will bring. Like the quilt in "Death of a Traveling Salesman," this one—and even its pattern has a suggestive name—"Delectable Mountains," carries sexual significance. Shelley senses that significance and backs "away each time she came forward" to see— and yet avoid close contact with—the quilt. Troy explains that this quilt will grace the marriage bed; he aims "for Dabney and me to sleep under it" almost always. Primrose reacts to this innuendo by darting "her little hand out, as if the quilt were hot and getting hotter" (113). Like Cousin Annie Flo in "Why I Live at the P.O.," these aunts will go to their graves "denying the facts of life." Their presence in these scenes emphasizes the changes and "eventualities" that will take place in Dabney's life after her marriage.

As in numerous Welty works, here water has symbolic properties. After her honeymoon Dabney seems still "timid of the element itself," and in her description of the river, she suggests that love becomes more mysterious with time: "In catching sight of love she had seen both banks of a river and the river rushing between—she saw everything but the way down" (244–45). Not yet finding her way, Dabney has taken only the initial steps into the river of marriage into which Mashula, Ellen, and Robbie before her have already waded deeply.

The aunts of *Delta Wedding* (most of whom are widows) have lost their spouses to war. Aunt Mashula Hines, Aunt Mac, and Aunt Shannon are all widows who survived pioneer tragedy and the Civil War to live out their lives alone. Aunt Mashula's night-light, which characterizes her long and fruitless wait for her husband, George, to return, is a symbol of loss just as much as a beacon of hope and commitment. That Dabney breaks this heirloom lamp just prior to her own wedding bodes ill for her marriage and measures her immaturity in matters of the heart. "Only this little night light" comforted Mashula through her dark hours, and all those around her envy the devotion conveyed by its burning "every dark night" (45). In breaking the night-light, as Ruth Vande Kieft notes, Dabney shatters "not only her innocence and childhood within the family, but a part of the family unity itself . . . all that the two aunts would like to preserve intact, along with their own and their niece's virginity" (*Eudora Welty* 106). The night-light represents the tradition of faithfulness and endurance of the Fairchild women in their marriages.

Faithfulness in the face of death also characterizes the two older sisters in *Delta Wedding*, Aunt Shannon and Aunt Mac. Old Aunt Mac, although stone deaf now and "little with age," after sixty years still dresses in mourning clothes for her husband, who was killed in the Battle of Corinth. The long decades are a testament to her loyalty—and remembered love—as is the glowing lamp for Mashula. Against this backdrop of perseverance and unshakable bonds, Welty establishes a clear theme for *Delta Wedding*. In their endurance and hardship in losing their war hero husbands, the aunts are role models for the young Fairchild generation.

In this novel, however, their lost loves also stimulate ceaseless bickering between Aunt Shannon and Aunt Mac. The two aunts had a "schism" as far back as Civil War days, in which an "ineradicable coolness had come between them—it seemed to have sprung from a jealousy between the sisters over which one agonized the more or the more abandonedly, over the fighting brothers and husbands. With the brothers and husbands every man killed in the end, the jealousy did not seem canceled by death, but extended by it" (118–19). Like Aunt Mac, whose outward symbol of mourning is her black clothing, Aunt Shannon enshrines her commitment to her lost love. By some means—senility or imagination—Aunt Shannon still lives with her husband, in her mind. She addresses him as if he were alive and present in the room, when she talks to "dearie," and she bends her head "as if he had come up behind her while she was knitting to give her a little kiss on the back of the neck, as indeed he had done often long ago." Her re-creations of the companionship preserve him in living memory. In her refusal to accept his death and let him go, Aunt Shannon shuns the specter of loneliness and keeps her husband alive, if only through her memory and imagination.

Shelley stands in *Delta Wedding* as a lonely figure in the novel, as does her nine-year-old cousin Laura, who visits for the wedding. Taken together, they may be autobiographical representations of Eudora Welty, who had the experience, as they do, of traveling to the Delta to visit a large family. Both are youthful and inexperienced girls considering love but who have yet to know it. Reminiscent of Josie in "The Winds," who is similarly expectant, Shelley senses the love around her, yet she fears initiation. She is in what Simone de Beauvoir calls the normal process of maturation: "Whether by slow gradations or all of a sudden, [a young girl] must undergo sexual initiation. There are young girls who hold aloof. . . . They may retain their childish repugnance for the male" (369).

Shelley feels such repugnance. She rejects imagining her mother and father as sexual partners: she "cannot think how it was when Papa and

Mama wanted each other" (85). She feels disgust at the thought of Troy, her sister's choice of a mate, and she knows that she could "never love him" (84). Shelley does, however, long for romance. She waits for the opportunity to read *The Beautiful and Damned* "and to read it in bed" (83), and she hopes secretly to understand what she sees going on around her in the relationships of couples: "But Shelley felt that George and Robbie had hurt each other in a way so deep, so unyielding, that she was unequal to understanding it yet. She hoped to grasp it all, the worst," but she still feels herself to be a "young, unmarried, unengaged girl" (88). Shelley expresses a similar reluctance in imagining Dabney's married life: "They all lay back in flowered chairs and ate busily, and with a greedy delight anticipated what was ahead for Dabney. . . . All except Shelley, who stared at George as he held the cake plate before her" (193). Ruth Vande Kieft summarizes the predicament: "Shelley responds with an initial terrorized retreat from experience, sexual involvement, mature relationships, and accident and death" (*Eudora Welty* 107).

With her back to the moon—a pose symbolic of her unreadiness for love—Shelley stands "shivering" in her nightgown, contemplating the wedding day and the relationships she observes. Her feelings about them take the foreground. She feels sympathy for her mother's pregnancy and is angry with her father for causing them: "Oh, Papa. . . . How could you keep getting Mama in this predicament?" (228–29). She apologizes to her mother for the pain Shelley's own birth must have caused—she was born with no help, and the doctor had trouble with the gas machine. She regrets her mother's experiences in giving birth to her: "This was Dabney's wedding night and the clock was striking. 'The gas machine,' Shelley tried to say through the noise, 'I'm so sorry, Mama'" (229). Marriage, sexuality, and birth converge in Shelley's imagination as she contemplates her own origin. Elizabeth Crews notes that "Shelley's journey moves her to sexual awareness" ("Cixous' New Woman" 67). Shelley also realizes that "some people . . . lived a lifetime without finding the one who relieved the heart's overflow" (223). The intense and austere presence of Shelley in *Delta Wedding* is a counterpoint to the busy wedding activities and a self-portrait of the author, who matured in her understanding of the interconnections of love, sexuality, marriage, and childbirth. Although she did have important and satisfying relationships, Eudora Welty seems never to have found "the one who relieved the heart's overflow."

Like her cousin Shelley, Laura is also an outsider at the family gathering. Laura, too, sees love swirling around her and hopes someday engage in it. Laura hugs the pickle barrel in a moment of eagerness: "All these things held the purest enchantment for her; once, last year, she threw her arms around the pickle barrel, and seemed to feel then a heavy, briny response in its nature, unbudging though it was" (237). Like Robbie's description of George asleep, with his "weight" and "unemanating" being (148), the pickle barrel suggests to Laura the "heavy" and "unbudging" quality that she may someday find in an embrace with a lover. Like the Welty characters of youth and inexperience from the early stories, Laura wants answers to "the heart's pull" and imagines that someday she will understand love as one of the mysteries of life, just as she has learned Newton's lessons on the pull of gravity: "She imagined that one day, maybe the next, in the Fairchild house—she would know the answer to the heart's pull, just as it would come to her in school why the apple was pulled down on Newton's head, and that it was the way for girls in the world that they should be put off, put off, put off—and told a little later; but told, surely" (237). Julia Eichelberger sees Laura as the embodiment of "Welty's artistic ambition and anxiety" but notes that Laura is "in danger of being swallowed up—or drowned—by the Fairchild clan" ("'Way for Girls'" 48).

Rose imagery has metaphorical significance in this novel, as in most other Welty writings. Howard does not see the beauty in roses—instead, he sees and feels the thorns: "I wish there wasn't no such thing as roses. . . . If I had my way, wouldn't be a rose in de world. Catch your shirt and stick you and prick you and grab you. Got thorns" (298). He implies all of the thorny political issues associated with plantation life. The white women have the leisure time to devote to flower adoration, but he cannot do so. The one who gathers the roses and works the gardens is the one who feels the prick of the thorns. As is typical of Welty, her stories and metaphors have serious political implications. Brannon Costello studies the language in the exchanges between the "paternalists" and "African American workers" as a symptom of strained race relations in Delta Wedding (30).

The brooch that Laura finds resembles a rose. Louise Westling notes: "Shaped like the flower traditionally identified with feminine beauty, the pin represents feminine sexuality even more obviously than the brooch Minta Doyle loses in *To the Lighthouse*." She adds that soon again the pin "is lost" and "this time in the fertile waters of the Yazoo" (116). The pin also may represent the ineffable quality of love that most in *Delta Wedding* seek but few can find.

In the great tradition of Shakespeare and Jane Austen, a wedding celebration brings Welty's novel to a close. The celebratory conclusion simultaneously reunites several couples. Robbie and George will renew their commitments to one another against a backdrop of the wedding. In reuniting: "Robbie knew that now, still, George in getting her back would start all over with her love, as if she were shy. It was his way—as if he took long trips away from her which she did not know about, and then came back to her as to a little spring where he had somehow cherished only the hope for the refreshment that all the time flowed boundlessly enough. . . . Well, she was always the same, the way a little picnic spot would remain the same from one summer to the next, under its south-riding moon, and he was the different and new, the picnicker, the night was the different night" (161). George and Robbie will "start all over" with each other, and the implication is that their marriage will endure.

The marriage of Robbie and George Fairchild has the vital, enduring component of Aunt Mashula's. Like a bride again, Robbie sits in "the middle of the whirl" of dancing bridesmaids and guests (182). During this reunion the whole family watches George and Robbie kiss, and India, especially fascinated, comes up "close on her toes to see if she could tell yet what there was about a kiss" (189). Ellen and Battle watch the festivities from their own "love seat" (185). As George and Robbie kiss, they now appear as compatible and well-matched dancers: "The bridesmaids . . . took the groomsmen and began to dance here in the room, and around George and Robbie there in the center. . . . While George was kissing Robbie, Bluet had him around his knees and kissed him down there, and with such fervor that she sat down, sighing. Then George and Robbie were dancing too—how amazingly together they went. In and out wove Litte Ranny, waving a pretend shepherd crook, shouting, 'I'm the wedding!' and stamp-ing the floral wreath in the rug" (189). The scene is resplendent with the reconciliation and communality of an Austen novel.

In *Delta Wedding* Welty embarks on her first full-length, realistic novel. Love and gaiety are featured prominently, but loss, jealousy, fear, uncer-tainty, loneliness, and waiting, as well as the issues of class and race, inter-play with the celebration. Ideas from earlier works recur: the endurance of successful relationships over time, the importance of balance between privacy and communal and familial roles, and the tension between inno-cence and experience. Along with them Welty depicts intimacy and the importance of loyalty and commitment as some of the eventualities of "the heart's pull."

CHAPTER 6

A "Little Sweetheart Rose in His Lapel"

The Heart of the Ponders

As is typical of Welty's fiction, comedy belies in *The Ponder Heart* a more serious philosophical rumination. The dark side, now well established as characteristic of her works, again here takes the form of death, loss, and loneliness. The Ponder family as a whole knows about love. Uncle Daniel is the
late baby: "Uncle Daniel was Grandpa's baby. They had him late—mighty
late" (9). Edna Earle says that Daniel has "been brought up in a world of
love" (143). The Ponder "heart" metaphorically implies the warmth, generosity, sweetness, and selflessness that Daniel Ponder always exudes.

The rose has cross-gendered associations in this novel. Usually adored
and worn by women, the roses in *The Ponder Heart* are favored by men.
They wear roses—on their lapels and hat brims. The male association with
roses here, combined with the heart as metaphor, is Welty's charming indication that Uncle Daniel is searching for love as well as of his good-
natured self and generosity in his relationships with the people around him
and they with him. Uncle Daniel appears with a red tie, Stetson, and a rose
in his lapel. He varies the roses that he wears, and Welty, who had great
familiarity with rose nomenclature, invokes an appropriate name for each
one of the roses. On one occasion Daniel has a "little Sweetheart rose in his
lapel" (12), and later he has an "Else Poulsen rose in the lapel" (86). The
other men wear roses too. "Around his hat" Big John wears "a bunch of
full-blown roses, five or six Etoiles in a row, with little short stems stuck
down in the hatband" (90), and Dr. Ewbanks wears an Else Poulsen
(107).[1] Edna Earle editorializes about these roses: "they're still growing in
Grandma's garden, in spite of everything" (90). Later "Old Gladney edges
up and takes a smell of Dr. Ewbanks' rose" (108).

Uncle Daniel's big, sweet, generous heart is fully on display in the novel.
His heart will be metaphorically construed here, much as it was for R. J.

Bowman in "Death of a Traveling Salesman," but Daniel will survive his hurts and disappointments in love, unlike the unluckier salesman. Edna Earle says he "loves society" and cultivates cheer wherever he goes: "As for Uncle Daniel, he went right ahead, attracting love and friendship with the best will and the lightest heart in the world. He loved being happy! He loved happiness like I love tea" (7, 14). Daniel continually sends people his love: "Give your grandfather my love," he says (132), and also sends his love to Judge Clanahan before the trial (138). Daniel's heart is so full that he can hear it beating (114). Edna Earle concludes that no one has the heart that Daniel does: "And it may be anybody's heart would quail, trying to keep up with Uncle Daniel's" (156).

Romance comes naturally to this lovable, caring, and generous man. In spite of his late start—he "had got clear up to his forties before we ever dreamed that such a thing as love flittered through his mind" (20)—Daniel as a middle-aged man dresses in clothing for an attractive, well-to-do male Welty character: he wears a white suit (as King MacLain does). Even as he participates in a Tom Thumb wedding in his childhood, Daniel makes a perfect bridegroom: "Everybody said it was the sweetest miniature wedding that had ever been held here. He was the bridegroom and I believe to my soul Birdie Bodkin, the postmistress, was the bride. . . . And here Uncle Daniel sat, with that first little bride right on tap" (34). Daniel is already prepared for what is to come.

Daniel's sojourn in the adult world quickly incudes love. His interest in the dancing girls is one of the first examples of his curious eye: "He kept telling me for a week after, that those dancing girls wore beyond compare the prettiest dresses and feather-pieces he ever saw on ladies' backs in his life, and could dance like fairies. 'They every one smiled at me,' he said. 'And yet I liked Miss Elsie Fleming very well, too'" (23).

Although Miss Teacake Magee sings "The Sweetest Story Ever Told" at her marriage to Daniel, the marriage dissolves all too quickly for several reasons: "What Uncle Daniel told me he didn't take to—I asked him because I was curious—was hearing spool-heels coming and going on Professor Magee's floor" (27). Daniel is uncomfortable with Miss Teacake's habits and also with the idea that he is an interloper in another man's house.

Even during her marriage to Uncle Daniel, Miss Teacake still dates every event from the time past "since [she] lost Professor Magee" (21).

The further adventures of Daniel Ponder into the world of romantic love lead him to Bonnie Dee Peacock. She "traipsed" into town with her "yellow, fluffy hair," which is "downy—like one of those dandelion puff-balls you can blow and tell time by" (34). Malnourished and insubstantial, she foreshadows Fay in *The Optimist's Daughter*. Bonnie Dee brings along her six-year collection of *True Love Story*, and Daniel falls in love with her immediately. His proposal of marriage is high-flown. Edna Earle recalls that Uncle Daniel "always makes everything sound grand. Home on the hilltop! Great big car! Negroes galore! Home-grown bacon and eggs and ham and fried grits and potato cakes and honey and molasses for breakfast every morning to start you off" (30–31). Although they agree on a "trial" marriage, the new couple nonetheless awakens jealousy in Teacake Magee: she "drove by Ponder Hill, pretending she was looking for wild plums," just to see Daniel and his new bride (37–38).

The trial marriage to Bonnie Dee engenders for Daniel heartbreak and sadness, however. When Bonnie Dee departs, she "was steadily breaking his heart." He tells and retells the story of her leave-taking, and in doing so, his pain intensifies: "And every night, when he'd come to the end, he'd screw his eyes up tight with fresh tears." Daniel even "broke down" in tears at the table one evening after his sad tale ended (51–52). He has all too soon known both the joy and despair of "the heart's pull."

His reunions with Bonnie are coy and playful, however, much as they are for Clyde and Ruby Fisher and Robbie and George Fairchild: "And when he reached for her, she went around to his other side. I believe she missed him. So I just politely turned on my heel, leaving them there" (60). Daniel sings a love song to honor Bonnie's return: "Oh, my bride has come back to me. Pretty as a picture, I'm happy beyond compare" (62). Bonnie enjoys and requites him, at least for a while; she declines a big trip to Memphis with her sisters because she is now "an old, married lady. And it was too late for her to go" (126).

When Bonnie Dee dies by a sudden lightning strike, Daniel allows his roving eye to wander again. First, he sees Johnnie Ree, Bonnie Dee's younger sister: Edna recounts that "all of a sudden Uncle Daniel *noticed* her. Noticed Johnnie Ree. . . . I heard his chair scrape. His eyes got real round, and I put my hand on his knee, like I do in church when he begins to sing too fast" (124). Next he asks Johnnie Ree for a date (152), and he also gives his ex-wife's knee a fond pat on his way out of the courtroom (149).

Only at the conclusion of the novel does Uncle Daniel appear at all deflated by these experiences. As always, Edna Earle analyzes his behavior: "And Uncle Daniel had got right back to where he started from. He went from giving away to falling in love, and from falling in love to talking, and from talking to losing what he had, and from losing what he had to being run off, and from being run off straight back to giving away again" (148–49). Robert Drake says that in Daniel, Welty depicts "love which never fails, never questions, but waits and is patient" (426). The final glimpse of Daniel at the close of the novel is poignant and sad. He "comes down a little later every night" from his room at the Beulah hotel. Edna Earle worries just enough about this solitary pattern to consider giving him "calomel-and-quinine." She knows it helps because she is "a pretty good doser" herself and has her own reasons to need it (155).

Edna Earle is the other essentially lonely character in the novel. Although she is a humorous, chatty person who says she can "hardly get a word in for myself," she nonetheless channels most of her narrative energy into expositions about the love status of other people. The narrative often centers on her point of view. Amid Edna Earle's funny remarks and self-ironies, however, Welty includes ideas about love. Daniel's world unfolds through the eyes of this niece, and yet much "gets told besides" Edna's own romantic history.

Edna Earle Ponder, like the previous manager of the Beulah Hotel, Cora Eubanks, is an old maid (13), but Edna does have a social life, albeit an erratic one, with the traveling salesman, Mr. Springer. Their relationship is unsatisfactory and haphazard, owing partly to Springer's restless profession but also to their lukewarm attraction to one another. Springer would "throttle into town and want that first-floor room . . . and count on me to go to the movie with him" (10). She blushes when she "had to come down" the staircase in front of Mr. Springer in her "kimono," on one of his trips to town. If she were trying an alluring ploy, it fails; the next week he comes through and does not stop to look for Edna Earle (58). In an even more dissatisfied moment, Edna complains that he never holds her hand at the right moments; Mr. Springer has no sense of the romantic timing: "I felt worn out, like when Mr. Springer stays over and makes me go to one of those sad, Monday night movies and never holds my hand at the right places" (73). Her patience with him wanes considerably in the courtroom scene when she says, "I didn't give a good continental" (153). The relationship with Springer disappoints Edna Earle on most levels.

Edna Earle expresses an interest in her romantic future. Certainly, she loves to talk, and as for Sister in "Why I Live at the P.O.," the ladies in "Lily Daw and the Three Ladies," and the maiden ladies in "Asphodel," talking and telling the story of love compensate somewhat for love that has not come along and provide a sense of vicarious participation. Edna Earle's obsession with talking, like Daniel's obsession with love, may simply buffer her against her lonely nights. John Edward Hardy focuses on Edna's talking: "one suspects that Edna Earle really does not want to be married, has never wanted it. . . . What Edna Earle wants is to talk. Marriage would seriously cramp her style as indefatigable and unchallenged narrator" (100).

Edna imagines marriage and the children and grandchildren that would naturally follow: "Suppose I'd even *attempted*, over the years, to step off— I dread to think of the lengths Grandpa would have gone to stop it. . . . I used to think if I ever did step off with, say, Mr. Springer, Uncle Daniel wouldn't mind; he always could make Mr. Springer laugh. And I could name the oldest child after Grandpa and win him over quick before he knew it" (27). She saves a poem in her drawer "to show her grandchildren" (59), but on the other hand, she talks insecurely of her place as the last of the Ponder bloodline: "anything Uncle Daniel has left after some future day is supposed to be mine. I'm the inheritor. I'm the last one, isn't that a scream? The last Ponder" (146). Her "scream" is an ironic indication of her lost hope for marriage and a family. Through her lighthearted chatter and banter, Edna's need for a mate and family emerge. Her later self-congratulations on not marrying Mr. Ovid Springer "too hastily" are finally just a rationale and camouflage for her disappointment at his never having proposed to her. Usually shielded by words, here Edna Earle's vulnerability is clear.

Uncle Daniel is the only man who understands and cares for her, and Edna reciprocates fully. Daniel needs care, and when he moves into the Beulah Hotel at the end of the novel, Edna Earle behaves as if she were his wife. She begins to call him "dear heart" and pampers him by "order[ing] off after" his favorite cigars. She "always keeps an extra supply on hand. And I'd light him one" (129, 53). She prepares his favorite meals at the Beulah and listens to his tales of woe. Edna's closeness to Daniel even during his marriage further secures a place for herself in Daniel's life: "Of course, I'm intended to look after Uncle Daniel and everybody knows it, but in plenty of marriages there's three—three all your life. Because nearly everybody's got somebody" (27). Again, Edna's protestations belie her true sentiments. She has no one, except her dear old relative. "Everybody's got somebody" is true for these two lonely figures, who ultimately care for each other.

Edna Earle pushes the boundaries of her relationship with Daniel more toward that of a spouse than a devoted niece: "I don't really think Uncle Daniel missed Bonnie Dee," Edna says after Bonnie's departure—"He had me" (56). "They knew where he was," she declares when people look for Uncle Daniel—"with me" (85). When his acquittal from the murder trial ends, Uncle Daniel comes to Edna for solace and shelter: "I've got good news for you. I'm coming to live with you for keeps" (153). "Come with me, Uncle Daniel," she says, "and [I] put my arm through his. . . . I'm here, and just the same as I will always be, but then he never was afraid of losing me" (152, 154). Edna Earle and Daniel are now companions, and their mutually supportive familial relationship buoys and sustains them both, even as it substitutes for romantic love.

Edna Earle's proclamations generally turn to love. Initially, she asserts that company is better than love: "There's something I think's better to have than love, and if you want me to, I'll tell you what it is—that's company" (56). Michael Kreyling points out that "the love that Edna Earle prefers is less physical and individualized than it is communal" (*Understanding* 158). Edna's rationalizations may have taken hold. Later she redefines her philosophy: "I don't know if you can measure love at all. But Lord knows there's a lot of it, and . . . : if the main one you've set your heart on isn't speaking for your love, or is out of your reach some way, married or dead or plain nitwitted, you've still got that love banked up somewhere. Love!

There's always somebody wants it" (69–70). Her solitary reality, however, belies these cheerful, aphoristic sentiments.

Edna Earle also opines that: "Love. . . . It's all in a way of speaking. . . . With some people, it's little threats. With others, it's liable to be poems" (117). Love for her has always been unattainable, and for Uncle Daniel love, like his riches, is inaccessible: "The riches were all off in the clouds somewhere, like true love is, I guess, like a castle in the sky, where he could just sit and dream about it being up there for him" (50). Edna nonetheless continues hoping that love will someday be coming, even though presently it is as elusive as a "castle in the sky."

As these three novels—The Robber Bridegroom, Delta Wedding, and The Ponder Heart—focus on matters of the heart, they emphasize love and marriage but with serious undertones that, taken together, provide one main dichotomy of Welty's fiction. The Robber Bridegroom, like the stories "A Memory" and "At the Landing," suggests that overidealized visions must give way to a more realistic approach to love. With settings often in the wild outdoors, on the verdant bank of the Mississippi River, Welty locates her southern landscape of the heart. The normalization and domestication of the carefree, charmed life in The Robber Bridegroom must occur: Rosamund starts the process by making her rough-mannered robber housemates wipe their feet on a doormat. The stains of the violence, including rape and death, in this story, must be reckoned with, however, even though the lighter tone of the novel claims center stage.

With its much more realistic setting, Delta Wedding builds upon the first novel and adds more complexity. The love relationships in this novel, like those of The Robber Bridegroom, are generally passionate and unabashed—they follow Mashula's formula of sustaining love through time and across the boundaries of death. The cycle of continuing love, which Mashula and the other widowed aunts have begun, becomes a tradition that the new generation can draw from and imitate. Love, desire, romance, and commitment combine in the marriage of George and Robbie Fairchild. They are similar to—yet even more realistic than—the bond between Jamie and Rosamund Lockhart.

In Delta Wedding Welty articulates ideas about what love means. Robbie wonders what to ask for in love. Welty's answer is that though mysterious and unexplainable, love cannot stop the course of life to death but can reach beyond death; it cannot overcome (and should not overwhelm) other obligations to family and community; marriage rarely alters the identity of the individuals. Robbie discovers there are "no eventualities" except perhaps to create new life; love has the power to regenerate itself (in some cases); and at the same time others never find the right mate to "relieve the heart's overflow."

In *The Ponder Heart* Welty again overlays a serious subject with a comic treatment. Edna Earle is at once a character who makes funny statements about life and also reveals herself to be aware of the limitations to happiness. Daniel, too, suffers the consequences of having dared to love. His attempts to combine happiness in marriage with his congenial generosity meet with bad luck. For both of the main Ponders in the novel, love is finally as elusive as money is to others. Edna Earle believes that the heart has an endless fund of love that someone always wants to receive. In her first three novels Welty puts forward the belief that Edna Earle confidently espouses—that love is "always banked up somewhere"—but then tempers these "castle in the sky" ideals with realistic depictions of solitary figures such as Welty herself.

CHAPTER 7

"With Rosettes"

The Golden Apples

During 1945–56 Eudora Welty published novels and volumes of short stories. Each book is distinct, yet she returns to familiar themes. *Delta Wedding* and *The Ponder Heart,* are primarily light in tone but all have dark undercurrents. *The Golden Apples* and *The Bride of the Innisfallen,* are more poetic and lyrical in style and more meditative in tone, on the whole, than earlier works. These later volumes of stories present wandering, lonely characters; adolescents experiencing the awakening of adulthood; and the emotional exhaustion of unrequited relationships. Adult figures such as Ran and Eugene MacLain grow to maturity yet find disappointment and then perhaps stimulation in loves old and new; Virgie Rainey and King MacLain find freedom from constraint and conformity. The familiar narrator appears again in *The Golden Apples*—in the figure of Katie Rainey, who in some ways resembles Edna Earle in *The Ponder Heart* and Sister in "Why I Live at the P.O." in her garrulousness and in continually pointing to the problems of everyone else. A story, Welty said, should be "like a string pulled taut," and her stories are succinct and deftly drawn portraits of relationships. Her novels provide ample space and time for full considerations and elaboration of themes, as in the tradition of Jane Austen, with a focus on the familial and the marital.

The Golden Apples and *The Bride of Innisfallen* echo the early volumes of short stories in themes of seeking, hoping, and finding love and/or knowing loss and disappointment. Relationships between men and women in *The Golden Apples* characteristically alternate between successful and unsuccessful. The later novel *Losing Battles* keeps with Welty's standard of a primarily lighthearted tone, but in her final novel, *The Optimist's Daughter,* she turns to the deeply psychological, sad, and highly autobiographical in her descriptions of pain and loss.

The marriage between King and Snowdie MacLain in *The Golden Apples* is by turns funny and troubling. Snowdie regularly expresses disappointment since the time when King long ago captured Miss Snowdie Hudson's heart. Katie Rainey explains his extravagance: "marrying must have been some of his showing off—like man never married at all till *he* flung in, then had to show the others how he could go right on acting" (4). Townsfolk expect Snowdie to "teach school: not marry" (5), but King courts her, and she falls in love with him: "She got took up by King MacLain all of a sudden. I think it was when jack-o'-lanterns was pasted on her window. I used to see his buggy roll up right to the schoolhouse steps and wait on her. He courted her in Morgana and MacLain too, both ends, didn't skip a day" (6).

The wedding day of Snowdie and King was predictable in traditional ways, with a bride as white as "your dreams." Katie describes the wedding: "It was no different—no quicker and no slower—than the like happens every whipstitch, so I don't need to tell you they got married in the MacLain Presbyterian Church before you could shake a stick at it, no matter how surprised people were going to be. And once they dressed Snowdie all in white, you know she was whiter than your dreams" (6). The marriage of King and Snowdie has a legal foundation, but very soon afterward King leaves on what becomes his pattern of staying away from home. Some of his absences last for years. The MacLain marriage takes a more unusual turn, however, when King asks his wife to meet him in the woods.

The woods again become the landscape of love and contrast with the regular domain that King and Snowdie have. Katie notes that the couple can be comfortable at home: "After all, they were married—they had a right to sit inside and talk in the light and comfort, or lie down easy on a good goosefeather bed, either" (4). The couple, however, begins to share another bed too—the floor of the woods.

The woods are a quiet, private, natural meeting ground in numerous Welty stories. In this one the couple will seek a compromise between the confining boundaries of matrimony and a more free approach to love and commitment, which King wants. Snowdie's flights to meet her husband in the woods please them both at first. They do not need the secretive woods in the way that Hester and Dimmesdale do in *The Scarlet Letter*—in which the woods is a place in which to camouflage their love from the condemning public. For King and Snowdie the floor of the woods is an escape from the routine of married life, which seems especially unappealing to the husband. He prefers pine needles to the "good goosefeather bed." In "Shower of Gold" Katie Rainey explains, all the while embroidering the tale, of the invitations King offers Snowdie: "he sent her word ahead: 'Meet me in the woods.' No, he more invited her than told her to come— 'Suppose you meet me in the woods.' And it was night time he supposed to her. And Snowdie met him without asking 'What for?'" (4). "'The woods' was Morgan's Woods. We would any of us know the place he meant, without trying—I could have streaked like an arrow to the very oak tree, one there to itself and all spready: a real shady place by *day*, is all I know. Can't you just see King MacLain leaning his length against that tree by the light of the moon as you come walking through Morgan's Woods and you hadn't seen him in three years? . . . Then, twins" (5). King may exemplify what Simone de Beauvoir calls the "conventional figure of man caught in his relations to woman: the father, the seducer, the husband, . . . the wayward son" (143). Only late in life does he return to live with Snowdie and rove no more. During his wandering years, however, his infidelities are widely known to the Morgana community; there are "children of his growing up in the County Orphan's, so say several, and children known and unknown, scattered-like" (4). He populates the landscape with evidence of his infidelities.

King's personality and activities have attracted much critical attention. Julia Demmin and Daniel Curley write that King "represents a natural force, strength, and regeneration, a pure elemental state of being" ("Golden Apples" 243). Ruth Vande Kieft notes that in his "pagan abandon and sensuality, his open defiance of sobriety and decorum, he is allied with such characters as Don McInnis of 'Asphodel' and Cash McCord of 'Livvie'. . . . King is widely adored for his mystery, his legend, his exoticism, his coming by surprise . . . his bringing of gifts, his sexual prowess; and above all, perhaps, for his ability to make of every woman a goddess, a queen, a legend to herself" (*Eudora Welty* 113–14). Robert Phillips says that "King and Snowdie have transcended the limitations of everyday, ritual bound, gossip-ridden Morgana to experience freely the primal joys of a fertile marriage" (59). Mary Catherine Buswell has pointed out that King is one of a pattern of infidels in Welty's stories whom "society accepts" (102). Patricia Yaeger sees him as "a roustabout who wanders through the forest, wild-eyed and white-suited, in search of maidens to distress"; he becomes the "muse" and "narrative subject in the fables the women of Morgana tell themselves as they go about their work" ("Because a Fire" 960). Barbara Ladd argues that the "resistance to the patriarchal narrative provides Welty with a strategy for making female experience visible, and audible," and she sees King as "the most talked about of fathers, the most mysterious, the most omnipresent, for all his wanderings" (*Resisting History* 60). Suzan Harrison adds that "King's absence makes him central to the community of Morgana" ("Other Way" 58).

Snowdie initially seems willing and content with the unusual arrangements out of town and in the knowledge of King's extramarital activities. Like Zeus, whose sexual visitations to Danae take the form of a sudden golden shower, King's romantic overtures to his wife thrill her even after long separations. She always answers her husband's call. When she goes to Katie to announce her pregnancy, Snowdie beams in the proud and satisfied way that Hazel does in "The Wide Net": "Me and Lady May both had to just stop and look at her. She looked like more than only the news had come over her. It was like a shower of something had struck her, like she'd been caught out in something bright. It was more than the day . . . she was looking out bold as a lion that day" (6). Michael Kreyling summarizes: Snowdie "assumes the challenge of his flesh and blood; she carries his twin sons" (*Eudora Welty's Achievement of Order* 80). In the brightness of the moment Snowdie is content.

The mythological bases of this and other Welty works have been well documented by Thomas McHaney, Rebecca Mark, Guy Davenport, and others.[1] Beauvoir's analysis of the Zeus—Danae myth also is suggestive of the roles King and Snowdie have in the story: "The origin of the grain and its verity lie in Zeus; woman's fecundity is regarded as only a passive quality. She is earth, and man the seed. . . . But [the earth] plays a necessary part: it supports the living germ, protects it and furnishes the substance for its growth" (144). The season of spring mirrors the process of regeneration that Snowdie brings about, just as seasonal cycles do in "Livvie" and other stories. "Her sunbonnet ribbons was jumping around her: spring-time" (6–7).

After a time, however, King's absences begin to take a toll on Snowdie, and the marriage, all things considered, gives her pain. Katie records Snowdie's mourning for King, during his years away from her, as if he were dead and she a widow: "Snowdie grieved for him, but the decent way you'd grieve for the dead, more like, and nobody wanted to think, around her, that he treated her that way." Then during the time of her pregnancy, Snowdie is guardedly content, as other Welty's pregnant characters tend to be: "She just went on keeping house, and getting fairly big with what I told you already was twins, and she seemed to settle into her content. Like a little white kitty in a basket, making you wonder if she just mightn't put her paw and scratch, if anything was, after all, to come near" (8). She is like a cat with paws ready to scratch.

Snowdie always responds to King's visits, but she raises her sons without him, and she names the twins for her parents and grandparents. Their names are "the only sign," Katie Rainey adds, "that maybe she didn't think the name King MacLain had stayed beautiful" (9). Nonetheless, as Gail Mortimer points out, "Katie herself was one of the community voices perpetuating the speculations about King MacLain that gave him increasingly mythic stature in Morgana" (135). Snowdie misses a Halloween visit with him, and that leads to a moment of frustration because her needs are basically unmet. King almost knocks on the door, but his sons, whom he has never seen, seem to scare him away: "He makes a little shadow knock, like trying to see how it would look, and then put his present behind his coat. Of course he had something there in a box for her. You know he constitutionally brought home the kind of presents that break your heart" (13). Only after she realizes he has come and gone does Snowdie fly to the door in an agonizing moment: "And Snowdie dropped her scissors on the mahogany, and her hand just stayed in the air as still, and she looked at me, a look a minute long. And first she caught her apron to her and then started shedding it in the hall while she run to the door—so as not to be caught in it. . . . She didn't stop at the door but run on through it and out on the porch" (15). Rebecca Mark has argued that Snowdie "does not need to cry. Yet in not crying she forfeits the ancient feminine power of the goddess, who weeps in the spring to bring her daughter, and later the fertility consort, back to life" (42). Nonetheless, in "the way her head held there" Snowdie's disappointment in missing King's visit is clear (15).

Katie shows her disapproval in hoping that King has slipped and "hit a stone and fell down running . . . and took the skin off his handsome nose" (18), but Snowdie's stoicism and pain are intense: "After he'd gone by, Snowdie just stood there in the cool without a coat, with her face turned towards the country and her fingers pulling at little threads on her skirt and turning them loose in the wind, making little kind deeds of it, till I went and got her. She didn't cry" (16). Katie and others in the community help Snowdie, and the communal relationships in this book are among Welty's most delicately drawn. Here the circle of people around Snowdie supports and sustains her: "We was every bit she had. Everybody tried to stay with her as much as they could spare, not let a day go by without one of us to run in and speak to her and say a word about an ordinary thing. Miss Lizzie Stark let her be in charge of raising money for the poor country people at Christmas that year, and like that. Of course we made all her little things for her, stitches like that was way beyond her" (8).

Plez, the old yard man, tries to protect Snowdie from the uncomfortable truth that her husband had come on Halloween but had not stayed to see her. Although he has seen King go to the house, he lies to Snowdie to shield her. "No'm, Mistis," he says when she questions him, "I don't recollect one soul pass me, whole way from town" (17). The truth emerges later when Mrs. Stark "got the truth out of him. . . . But of course he wasn't going to let Miss Snowdie MacLain get hurt now, after we'd all watched her so long. So he fabricated" (18). The community tries to buffer her pain.

For all of her talk, nosiness, and disappointments of her own, Katie Rainey is a character with a narrative purpose. Like Sister in "Why I Live at the P.O.," Edna Earle in *The Ponder Heart,* and the ladies in "Asphodel," Katie talks to compensate and to experience vicariously the world around her. Her own marriage contrasts with the freer lives of the MacLains, and her husband, Fate, may resemble Leota's lazy Fred in his unwillingness or inability to fulfill her. In sharp contrast to Snowdie's husband, King, Fate "ain't got a surprise in him" (6), which accounts at least in part for

Katie's fascination with King. "With men like King," she says dreamily, "your thoughts are bottomless" (17). Fate Rainey may offer stability for Katie's domestic environment, but she clearly fantasizes about King's alluring surprises.

Katie also understands King's deceptive ways. She prides herself as a woman of experience who can recognize truths about men like King: "But it didn't seem to me, running in and out the way I was, that Snowdie had ever got a real good look at life, maybe. Maybe from the beginning. Maybe she just doesn't know the *extent.* Not the kind of look I got, and away back when I was twelve year old or so. Like something was put to my eye" (7). Her realistic apprehension of how life inflicts pain is one of Katie's hardearned lessons. Her daughter, Virgie, whom many see as the heroine of the book, inherits Katie's perspective. Even after her diatribes against him, however, Katie's vision of King MacLain continues to evoke fantasy. She imagines him escaping to California, a metaphorically "gold" place: "I believe he's been to California. Don't ask me why. But I picture him there. I see King in the West, out where it's gold and all that. Everybody to their own visioning" (11). Katie's talking and "visioning" compensate in part for her own unrealized dreams.

Miss Eckhart in "June Recital" and the twins Ran and Eugene MacLain in "The Whole World Knows" and "Music from Spain" join Katie Rainey as characters from *The Golden Apples* whose dreams of happiness seem not to materialize. Like "lost beasts," they wander without places to dwell contentedly (96). Welty has said that "June Recital" shows "most acutely" the inner life of Miss Eckhart (*One Writer's Beginnings* 101). Welty also acknowledges that Miss Eckhart has an autobiographical origin. In Miss Eckhart, Welty says, "[I] found my voice in my fiction":

> As I looked longer and longer for the origins of this passionate and strange character, at last I realized that Miss Eckhart came from me. There wasn't any resemblance in her outward identity: I am not musical, not a teacher, nor foreign in birth; not humorless or ridiculed or missing out on love; nor have I yet let the world around me slip from my recognition. But none of that counts. What counts is only what lies at the solitary core. She derived from what I already knew for myself, even felt I had always known. What

I have put into her is *my passion for my own life work, my own art.* Exposing yourself to risk is a truth Miss Eckhart and I had in common. What animates and possesses me is what drives Miss Eckhart, *the love of her art and the love of giving it, the desire to give it until there is no more left.* . . . Not in Miss Eckhart as she stands solidly and almost opaquely in the surround of her story, but in the making of her character out of my most inward and most deeply feeling self, I would say I have found my voice in my fiction. (*One Writer's Beginnings* 101; emph. added)

Late in "June Recital" the actions of Miss Eckhart take on their full tragic meaning, but when Welty first introduces this character, she is carefully decorating the piano in the old (now abandoned) MacLain house. She had rented the studio and had given piano lessons throughout her life. The act of decorating now includes draping the top with greenery and a magnolia blossom. Miss Eckhart intends to burn the piano, the symbol of her life's work, and destroy the house as well. Only Cassie Morrison and Virgie Rainey, two of her piano students who witness the old woman's crazed attempts to destroy the house, understand the full significance of her actions.

The magnolia blossom, the metronome, and the greenery that Miss Eckhart places on the piano all suggest her former dreams, which are now but memories. Virgie Rainey, Miss Eckhart's star pupil, and the girl in whom the teacher places her vicarious hopes for success, brings a magnolia blossom as a gift to Miss Eckhart before her music lessons: "Virgie carried in the magnolia bloom like a hot tureen, and offered it to Miss Eckhart, neither of them knowing any better: magnolias smelled too sweet and heavy for right after breakfast" (41). The oversweet scent of the magnolia suggests both Virgie's hope for the future and the lost dreams of the artist in her presence. Barbara Ladd argues that Virgie, "like Welty, resists victimization and identifies the 'kernel,' speaks the open secret of History, and reclaims imaginative power" (*Resisting History* 65). The metronome represents what Vande Kieft calls Miss Eckhart's "last hope for vicarious fulfillment"—through Virgie (*Eudora Welty* 118). Rebecca Mark engages in an extended discussion of Medusa and Miss Eckhart: "By pulling together the fragments of myth and symbol, she creates meaning where there would have been silence" (60).

Miss Eckhart's star student not only disappoints her teacher by failing to become a great pianist; she also deliberately and repeatedly hurts Miss Eckhart. She insults her teacher by refusing to use the metronome that Miss Eckhart "worshipped" (45–46); she "mistreats" her by telling the community about Mr. Voight, the other renter in the house who exhibits himself naked to the piano students (47): "Anybody could tell that Virgie was doing something to Miss Eckhart. She was turning her from a teacher into something lesser. And if she was not a teacher, what was Miss Eckhart?" (41). Virgie's unwillingness to develop her full potential disappoints Miss Eckhart, whose own missed opportunities contribute to her final madness. For Eckhart the memory of past opportunity replaces the hope for it.

Perhaps because she has pretty ankles, Miss Eckhart attracts a suitor— Mr. Sissum, the clerk in the shoe department of Spight's store. "When she came in she took her seat and put her foot earnestly up on Mr. Sissum's stool like any other lady in Morgana and he spoke to her very nicely . . . about her feet and treated them as a real concern; he even brought out a choice of shoes" (50). The relationship never grows, however, because neither one seizes the opportunity: "Miss Eckhart might have come over to his aisle more often, but she had an incomprehensible habit of buying shoes two or even four pairs at a time, to save going back. . . . She didn't know how to do about Mr. Sissum at all" (44).

Miss Eckhart's feelings for Mr. Sissum emerge when he gives her a doll that she likes and that makes her laugh. Her intense laughter belies her heightened emotionalism: "Never had Miss Eckhart laughed so hard, and with such an unfamiliar sound as she laughed to see Mr. Sissum's favor. Tears ran down her bright, distorted cheeks every time one of the children coming into the studio picked the Billikin up" (53). When he drowns, she displays her grief fully at his funeral. Carol Ann Johnston sees Miss Eckhart's "silent but powerful outpouring of grief" as an indication of her "powerful feeling for Mr. Sissum" (28). The magnolia appears in motif: "But when the coffin was lowered into Mr. Sissum's place in the Sissum lot under a giant magnolia tree . . . Miss Eckhart broke out of the circle. . . . She pressed to the front, through Sissums from everywhere and all the Presbyterians, and went close to get a look; and if Dr. Loomis had not caught her she would have gone headlong into the red clay hole. . . . As she struggled, her round face seemed stretched wider than it was long by a feeling that failed to match the feelings of everybody else. It was not the same as sorrow" (47). Welty carefully distinguishes between common sorrow and intense grief.

The magnolia suggests Miss Eckhart's lost dream as it shelters the body of the man she should have married. The metronome becomes significant again too. In her grief Miss Eckhart nods her head "increasing in urgency. It was the way she nodded at pupils to bring up their rhythm," and "helping out the metronome" now seems like Edna Earle's "castle in the sky." The recitals Miss Eckhart gives for her students every spring also suggest her passion for art, even in discouraging circumstances. Her own single musical performance in the story illustrates her violent emotions redirected into art: "Coming from Miss Eckhart, the music made all the pupils uneasy, almost alarmed; something had burst out, unwanted, exciting, from the wrong person's life. This was some brilliant thing too splendid for Miss Eckhart, piercing and striking the air around her the way a Christmas firework might almost jump out of the hand that was, each year, inexperienced anew" (49–50).

Miss Eckhart's face is one "for music only" as she finishes the Beethoven sonata (56), and to describe her transport, Welty uses sexual connotation. Her playing reveals her "stiff delight" and "curious anguish" (53): "Performing, Miss Eckhart was unrelenting. Even when the worst of the piece was over, her fingers like foam on rocks pulled at the spent-out part with unstilled persistence, insolence, violence. . . . Then she dropped her hands" (54). Faulkner similarly expressed the act of artistic creation in the language of sexual experience.

The students' recitals, with their elaborate preparation, are suggestive of the celebration of a traditional wedding. Preparations for the event consume "many hot, secret weeks" (59), the recital itself is a "ceremony" (62), and the recital dresses look "like a flower girl's dress in a wedding" (60). Miss Eckhart's dress, too, resembles a wedding dress, an aged one that has been kept for a long time, and she is "white-shod" by Mr. Sissum: "She was wearing her recital dress. . . . It was an old dress. . . . People would forget that dress between times and then she would come out in it again . . . it was a tawny crepe-back satin. There was a bodice of browning lace. . . . Miss Eckhart, achieving silence, stood in the shadowy spot directly under the chandelier. Her feet, white-shod, shod by Mr. Sissum for good, rested in the chalk circle previously marked on the floor" (64). Reminiscent of Emily Dickinson, Miss Eckhart is the perpetual, unmarried bride of whiteness at this recurring, wedding-like ceremony: "A blushing sensitivity sprang up in her every year at the proper time like a flower of the season" (62). The studio is "decorated like the inside of a candy box, with 'material' scalloping the mantel shelf and doilies placed under every movable object . . . with streamers of white ribbons and nosegays" (63). Miss Eckhart is bride-like in the anticipations and fulfillment the occasions provide.

The story takes on a darker complexion, however, when the community begins to disinherit Miss Eckhart, as they do Mrs. Larkin in "A Curtain of Green." If Virgie Rainey brings Miss Eckhart good luck (42), the girl's waning interest in her teacher still bodes ill for the future. Carey Wall argues that "Miss Eckhart is certainly to be pitied, as Cassie pities her, for being a suffering outcast whose one love, Virgie, does not return the passion" (21). Patricia Yaeger sees Miss Eckhart as "the immigrant outsider" (*Dirt and Desire* 144) who "represents new and frightening parameters for Southern women's lives" (122). Somehow Miss Eckhart's love "never did anybody any good" (65), and she falls in reputation, largely due to the gossips' tales about her: "Then stories began to be told of what Miss Eckhart had really done to her old mother. People said the old mother had been in pain for years, and nobody was told. . . . But they said that during the war, when Miss Eckhart lost pupils and they did not have very much to eat, she would give her mother paregoric to make sure she slept all night and not wake the street with noise or complaint, for fear still more pupils would be taken away. Some people said Miss Eckhart killed her mother with opium" (57). The autobiographical implications emerge. Welty, who cared for her aging mother for many years, may be exploring her suspicions of what the townspeople said of her. She would draw a similar portrait of her mother in *The Optimist's Daughter*, when the townsfolk say Laurel's mother "died a-crazy."

The ladies in town say that Miss Eckhart's demise might have been prevented by one of several means. Had she allowed herself "to be called by her first name, then she would have been like other ladies"; she might also have belonged to a church, so the ladies could invite her to their affairs there; and if only "she had been married to anybody at all, just the awfullest man—like Miss Snowdie MacLain, that everybody could feel sorry for" (66), then perhaps they could have found reason to sympathize with her and accept Miss Eckhart. In their inflexibility, however, these neighbors and friends shun her and remove their children from her influence. The community thus breaks her spirit and surely hastens her descent.

The opening scene, in which the crazed Miss Eckhart decorates her piano with the magnolia blossoms of her past—only to burn them—is a tragic one, indeed. Almost no one in town recognizes Miss Eckhart now, except Virgie, who ignores her, and Loch and Cassie, who observe her dispassionately. The lonely artist adheres to her dreams and is unwilling to see them dissolve; she would instead burn them in a pyre. As Mr. Moody and Mr. Bowles slowly escort her to the insane asylum in Jackson at the end of the story, she wears a gray housedress, "prophetic of an institution" (89), and here resembles Blanche DuBois in *A Streetcar Named Desire*. Her face is the Yeatsian "face that was in the poem" and is "old with wandering" in search of dreams (34). In her drab institutional gray, Miss Eckhart finally is without art or love but retains her own "dream world" (*Conversations* 332).

Patricia Yaeger argues that Miss Eckhart's "giant body becomes a symbol of female artistry and self-empowerment threatening beyond words, but her gigantism also becomes a battlefield for the social violence that is ordinarily scripted onto the body of the romantic white girl" (*Dirt and Desire* 123). If Welty heard in Miss Eckhart the "voice of my own fiction," however, then she may be projecting her worst fears—of herself—as a woman too tall and awkward to be noticed, respected, or admired and one who knew rejection in love.

Love continues as a prominent topic in "June Recital." Virgie Rainey and Loch Morrison typify Welty's characters who anticipate or know first love. From the beginning of "June Recital" Virgie appears as a sexual creature: "She looked like a tomboy but it was not the truth. She had let the sailor pick her up and carry her one day, with her fingers lifting to brush the leaves. It was she that had showed the sailor the house to begin with, she that started him coming" (24). She initiates a sexual relationship with her sailor boyfriend. Michael Kreyling writes, "Sex is a significant part of the 'power and emotion' in which Virgie moves" (*Eudora Welty's Achievement of Order* 84). Elaine Upton Pugh adds: "Although young when we meet [Virgie] in 'June Recital,' she is sexually precocious. She has a lusty relationship with the young sailor. . . . She does not linger in adolescence, but has somehow resigned herself to or seized the fate and responsibilities of an older woman. . . . She delights in eating figs, and figs are an important symbol of sexuality" (439).

Virgie's vitality and sense of abandon are her most remarkable qualities (along with her musical gift). The bicycle that she rides to her lessons suggests her desire for freedom: "she would ride it up into the yard and run the front wheel bang into the lattice, while Cassie was playing the 'Scarf Dance.' . . . Miss Eckhart would put her hand to her breast, as though she felt the careless wheel shake the very foundation of the studio" (41). Virgie is "as exciting as a gypsy"; she is "full of the airs of wildness"; she smells of sweet flavors; and she has a strong pallet—she drinks "vanilla out of the bottle, she told them, and it didn't burn her a bit" (44). The people around her sense that she "would go somewhere, somewhere way off" (43), and their predictions are accurate. Welty says of Virgie that at the end of the book "I think she's got it in her to do something else." Virgie is leaving and "saying good-bye to the life there in Morgana" (*Conversation* 305). She has an independent spirit.

Loch Morrison, Cassie, Nina, and Easter resemble Josie in "The Winds" in their budding sexuality. Loch's voyeurism by means of his telescope enables him to witness love, though he does not yet experience it. Through his magnifier he views the old MacLain house, with its upper back room. The bed, which faces his, is the location that Virgie and her sailor choose as their meeting place, and Loch views them through the telescope: "The foot was gone, and a mattress had partly slid down but was holding on. A shadow from a tree, a branch and its leaves, slowly traveled over the hills and hollows of the mattress" (21). Barbara Ladd notes that "Loch Morrison's summer afternoon in bed in 'June Recital' is filled not only with familiar people and familiar routines but with the spaces for watching and daydreaming" (*Resisting History* 67). Loch anticipates the day when he, like the sailor, will experience sex: "He was waiting for the day when the sailor took the figs." The figs outside his window suggest his ripening desires: "They were rusty old fig trees but the figs were the little sweet blue. When they cracked open, their pink and golden flesh would show, their inside flowers, and golden bubbles of juice would hang, to touch your tongue to first. Loch gave the sailor time, for it was he, Loch, who was in command of leniency here; he was giving him day after day" (21).

Loch's dreaming of figs continues to invoke images of fertility and sexuality: "The big fig tree was many times a magic tree with golden fruit that shone in and among its branches like a cloud of lightning bugs—a tree twinkling all over, burning, on and off, off and on. The sweet golden juice to come—in his dream he put his tongue out, and then his mother would be putting that spoon in his mouth" (22–23). Rebecca Mark says that Loch "does not have the power to perceive what Virgie and the sailor are doing" (61). Later he senses the presence of sexuality, although he may not be ready for it: "Something was coming very close to him, there was something he had better keep track of. . . . he might give a yell, like 'Coming, ready or not!'" (26). When Loch views the lovers through his telescope, the scene (like a later one in *Losing Battles* in which Vaughn spies Gloria and Jack together in the woods) unfolds from the perspective of an uncomprehending child. The lovers look to him like paper dolls: "And then, like the paper dolls sprung back together, they folded close—the real people. Like a big grasshopper lighting, all their legs and arms drew in to one small body, deadlike, with protective coloring" (30). Likening this lovemaking to insect behavior may be the perspective of inexperience or a sly, ironic commentary on the part of the adult author. In the last scene Loch is "lying stretched and pointed in the four directions. His heart pumping the secret anticipation that parted his lips, he fell into space and floated. . . . He dreamed close to the surface, and his dreams were filled with a color and a fury that the daytime that summer never held" (84). His readiness again evokes Blakean themes of "innocence and experience."

Sexual awakening also applies to Nina, whose descriptions of pears in "Moon Lake" is suggestive of sexuality: "Again she thought of a pear . . . beautiful, symmetrical clean pears with thin skins, with snow-white flesh so juicy and tender that to eat one baptized the whole face." The process of fruit ripening indicates her physical maturation: "To all fruits, and especially to those fine pears, something happened—the process was so swift, you were never in time for them. It's not the flowers that are fleeting, Nina thought, it's the fruits—it's the time when things are ready that they don't stay. She even went through the rhyme, 'Pear tree by the garden gate, How much longer must I wait?'—thinking it was the pears that asked it, not the picker" (116). The rhyme from Welty's childhood storybooks reappears again here and heralds, as it did in "The Winds," the young girl's readiness for sexuality.

Another provocative encounter in the volume involves Mattie Will Sojourner and her own woodland escapades with the MacLains in "Sir Rabbit." Rebecca Mark fully interprets Mattie Will's encounter with the MacLain twins as it relates to Yeats's "Leda and the Swan" (103–9). Mattie's first encounter occurs when she is fifteen years old; the MacLain twins overtake her while she is hoeing. She feels no terror as they roll together over the "turned-up mold" of the earth, but later on, after her marriage, she reflects upon the event: "Who had the least sense and the least care, for fifteen?" (100). The incident is not one she feels ashamed of—but she does feel perhaps a little foolish about the youthfulness of them all. The moment also prefigures her encounter with King, which occurs in the second section of the story.

The narrative perspective Welty uses to describe the trysts with King are from a female point of view, as are most of the intimate portraits Welty writes. Michael Kreyling calls the "Sir Rabbit" story a "reprise of the idyll in 'A Shower of Gold'" (*Eudora Welty's Achievement of Order* 87). MacLain is as elemental as "the preternatural month of June" (*Golden Apples* 107). Mattie imagines that such a moment would have "terrified [her] for the rest of her life" (99), but as the scene unfolds, she feels no terror. Mark points out that "Mattie Will does not need or want saving" (106). MacLain is enchanting in his white linen suit and looks like a "white glimmer." She notices that he even whistled with manners: "Nobody could have told her how sweet the old rascal whistled, but it didn't surprise her" (90). Kreyling comments that the encounter leaves Mattie "enriched" (*Eudora Welty's Achievement of Order* 93): "When she laid eyes on Mr. MacLain close, she staggered, he had such grandeur, and then she was caught by the hair and brought down as suddenly to earth as if whacked by an unseen shillelagh.

. . . But he put on her, with the affront of his body, the affront of his sense too. . . . She had to put on what he knew with what he did. . . . Like submitting to another way to talk, she could answer to his burden now, his whole blithe, smiling, superior, frantic existence. . . . Now he clasped her to his shoulder, and her tongue tasted sweet starch for the last time. . . . she was Mr. MacLain's Doom, or Mr. MacLain's Weakness, like the rest, and neither Mrs. Junior Holifield nor Mattie Will Sojourner; now she was something she had always heard of" (95). MacLain is captivating, and his actions lend excitement to Mattie Will's life, as they did to Snowdie's. Although neither woman is happy, neither greatly regrets having understood the dance in the wood.

The Golden Apples portrays its most complex figures in their late adulthood. Miss Eckhart, Katie Rainey, Ran, and Eugene all reach older age in this book, and all of them are finally dark, if not tragic, characters. "Sex" in "The Whole World Knows," Kreyling says, "means pain and discord" (*Eudora Welty's Achievement of Order* 93). Eugene and Ran as adult men are alike, Vande Kieft adds, "only in a common woe: marital discord, failure in love" (*Eudora Welty* 128). The community in this story intervenes intrusively as the marriage of Ran and Jinny MacLain weathers a crisis of commitment. Jinny has been the adulteress first, but the town blames Ran for her infidelity. Ran instinctively senses the town talk; he knows the difficulty of getting "away in Morgana. Away from anything at all": "I could listen to women and hear pieces of the story, of what happened to us, of course—but I listened to the ferns. . . . No matter, it was being told. Not in Miss Lizzie's voice, which wouldn't think of it, certainly not in Jinny's, but in the clear voice of Maideen where it had never existed—all the worse for the voice not even questioning what it said—just repeating, just rushing, old—the town words. . . . Telling what she was told she saw, repeating what she listened to—young girls are outlandish little birds that talk. They can be taught, some each day, to sing a song *people* have made" (143). Ran's internal monologue conveys the embarrassment he feels as he imagines what the gossipers say: "Jinny was unfaithful to Ran—that's the up and down of it. There you have what it's all about. That's the brunt of it" (164). He thinks of all of the permutations the town speculation will include: "He walked out on her and took his clothes down to the other end of the street. Now everybody's waiting to see how soon he'll go back. They say Jinny MacLain invites Woody out there to eat, a year younger than she is, remember when they were born. Invites, under her mama's nose. Sure, its Woodrow Spights she invites. Who else would there be in Morgana for Jinny Stark after Ran, with even Eugene MacLain gone? She's kin to the Nesbitts. They don't say when it started, can anybody tell? At the Circle, at Miss Francine's, at Sunday School, they say, they say she will marry Woodrow: Woodrow'd jump at it but Ran will kill somebody first. And there's Ran's papa and the way he was and is, remember, remember?" (144). Even later in his life, after the incidents of Jinny's adultery and Ran's involvement with the suicidal Maideen, the community first censures but then adores Ran because of (rather than in spite of) his reputation and colorful history. The story of his life, which the townsfolk tell and retell, becomes a part of the "public domain," just as he predicted: "They had voted for him for that—for his glamour and his story, for being a MacLain and the bad twin, for marrying a Stark and then for ruining a girl and the thing she did. . . . They voted for the revelation. It had made their hearts faint, and they would assert it again" (210).

Ran's private affairs assume almost heroic dimensions, as they do for Don McInnis in "Asphodel," and the passionate nature and glamour of his story perpetuate the mystery of the man. Peter Schmidt says that "The Whole World Knows" and "Music from Spain" are "Welty's most daring exploration of the tragic causes and consequences of male misogyny." Ran's problems, Schmidt adds, stem from the fact that "shared, mature sexuality intimidates [Ran], as does maternal consolation, but rape is restorative; it reaffirms his deflated manhood and reasserts his right to turn women simply into objects of his desire" (79, 72). Ran pays a price for his reputation, however. After he is with Maideen Sumrall in Vicksburg, he cries out in the loneliness of the moment: "Father, Eugene! What you went and found, was it better than this? And where's Jinny?" (181). Mark sees the encounter between Ran and Maideen as a rape (145), as do Schmidt and others.

Eugene, however, has a complicated life, though perhaps one that includes joy. Eugene's marriage flounders in "Music from Spain." After he suddenly slaps his wife, apparently without warning, and walks out, Eugene spends the day wondering, as Kreyling puts it, whether "life is to have its way with each of us, to decree relinquishment of youth, hope, beauty, to leave only a dry and thin age to be trussed and braced against inevitable ruin?" (*Eudora Welty's Achievement of Order* 96). Later with his Spaniard friend, by the light of the willful, "racing moon," Eugene explores the freedom his companion has. The moon also is alluring to Eugene, who seeks new experiences and love outside the marriage bond.

Scholars have analyzed this story in detail. Elaine Upton Pugh sees the moon in this passage as a reference to Celtic and Greek mythology, which associates the moon with the cow, "the horned wanderer of the night" (440). Mark notes that Eugene is "entering another dimension" and also the "full range of masculinity—both its projections and fantasies and its dreams and myths (197, 208). Barbara Ladd discusses unexpected recognitions in "Music from Spain" and the role of female aspiration in the story (*Resisting History* 69). Matt Huculak details the journey of self-examination that Eugene makes as he walks through town and points to the "life changing" experience that Eugene undergoes as he is coming to understand his awakening homosexuality. Huculak interprets Eugene as moving through the "dark, previously unexplored pathways of his soul" and says that Welty is "seeking understanding" (317). Thomas McHaney writes that "the tubercular Eugene experiences—and King must face—the fate of those who return to see their homeland after a sojourn in the timeless otherworld of the Celtic myths: annihilation or old age." He sees Ran as one whose "travels are much closer to home but just as perilous for him and others despite the ironic diminution, [and he] is forgiven for the sham of his life by being made into a 'smiling public man,' to use Yeats's phrase from 'Among School Children'—the town elects him mayor" ("Falling into Cycles" 185). Vande Kieft argues that the twin sons are as "as much victims of their differently dominating wives as they are victimizers" ("'Where Is the Voice'" 193). Mark notes, "As soon as Eugene spotted his male guide, 'a gate opened to Eugene.'" She adds that Welty, like Joyce, describes the [San Francisco] scene as a wasteland, but in "Music from Spain" from this empty beach "the potential for something new emerges" (198, 214).

Eventually, like his father, Eugene returns home to his wife. He imagines as he is going there that she will be waiting "like a bride," standing at the window "with the white curtains of the bay window hanging heavy all around her" (197). Like his father, too, Eugene's forays into the possibilities of San Francisco have lured him back to his wife this time, but whether his stay is permanent or fleeting is ambiguous at the end of the story. Scholarly interpretations have suggested convincingly that Eugene's relationship with the Spaniard is a homosexual encounter. This reading may correspond to the biographical facts surrounding Welty's visits and stays in San Francisco, where she joined John Robinson, her longtime friend and companion from Jackson, Mississippi. Although she had hoped to marry Robinson, his latent homosexuality emerged. The depiction of Eugene and the Spaniard may be a step in her working through the shift in her relationship with Robinson and her coming to terms with his sexuality.

The stories in *The Golden Apples* portray mainly those who dream of or search for a better life. Chester Eisinger summarizes that in the collection Welty "reaches for and grasps a deeper strain, and she confronts the pain of loss, the powerful frustration of unfulfilled quest, the high cost of isolation for the outsider, and the terror of life" (17). Welty explains her intent as well: "What had drawn the characters together there was one strong strand in them all: they lived in one way or another in a dream or in romantic aspiration, or under an illusion of what their lives were coming to, about the meaning of their (now) related lives" (*One Writer's Beginnings* 99).

CHAPTER 8

"Roses as Headlights"
The Bride of the Innisfallen

The Bride of the Innisfallen alternates, in much the same way as *The Golden Apples* does, between the stories of thwarted and anticipatory relationships. "No Place for You, My Love" and "Circe" both concern missed opportunities or failed attempts at love; "Ladies in Spring" and "Going to Naples" focus on anticipation; and "The Bride of the Innisfallen" and "Kin" depict characters who either expect to have or have not had successful relationships.

"The Naked in Heart": "No Place for You, My Love"

An unsuccessful encounter between a man and woman who have a brief but intense experience together occurs in both "No Place for You, My Love" and "Circe." An attempt at romance is the main focus of "No Place for You, My Love," in which a recently acquainted couple takes a day trip together to the Gulf, south of New Orleans. The story weaves together motifs of exposure and vulnerability to show the subtle emotional risks the two people take as they try to know each other better. Even though they claim to be only "two Northerners keeping each other company" (4), what they consciously seek is love.

Welty offers the keynote for the story: "Of all human moods, deliberate imperviousness may be the most quickly communicated—it may be the most successful, most fatal signal of all. And two people can indulge in imperviousness as well as in anything else" (4). The story will trace the "fatal signal" that the two people give and receive from one another as a relationship between them grows more and more remote. The point of view in this story alternates frequently between the male and the female perspective and vividly reveals the thoughts of each as they become acquainted in conversation, as if in two parts of a duet.

The two people meet each other at the bar in Galatoire's restaurant in New Orleans. While they are still "strangers to each other," they both begin wondering about what the other is like and what the other is thinking. The man thinks that the female is "a woman who was having an affair," and almost at the same time she reveals her feelings of self-consciousness: "It must stick out all over me . . . so people think they can love me or hate me just by looking at me" (3–4). Through this shifting perspective the nuances of their early relationship and the theme of vulnerability come to the fore.

The image patterns modulate between concealment and revelation. The exposure and vulnerability that (primarily) the woman feels as she agrees to and undertakes a day trip with her new acquaintance and then their mutual retreat into protective concealing are the pivotal points upon which the story turns. Images of light—of naked or partly revealed skin (including faces and heads) and flesh colors—suggest the vulnerability and exposure that the couple has and the risks they take with each other as their acquaintance progresses. Shadow, darkness, animal hides, and instruments of penetration (such as mosquitoes with sharp noses) all indicate the more somber themes of concealment, threat, and retreat to which the both individuals eventually turn.

As in "Clytie," faces in "No Place for You, My Love" are an important index of vulnerability. Through facial expression others can partly apprehend clues to identity. The physically exposed faces, heads, and nakedness of the body represent the psychological risks these individuals have taken in journeying into knowledge of one another. Like strangers leaving New Orleans, each person follows the "clues in a maze" to know the heart of another (6).

The unrelenting New Orleans heat and light and near-nakedness of the local people parallel the vulnerability in emotional risk the couple takes in discovering one another. Hers is a "blunt, fair face" with which the wind and sun will play havoc (3). The farther the man and woman travel south of the city, the hotter the weather becomes, and consequently the natives have on fewer and fewer clothes: "As time passed and the distance from New Orleans grew, girls even darker and younger were exposing themselves over the porches and porch steps, with jet black hair pulled high, and ragged palm-leaf fans rising and falling like rafts of butterflies. The children running forth were nearly always naked ones" (7).

The exposure of the face and skin tones further reinforces the themes of vulnerability, openness, and insecurity. A black man raises his hand and reveals its "pink and black" cover (6); his hand looks dark and obscure on the top, but the underneath is exposed in its light color. A man they pass who is asleep in a truck has a "raw, red look." As they travel, "by rushing through the heat at high speed, they brought themselves the effect of fans turned onto their cheeks" (7). Even the iron swans they see in yards are painted "flesh color" (6), and the skin of the natives alternates between an olive and pink shrimp color, a rich association in which the rawness of shrimp flesh suggests sunburned human skin. The shells along the road have a "pink-tinted" color. Later they pass "a Negro couple, sitting on two facing chairs in the yard outside their lonely cabin—half undressed, each battling for self" against the heat (24).

The human face is always important in Welty's writings, and that is true in this story. The tombs in the cemetery they visit are as "brilliant as faces" (14); the men on the ferry have "searchlight faces" (10). On the way home the earth takes on the appearance of having a face and body. The man senses that "they had been riding for a long time across a face—great, wide, and upturned. In its eyes and open mouth were those great fires they had had glimpses of, where cattle had drawn together: a face, a head, far down here in the South—South of South below it. A whole giant body sprawled downward then, on and on" (25). The "searchlight faces" metaphorically represent the theme. As if exposed by a bright searchlight, the couple uncover their feelings, for better or worse, as the story progresses.

The woman's face and cheeks carry the image pattern further. As she stares down into a clustering of water hyacinths, she feels "exposed": "up to her face under the brim of her hat; her own cheeks felt like the hyacinths to her, all her skin still full of too much light and sky, exposed" (17). Welty explains the theme plainly in "How I Write": "The vain courting of imperviousness in the face of exposure is this little story's plot" (*On Writing* 36).

Bestial skins and hides emphasize the theme of vulnerability and protection. The concrete road the couple travels on has "dead snakes stretched across . . . like markers." Their skins are like "inlaid mosaic bands, dry as feathers" (13). Even the houses they pass are "spotted like the hides of beasts faded and shy" (6). The road narrows to a shell road, and the shell creatures "littered their path, scuttling or dragging" (8). Noel Polk notes the teeming "hordes of crayfish, and shrimp and terrapins and turtles and alligators, 'crawling with hides you could not penetrate with bullets.'" The shells and hides of these creatures are, Polk writes, the reminder "that they are not armor-plated, but are in fact two very vulnerable and hurtable human beings. So she has retreated into a thickened hide of 'deliberate imperviousness,' her only protection" ("Water" 107).

The alligator, previously a symbol of mysteriousness in "The Wide Net," here represents imperviousness. The boys on the ferry see an alligator: Welty describes the alligator as "a hide that could walk"—no identity or clue to its sensibility exists in this thickly clad beast. As she is watching the alligator, the woman thinks the hide it has is "respectable and merciful" because it shelters him from penetration from outside menace and allows him to keep a safe distance from anyone he chooses. She says to herself, "Deliver us all from the naked in heart," a line that combines the images of nakedness and of protective shields to emphasize the rawness of the woman's nerves in her feeling of exposure (12).

The alligator can also snap as a weapon. Although the boys laugh, the alligator suggests evidence of its "heroic horror": "the last worldly evidence of some old heroic horror of the dragon," the woman calls it (10). The alligator may also indicate her alienation from her traveling partner. She similarly distances herself from the reptile: "Her distance was set—the number of feet and inches between herself and it mattered to her" (11). The same holds true for the relationship in which she finds herself on this daytrip. Michael Kreyling observes: "Both the people on this pilgrimage are keeping their distance . . . Individual hearts remain separate behind impenetrable barriers unless the call to place them in the balance is heeded" (*Eudora Welty's Achievement of Order* 198).

The biting of the alligator and bites by mosquitoes suggest puncturing the shields of concealment and protection. Mosquitoes are everywhere in this story, encouraged by the landscape of heat and water, and natives and strangers alike fend off attacks as best they can. A family of eight who lives along the road beat themselves with wild palmettos to prevent mosquitoes from biting: "Heels, shoulder, knees, breasts, back of the heads, elbows, hands, were touched in turn—like some game each playing it with himself." The man strikes himself "on the forehead" for the same preventative measure. His wife, he thinks, would "not be at her most charitable if he came bringing malaria home to the family" (8). Later a "horde of mosquitoes and gnats came singing and striking at them first" (17). Even a kiss is interrupted by mosquitoes, which "coat their arms and even their eyelids" (24). "A boy with shrimp-colored arms capered from side to side, pretending to have been bitten" (11).

The alligator also suggests the degree of vulnerability and exposure the woman feels among the people around her. Roped by the boys, the alligator is "paraded in capture before the eyes of country clowns" (11). The woman has similar moments of repulsion for the men whose eyes seem constantly focused upon her and who call attention to her and reveal her. The most obvious example occurs when her hat blows off onto the ferry. Although her friend retrieves her hat, she calls it "useless" once it has uncovered her head, left her vulnerable, and attracted attention to her. She thinks, "What they were saying below was more polite than their searchlight faces," and they all look at her "holding her hands to her head" (10). She fears even exposing her earrings; the revelation of herself to others is risky and dangerous. To her the river looks "like an exposed vein of ore" (11). To reveal her heart, or even part of it, is too risky. She wishes to be "delivered" from those who too readily expose their hearts. The story has its autobiographical origin in a trip south of New Orleans that Welty took with Carvel Collins and as such may well be another intimate look into the protected heart of Eudora Welty.

Light and shadow—and the gradations in between—including sunrise, high noon, sunset, "shadowless and sunless" twilight, moonlight, and dark night—emphasize the themes of concealment, exposure, and revelation. The light at Galatoire's intriguingly alternates with the turns of the fan, revealing, concealing, and alluring the couple toward each other. The internal mirrors and lights of the downstairs floor of the famous restaurant are recognizable: "mirrors and fans were busy agitating the light, as the very local talk drawled across and agitated the peace." As is typical in Welty's writing, the light becomes metaphorical and revelatory: "Then suddenly, as she took her hand down, the secret fact was still there—it lighted her. It was a bold and full light, shot up under the brim of that hat, as close to them all as the flowers in the center of the table" (4). Exposure will have its unpleasant consequences later.

Illumination in Welty's stories usually signifies epiphany or under-standing. The same is true in this story. The harsh sun exposes too much as the two people continue on their excursion. In the light on the ferry—and without her protective hat—the woman again feels self-conscious and thinks "they all must see that with her entire self all she did was wait." Her hands and purse seem to be "objects bleaching there" in the sun (10). The "incredible brightness of four o'clock"—and the exposure it provides—causes the woman to articulate her conclusions about risk: "Her eyes over-come with brightness and size, she felt a panic rise, as sudden as nausea. Just how far below questions and answers, concealment and revelation, they were running now—that was still a new question, with a power of its own, waiting. How dear—how costly—could this ride be?" (13). The ride becomes less risky, however, when the couple chooses to recede into im-perviousness and resists the challenge to plunge into a closer relationship.

After sunset and nightfall the moon appears to change in size and color. This alteration signifies the retreat of the couple away from one another. At first the moon seems like "a fire burning somewhere now." The moon is "enormous," and "tangerine-colored." The color of shrimp, flesh, and of the orange sign announcing the natives' wild shrimp dance, the moon oversees the sexuality that the couple explores briefly. They have reached the "jumping-off place" for their relationship; either they will plunge ahead or retreat (16). They choose to withdraw, like an an-guished cry: "Something that must have been with them all along sud-denly, then, was not. In a moment, tall as panic, it rose, cried like a hu-man, and dropped back" (26).

The fading of the moon to "ash-white" and faintness of the stars corre-spondingly reflect the demise of what might have been between them: "Un-der the now ash-white moon, the world traveled through very faint stars" (24). The opportunity for a romantic time has waned. Finally, the man recalls his student days when the "shriek and horror and unholy smother" of the subway means the "lilt and expectation" of love (27). Although this couple may have met with "lilt and expectation" at Galatoire's, impervious-ness finally seals them in an "immunity" that Cupid's arrow cannot pierce.

"Some Future and Secret Joy": "The Bride of the Innisfallen"

"The Bride of the Innisfallen" and "Circe" continue the theme of unsuccessful love. The first story considers a random group of people riding together on a train to Fishguard and then a boat to Cork, Ireland. Almost all of the passengers identify themselves by their status in or out of a relationship. The lady in a salmon and yellow raincoat says "farewell" to someone in the ominous "spring that refused to flower" (47). A pregnant wife smiles in her "calm blue coat"; her face shows "degrees of maternity, and other faces show degrees of love or anger" (50); an American wife "leaves London without her husband's knowledge" (48); even Victor, a little boy, has been to his brother's wedding; a pair of lovers lament that "Love was amazement now," but they are "the one subject nobody was going to discuss" (70). These journeys will be those of love and loss.

Scholars have scrutinized this enigmatic story. Michael Kreyling focuses attention on the American wife, who is, he says, "surrounded by mates alone or in pairs, emphasizing the bond she has just unilaterally begun to dissolve by leaving." "Courageously," he adds, "her heart turns to embrace the world in its complex and inevitable rhythm of love and loss. . . . In love and faith the woman consents to be the world's partner, its bride, in this paired existence" (Kreyling, *Eudora Welty's Achievement of Order* 135, 134). Ruth Vande Kieft also adds that the American girl's only excess has been one of "hope, joy, and the wonder at the mystery and glory of human life" (*Eudora Welty* 49). The American girl recovers what Alun Jones calls "the joy of innocence and the sense that life will endure" ("Travelling Coincidence" 44).

Journeys have a special significance in Welty's stories. In *One Writer's Beginnings* she writes of the importance of journeys in her life, in which "Travel itself is part of some longer continuity": "Taking trips tore all of us up inside, for they seemed, each journey away from home, something that might have been less selfishly undertaken, or something that would test us, or something that had better be momentous, to justify such a leap into the dark. The torment and guilt—the torment of having the loved one go, the guilt of being the loved one gone—comes into my fiction as it did and does in my life. And most of all the guilt then was because it was true: I had left to arrive at some future and secret joy, at what was unknown . . . waiting to be discovered" (94). The train ride through the Welsh landscape with the colorful passengers aboard hurtles the passengers onward toward the "unknown waiting to be discovered" future. The travelers are, as Don Harrell puts it, "bound on a spiritual journey of the soul" (2).

The harbinger of the future is perhaps most clearly identified by the bride, who emerges at the end of the trip, complete with delight and ringing bells typical of a Jane Austen novel: "Sure enough, a girl who had not yet showed herself in public now appeared by the rail in a white spring hat and, over her hands, a little old-fashioned white bunny muff. She stood there ready to be met, now come out in her own sweet time. Delight gathered all around, singing began on board, bells could by now be heard ringing urgently in the town" (79). She represents the joys and expectations of other travelers. The sense of anticipation characteristic of a bride renews the promise of "something momentous" that might happen to the rest to "justify" their "leap into the dark." The expectancy of this moment renders the conclusion of the story more optimistic. Although the American woman's husband has said, "You hope for too much," she has continued to hope, but she hides her joy "for fear it is promiscuous" (82). As the others move on to various destinations, the American woman faces the unknown in her future with hope and joy. Kreyling says that she "participates in the vital rhythm simply by going on into the world and into the life she has" (*Eudora Welty's Achievement of Order* 139). The end of the journey is to be applauded, not because the ending is certain but because in the uncertainty lies the secret of possibility.

"Grief, That Couldn't Hear Me": The "Black" Heart of Welty's "Circe"

Secrecy and the mystery of the unknown are the central topics of "Circe." This story is typical of Welty's choice of narrative stance: she writes again from the female perspective, and the story is vintage Welty in theme too—the protagonist, even though she is a mythological creature with vast power, simply seeks love. Welty's twist on the old myth humanizes and personalizes the character of Circe and presents her story from the female perspective, instead of the male perspective that surrounds her. Circe remains the conquering, spellbinding goddess of old, but Odysseus is the more victorious in the end. His mortality, though flawed, is preferable to godliness because he feels the human emotions of love and grief.

The story has tragic elements, but comic moments relieve the seriousness of Circe's unenviable fate. Welty's Circe is the perfect housekeeper and hostess—gracious in the southern style of the "hospitality" she offers her guests (108–9). This characterizing of Circe with southern etiquette engenders incongruity—Circe of old mythology is exotic, intoxicating, and magical. This shift creates a comic tone. Circe has her "Needle in air"— sewing—when Odysseus's men arrive on her rocky shores, and bread bakes in the oven (102). Like Rosamund in *The Robber Bridegroom*, the scene is a domestic one, albeit laced with magical realism. Circe is an immaculate housekeeper and well trained in the art of housecleaning. She wields her wand "like a broom"; becomes angry when the sailors are "tracking the clean floor" (107); oversees the kitchen servants; and at night gives a final check: "I went my way over the house as I do by night to see if all is well and holding together" (109). Like an angry wife, Circe admonishes the sailors not to dirty her house: "'Outside!' I commanded. 'No dirt is allowed in this house!' In the end, it takes phenomenal neatness of housekeeping to put it through the heads of men that they are swine. With my wand seething in the air like a broom, I drove them all through the door" (103). This Circe appears to be a homemaker who keeps her house clean.

The magic broth she concocts is also regionally oriented: she makes a good Cajun gumbo—with oysters and pork—and in keeping with southern custom, she shares the recipe with no "other woman": "I tasted, and it was perfect—swimming with oysters from my reef and flecks of golden pork, redolent with leaves of bay and basil and rosemary, and with a glass of island wine tossed in at the last: it has been my infallible recipe. Circe's broth: all the gods have heard of it and envied it" (103). Welty's Circe is in these pages a domestically oriented woman and good cook, much like Ellen Fairchild in *Delta Wedding*, who keeps to her old family recipe.

Circe is nonetheless still a goddess of magical powers who apparently hates men. She imagines men as swine before she transforms them bodily. When, for instance, the sailors land and disembark, the men have porcine appearance and behavior: "Heads lifted to the smell of my bread, they trooped inside—and with such a grunting and frisking at their heels to the very threshold" (102). The animal nature of the humans, rather than their humanity, attracts Circe's attention. Her assessment of men and plans for them will be animalistic in nature.

Circe dehumanizes the men and re-creates them as animals: "What tusks I had given them!" They are "filthily rivaling" and have "twice as many hooves as there had been feet before" (103). Even when she lifts this spell, she describes them "treading on their napkins, tracking the clean floor," the way animals, not humans, would (107). With her power she bestializes and trivializes these unclean men.

Odysseus's power to resist Circe's magic proves him heroic: "If a man remained unable to leave that magnificent body of his, then enchantment had met with a hero" (103). Michael Kreyling observes that "she feels her spell counteracted by one that Odysseus has cast upon her. She falls in love with him," but she "desires reciprocal passion, a passion to bring her self into being" (*Understanding Eudora Welty* 126, 169). The moment neutralizes Circe's power and brings a good man into the life of this magician. When Odysseus arrives, Circe feels passion, but she is unaccustomed to it and cannot define or identify her feeling: "I threw open the door. A shaft of light from the zenith struck my brow, and the wind let out my hair. Something else swayed my body outward" (102). She feels the undefinable tug of passion again later: "I felt something from behind press like the air of heaven before a storm, and reach like another wand over my head." She says, however, "Before everything, I think of my power," and she is angry that other powers are operating beyond her control (103). Odysseus's attractiveness overpowers her own magic, invincible though she seems: "There is no mystery in magic! Men are swine: let it be said, and no sooner said than done." Circe wishes she could crush Odysseus's power "like an island grape" (105). His "secret" challenges Circe to capture, seduce, and hold him near, as she does her swine.

Their scenes in bed together are enchanting. In her luxurious chambers she baths him, dries him by her fire, rubs oil on his "shadowy shoulders, and on the rope of curls in which his jaw was set," and then in acquiescence, if not submission, she kisses his hand: "He fell among the pillows, his still-open eyes two clouds stopped over the sun, and I lifted and kissed his hand" (104). The couple finds their island paradise: "Passion is our ground, our island—do others exist [?]" (107).

Odysseus feels human emotions—and that is his secret that Circe discovers and covets most dearly. The sailors show their thanks to Circe before they depart, but she is inhuman and emotionless. They also show joy upon their reuniting with others in their group. Odysseus lovingly counts and names each man as he reenters his former state of being. The men shout and embrace in the reunion, and Circe allows them a feast. Ruth Vande Kieft points out that "Circe envies the human condition" (*Eudora Welty* 50), and Andrea Goudie notes Circe's inability to grieve (488). Gail Mortimer adds, "By any definition, Circe does not understand the emotions that follow from human finitude: the poignancy of what might have been, the sorrow of what is now over, the pleasure of what is" (89).

The group of men also grieves when Elpenor, the youngest of the sailors, falls to his accidental death from the rooftop: "They all ran from the table as though a star had fallen. They stood or they crouched above Elpenor fallen in my yard, low-voiced now like conspirators—as indeed they were. They wept for Elpenor lying on his face, and for themselves, as *he* wept for them the day they came, when I had made them swine. . . . He knelt and touched Elpenor, and like a lover lifted him; then each in turn held the transformed boy in his arms" (110). They "conspire" against Circe in that they have keen emotions, which torment her because she knows none of it. When she cries out to them, "When you dig the grave for that one . . . write on the stone: 'I died of love.'" They all run from her because she speaks sarcastically and ironically, with no feeling or knowledge either of mortality or love. Circe admits, however, that her language now is becoming essentially human: "I spoke in epitaph—in the idiom of man" (110).

Circe slowly apprehends human qualities. She exhibits signs of loneliness and possible despair. Just before Odysseus leaves, she describes her "black" heart: the "lonely dull mornings when mist wraps the island and hides every path of the sea, and when my heart is black" (107). She identifies briefly with Cassiopeia, "who sits there and needs nothing, pale in her chair in the stream of heaven" (109), but Circe doubts her magic. "The old Moon was still at work. 'Why keep it up, old woman?'" she asks.

She longs for human grief and "could shriek at the rising Moon": "I stood on my rock and wished for grief. It would not come. Though I could shriek at the rising Moon, and she, so near, would wax or wane, there was still grief, that couldn't hear me—grief that cannot be round or plain or solid-bright or running on its track, where a curse could get at it. It has no heavenly course; it is like mystery, and knows where to hide itself. . . . I cannot find the dusty mouth of grief. I am sure now grief is a ghost— only a ghost in Hades, where ungrateful Odysseus is going—waiting on him" (111). Although Circe wishe[s] for grief, she cannot feel it. She senses that grief is "like mystery"—hidden to her but open to humankind. In this story of myth and mysteries Welty identifies the distinctly human characteristics of feeling and emotion—and contrasts them with a darker, colder, emptier, less fulfilling life of a goddess for whom emotion is elusive.

Roses in "Kin": Souvenir de Claudius Pernet, Mermaid, Mary Wallace, Silver Moon, Étoiles, Duquesa de Penaranda, Gruss an Aachen, Climbing Thor

Roses help create the tone of "Kin," a thoughtful mood piece about the importance of family set in Mississippi. The protagonist, Dicey, is likely another autobiographical rendition of the author. Visiting relatives in the country, and then going beyond them deeper out in the country to visit even older relatives, gives Dicey a chance to reflect on family, roots, and her place among the relatives, as well as apart from them, and she has the opportunity to see how the extended family lives, what their values and customs are, and how they are caring for their elder relative, Great Uncle Felix, who is suffering from a dementia-like disorder. Although the portrait of Uncle Felix is troubling, Welty balances the tone with her portrait of Dicey, who is engaged to be married soon. The two narratives temper the mood of the story and prefigure characters and situations in *The Optimist's Daughter*.

Dicey has returned to Mississippi, from which she has been "gone almost [her] whole life, except for visits" to see family (112). The others in the family complain that Dicey's visits even now are incomparable to those of days past: "When your mother was alive and used to come bringing you, visits were different. . . . She stayed long enough to make us believe she'd fully got here" (115). Welty again explores these topics of the guilt associated with leaving home in her depiction of Laurel Hand's returning to Mount Salus for her father's funeral in *The Optimist's Daughter*. Felix in "Kin" foreshadows Judge McKelva in his late-life rumination on past love. Both works focus on marriage as it affects ties and responsibilities to "kin" and the point of view of a "grown woman" who is now a "stranger" in her own family and who is bound and determined that she "was not going to be an old maid" (114, 113). She thus sets the theme of the story and identifies herself, in some ways at least, as another potentially autobiographical rendition of the author.

With this marital goal firmly in mind, during her visitation to Mingo, the old homeplace, Dicey reluctantly delves into the lore of her kinfolk. Michael Kreyling points out that the story concerns four women in response to marriage: "the pilgrimage traditionally prescribed for the women" (*Eudora Welty's Achievement of Order* 130). Dicey waits impatiently for the chance to announce the "news" of her engagement (112). Instead, the family insists that she become reacquainted with her kin. At first she is "not that anxious to claim kin" (116). She makes fun of Sister Anne, who was "going to marry and [was] stood up in church. . . . And she was about forty years old!" (117). A little later she argues that "falling in the well, and being an old maid, that's two things" to be "poor about" (118).

The family lore affects Dicey's view of marriage. The members of her family tell the story of Aunt Ethel, whose grief for her husband overwhelmed her: "ever since his death seventeen years ago, Aunt Ethel could not bear to hear the name of her husband spoken, or to speak it herself" (119). Dicey has not yet felt the power of emotions like these. Ethel explains that Sister Anne may have been wise to choose a life without marriage: "maybe a girl might do well sometimes *not* to marry, if she's not cut out for it" (120). This remark surprises Dicey, and she cries out, "Aunt Ethel!" in her amazement that not marrying might be a sensible option for a woman. Eudora Welty, who says she based some stories on what she heard and observed, may have heard such advice and taken it to heart in her own life.

After a time Dicey visits Sister Anne and Uncle Felix. Having heard their stories, she is more impressed with them. When she sees Sister Anne, the woman who was jilted in church, she feels empathy: the look on her face is "as fond and startling as a lover's" (130). The scene of reacquaintance with Uncle Felix—and the revelation of his own love story—is central to the tale. Reminiscent of Solomon in "Livvie," Felix reclines motionless in his big featherbed with its black iron bedstead. His memory, slowly awakened by the rose scent of Dicey's handkerchief, returns to former days of love. The inscription that he pencils slowly on a note for her reads, "River—Daisy—Midnight—Please" (148). Perhaps he is intending to say "Dicey" instead of "Daisy," but in any case his inviting her to the river at midnight seems to have awakened in him a memory of love on the riverbank. In either case the scent of roses recalls to Felix a romantic idea in the confines of his sickroom. Alfred Appel concludes, "For Dicey . . . the experience has underlined her own deep sense of loss—'it was the "please" that had hurt me'" (241). Michael Kreyling summarizes that "Dicey understands the implications, hears the solitary note, like Dewey." Felix, who has "red roses on his suspenders" is "still nurturing in his parched age a moment of communion and touch, a voluntary surrender of his immunity from the world" (*Eudora Welty's Achievement of Order* 131). Even in advanced age, he is a fellow pilgrim in the world of love.

Rose-growing instruction, the customs of rose growers, and rose lore are fully apparent in this story, and Welty presents them literally and as metaphorical suggestions: "and everywhere, the yawning, inconvenient, and suddenly familiar rooms were as deep and inviting and compelling as the yawning big roses opening and shattering in one day in the heating gardens" (114). The big, drooping, inviting, and compelling roses in this description are but short-lived. Like the beautiful and spacious rooms of the old family home in which Dicey finds herself, they allude to her attachment there as tenuous.

The ladies in this story all clearly are accustomed to growing, admiring, appreciating, and discussing roses, as were Eudora Welty and her mother: "Aunt Ethel's roses were at their height. A look of satisfaction on Rachel's face was like something nobody could interrupt. To our sighs, for our swooning attitudes, she paraded the vase through the room and around the bed, where she set it on the little table." Rose growers such as these women know the names of the roses they have in their gardens. Ethel is no exception: "Souvenir de Claudius Pernet—and *that's* Mermaid—Mary Wallace—Silver Moon—those three of course Étoiles—and oh, Duquesa de Penaranda—Gruss an Aachen's of course his cutting he grew for me a thousand years ago—but there's my Climbing Thor!" (122). Giving the gift of roses is an activity in which Mrs. Welty and her daughter, Eudora, engaged.

Tips for rose growing and instruction are embedded in the language of the story. The best practice among rose growers is to cut them either in the coolness of an early morning or after the intense heat of the late afternoon. Rachel overturns those best practices: "Rachel, who believed in cutting roses in the heat of the day—and nobody could prevent her now, since we forgot to cut them ourselves or slept through the mornings—came in Aunt Ethel's room bearing a vaseful" (122). Her contrary actions about the rule of thumb for cutting roses position her in willful disregard of rose gardening tradition. She will not be the wise one in this story. Sister Anne also does not understand what to do with roses: "she began sticking the roses into a smoky glass vase too small for them, into which she'd run too little water" (132). Her incompetence in rose care is apparent and marks her.

The roses again serve metaphorically—this time as headlights—which illuminate the path: "Kate took the cake and I took the flowers—the roses going like headlights in front of us" (126). The roses light the way toward clarity of vision and understanding. Later, in carrying the roses to "Great-uncle Felix," Dicey sees the roses again as "lights" carried between them: "those head-heavy lights of Aunt Ethel's roses smothered between our unequal chests" (128). Anne knows that Uncle Felix's time on earth is limited. She takes the roses to him and places them so that he may see them: "Sister Anne bore the roses to the window and set them down on the window sill in his line of sight" (136). The roses are "in his line of sight," and on the literal level he may admire their beauty. Symbolically, however, they also portend his death, and his line of sight is now focused outward, or perhaps heavenward. Seeing and vision in the broader sense of the word have been prominent themes in Welty's fiction. With this emphasis on headlights, vision, and line of sight, the story builds toward epiphany or clearer understanding on the part of the protagonist. Roses will light the way; the protagonist will see her family in a new light.

The image of garish roses also controverts the traditional trope. Welty anthropomorphizes the roses: they "glare back at" the girls who carry them: "Our roses glared back at us as garish as anything living could be, almost like paper flowers, a magician's bouquet that had exploded out of a rifle to shock and amaze us" (137). Later "their heads hung" (144). The roses, which appear garish and shocking, with heads hanging down, surely point the way to Uncle Felix in his state of dementia, in which he appears to the girls as grotesque.

Ethel admires her roses but sees their pale thorns through the cut-glass vase. She knows they will inflict pain: "Still looking at the roses she waited a moment. Pressing out of the vase, those roses of hers looked heavy, drunken with their own light and scent, their stems, just two minutes ago severed with Rachel's knife, vivid with pale thorns through cut-glass" (122). The knife and pale thorns imply pain, injury, danger, and death.

The knife and thorns that end the passage contrast with the "light and scent" of the roses. This duality keeps to Welty's early established pattern of creating clear dichotomies: the roses, with their characteristic beauty and scent, also inflict hurt and injury; they appear drunk with their "own light and scent," even at the moment that a knife causes their destruction. Beauty coexists with pain and death. Later Dicey notices "with reluctance that Sister Anne's fingers were bleeding from the roses" (135). The roses have beauty and a scent that all enjoy, but the "pale thorns" cut—and that grotesque image portends death. Anne senses the nearness of Felix's death. "If I know the signs," she says, "we're losing him fast" (149). Like headlights, the roses illuminate the path to understanding, but their thorns are sharp. With hands bloodied by thorns, Anne interprets the signs.

Like headlights, roses illuminate Dicey's path toward understanding her place in the family. She empathizes with her great-uncle, but the time is a contemplative one as her thoughts also turn to her forthcoming marriage. She has time to reflect on her kin, their lives, and the closeness of their relationships. She notices Uncle Felix's roses: "On either side of us were Uncle Felix's roses—hillocks of bushes set in hillocks of rank grass and ragged-robins, hung with roses the size of little biscuits" (126). Like "little biscuits," these roses contribute a distinctly southern metaphor.

When she departs, Dicey notices the faces of the family and friends as they gather on the porch, and she begins to assess her visit with them. As she is leaving, the landscape appears fragrant and resplendent: "the fragrances winding up through the luster of the fields and the dim, gold screen of trees and the river beyond, fragrances so rich I once could almost see them, untransparent and Oriental? In those days, fresh as I was from Sunday School in town, I could imagine the Magi riding through, laden" (151). Like the Magi, the landscape around her is laden with gold.

As her visit ends, images become dark, and Dicey's family appears to her as obscure and unknowable. She blends in smoothly with the velvety landscape, too, as she recedes from her family to her own separate future. She has to some extent rejoined them, however briefly, but now begins to distance herself from her kin, who have opened their home and their hearts to her during her visit. Her relatives and friends appear "quiet and obscure and never-known as passengers on a ship already embarked to sea. . . . Their faces were like dark boxes of secrets and desires to me, but locked safely, like old-fashioned caskets for the safe conduct of jewels on a voyage" (154). They are ultimately unknowable, and each is preserved with "secrets and desires" in that time and place in Mingo, Mississippi, framed, as if in a portrait the photographer took that day, against the darkening sky. In her reflective ride back home, the sky becomes "all one substance now, one breath and density of blue," as the evening stretches out along the "dark blue country road"; soon "all was April night." She thinks of her "sweetheart, riding, and wondered if he were writing to me" (155). With the future before her and her relatives receding behind her, she has learned more about them—who they are and what they stand for, how they live and treat their elders—and has realized more fully the strength of family ties through time and across the generations.

The "Dove-Call of April or May": A Promise of Love in "Ladies in Spring"

"Ladies in Spring" and "Going to Naples," each written from different perspectives, treat what "Kin" hints at—a youthful initiation into love. In its recollections of first love "Ladies in Spring" is reminiscent of "A Memory," but this story presents a male protagonist whose fifteen years distance in hindsight offer him a keen perspective. Looking back in time, Dewey recalls that his father's lover tried one day to meet him in the woods. Dewey begged his father to join him in his supposed fishing trip (with his two poles) and unwittingly interrupts the lovers' meeting. Welty alludes to the tryst in the first line of the story: "The pair moved through that gray landscape as though no one would see them" (84). The words foreshadow their later discovery by others as well as the implication that no one would have seen Blackie and his lover if Dewey had not requested (and been denied) the privilege of tagging along.

Blackie's lover calls to him through the woods like a "dove-call of April or May," but her call will receive no answer. The innocent Dewey, uninitiated in the world of such love-calls, misinterprets the sorrow and urgency of the voice. He assumes the lady is grieving for the dead: "such a complaint she sent over, it was so sorrowful. And about what but death would ladies, anywhere, ever speak with such voices—then turn and run?" (88). Later he instinctively suspects that this lady and her lover will not unite: "Dewey . . . believed that the one that lady waited for was never coming over the bridge to her side, any more than she would come to his" (89–90).

Blackie is a dark man, "the darkest Coker of the family, much darker than Uncle Lavelle, who had run off a long time ago" (94–95). Like George Fairchild in *Delta Wedding*, whose coloring is "almost Spanish," Blackie's deep skin color suggests his passionate nature. His name corroborates this image: "his father looked very black, trapped under the umbrella. Had Miss Hattie looked at him, that showed what his name was and how he got it!" (92). Dewey's presence at the scene inaugurates, as Margaret Bolsterli notes, "participation and marks his entry into the adult world." "Dewey," she adds, "is accepting his role as a 'dark' Coker. He will behave the same way when his turn comes. Fertility will always be assured" (Bolsterli, "Mythic Elements" 69, 72). He charms his dovelike friend, whose face by contrast is "white and still as magic" (88).

Miss Hattie, the rain dancer, takes on the characteristics of a rain or fertility goddess: she produces the needed rain. She also has that essential, communal role as postmistress. Hattie first calls the name of the presumed lover—her niece, Opal: "Opal Purcell slipped sideways through the elder-berry bushes at the creek bank, with both hands laid, like a hat, on top of her head." Hattie knows Opal has been in the rain and prides herself on having conjured it. She touches Opal's hair and says, "Has it rained that much?" (92). Her powers as goddess are limited, however. She does not realize the connection between the lovers that her sudden rain has fer-reted out of the woods.

Only in retrospect does Dewey realize the significance of the day's events: "Fifteen years later it occurred to him that it had very likely been Opal in the woods" (99). The last images of the story invoke fertility: the plum tree has flowered; next it will bear fruit. His newfound friend, the black dog, suggests play and frolic, and the moon has risen but "not yet taken light" (101). Life holds the promise of fulfillment for Dewey, but his understanding of mystery is just awakening, like the "white blooms" of spring. Ambiguity compromises his anticipation, though, as Dewey hears "the lonesomest sound in creation, an unknown bird singing through the very moment when he was the one that listened to it" (100). For Michael Kreyling, Dewey hears the note of "longing and loneliness," and he points to the ship's name, *Pomona,* the "goddess whose special attention is fruits and orchards" (*Eudora Welty's Achievement of Order* 128, 132). Spring her-alds anticipation, but like the poet in Keats's "Ode to a Nightingale," bird-song invokes a note of sadness.

The "Still-Hidden Heart" in "Going to Naples"

Ambiguity also characterizes the final story, "Going to Naples." Like "Ladies in Spring" and "Kin," this story depicts the anticipation of love or the sepa-ration from it—and from the perspective of a number of people, primarily a young woman, Gabriella. As in "The Bride of the Innisfallen," "Going to Naples" depicts a journey that emphasizes an unknowable future but one that is ripe with possibility. Like the train in "The Bride of the Innisfallen" and the ship in *The Ship of Fools,* this boat sailing for Palermo and Naples provides a venue for a gathering of people at different stages of life.

The scene is ripe with potential: Mrs. Serto seeks a husband for her daughter; Poldy, the Polish American, is "on his way now to marry a girl in

Italy that he had never seen" (157); and two black men have feet pointing outward, forming an M shape, which stands for "getting married" (159). Gabriella Serto gives in to temper tantrums about leaving American life. They show her poor manners and immaturity; older people remember their loves when Gabriella's cavortings reawaken their senses; and other travelers seek various destinations and hopes.

Sexual imagery abounds: the flesh pops through Gabriella's ripped stocking "like a tear" (156); her "flying dark hair" and "contending body" make Gabriella appear "as though some captive, that had never had news of the world, land or sea, would sometimes stand there and look out from that pure arch" (161). She springs forward, like a cat, with all the tension within her. Aldo sprawls on a deck chair "like a man pining to be teased" (164), and he retrieves his toothpick "as though he drew a gun from a holster" (165).

When the two potential lovers come together to play, they are immediately, physically close: "Gabriella drove her face into Aldo's warm shirt. She set her teeth into his sleeve. But when she pierced that sleeve she found his arm—rigid and wary, with a muscle that throbbed like a heart. She would have bitten a piece out of him then and there for the scare his arm gave her, but he moved like a spring and struck at her with his playful weapon, the toothpick between his teeth. In return she butted his chest, driving her head against the hard, hot rayon, while, still in the character of an airy bird, he pecked with his little beak that place on the back of the neck where women no longer feel" (165). The scene prompts the older people on the ship to reminisce: "Looking, dreaming, down at Gabriella, they felt something of an old, pure loneliness come back to them—like a bird sent out over the waters long ago, when they were young. . . . Only the long of memory, the brave and experienced of heart, could bear such a stirring, an awakening—first to have listened to that screaming, and in a flash to remember what it was" (167). In this poignant moment Welty juxtaposes two dreams in one scene: on the one hand, Gabriella and Aldo cavort and play, their hands interlocked and their hopes high; on the other, the older people, for whom the memory of love may be all that remains, can only "bear such a stirring, an awakening" of forgotten feelings. The contrast is stark, and the result is powerful: for the young, dreams may still come true, but the old sometimes can only recall its dramatic impact through memory. As in "Livvie," this story offers a compelling contrast between the vigorousness of youth and the haunting memory of it in aging years.

Not all expectations lead to fulfillment in "Going to Naples." Kreyling sees the tale as illustrating "the heart again denied its refuge in the other, but stronger for the denial" (*Eudora Welty's Achievement of Order* 134). The story ends as the passengers depart for their separate ways. As in "The Bride of Innisfallen," this story depicts partings and future uncertainties. The characters fade into the "sliding life of the streets" (206), but the future is still all "ahead of them," like a "bubble." The unknown holds its secrets, much like the "still-hidden heart of Naples," and all that stands in the way of full experience is the apprehension about plunging into it (207).

As a collection, *The Bride of the Innisfallen* carries forward Welty's focus on human relationships, particularly coming to know love and remembering it wistfully. Compared with their previous counterparts, fewer characters in this volume die, commit suicide, go mad, or by the same token, find lasting happiness, fruitful marriage, or enjoy a smooth combination of romance and love. This book offers a more tempered view and is the only one that Welty wrote in which only one death occurs (Elpenor dies in "Circe"), no one marries, and few tragedies or ecstasies of extreme dimension occur. Several characters almost die (such as Felix in "Kin"), and several are about to marry (Dicey in "Kin" and the bride in the title story). In these dense but quiet works Welty concentrates on the subtle gradations of emotion that have less dramatic consequences for plot but more intensity in overall impact.

The mysteriousness of identity—a topic present in earlier works—provides a general theme for this volume. Discovering the secret identity of another individual becomes in "No Place for You, My Love" a task with risk and difficulty. For "Circe" knowing the lover's consciousness is still paramount but veiled by the dueling powers of passion and magic. The journeys in "Kin," "The Bride of the Innisfallen," and "Going to Naples" offer the occasions for anticipating or finding the unknown in relationships: "some future and secret joy, at what was unknown" (*One Writer's Beginnings* 94). "Ladies in Spring" and "Kin" focus on the carefree views of immaturity that clarify upon maturation. Most of these stories depict young characters seeking fulfilling relationships but not necessarily finding them. Older characters who once knew them sense such relationships almost palpably through memory. *The Bride of the Innisfallen* offers nuanced possibilities and boundaries in relationships.

CHAPTER 9

"Like the Stamens in a Dainty Bess Rose"

The Love Story in Losing Battles

Welty said of her novel *Losing Battles:* "I wanted to show that relationships run the whole gamut of love and oppression. Just like any human relationship has the possibilities of so many gradations of affection, feeling, passion, resistance, and hatred" (*Conversations* 221–22). These infinite "gradations" form the bases for most of her stories. Welty considers the many "alternatives and eventualities" in the world of relationships. Some couples know the "ancient communication" between two people, or the deep and time-tested commitment of Ellen and Battle Fairchild or Becky and Judge McKelva. Others face the harsh consequences that loss and death force people to confront.[1] Those who know love but must relinquish it are among Welty's most compelling characters. Laurel Hand is one such figure, who has known and lost a marriage that was near-perfection in its wholeness, was enriching and educating for both partners, yet simultaneously presented challenge and security.

Welty's late novel *Losing Battles* continues the tested themes and narrative techniques of earlier works. She writes of romance, domesticity, and familial orientation. Again in *Losing Battles* she relies on the "by ear" storytelling strategy, in which dialogue and dialect are almost as important to the story as the plot line. Welty considers here, as in *The Optimist's Daughter,* complex questions about love and reaches deeply for answers, emotionally and philosophically, in her late novels.

Losing Battles considers love of different kinds. Joyce Carol Oates has termed it "a book about domestic love" in which "we hear about the young hero, Jack; we hear about his exploits, his courage, foolishness, his falling in love with the young girl who is his teacher; hear about the bride herself and about her infant girl; gradually . . . understanding how the hero and his bride came to be separated and how they will be joined again." In a larger sense, she adds, the book concerns the importance of family life: "What is important is love—the bonds of blood and memory that hold people together, eccentric and argumentative and ignorant though these people are. The basic unit of humanity is the family, the expanded family and not the selfish little family of modern day."

Loyalty, allegiance, and commitment to family, even at the expense of community involvement, are topics Welty has considered before and takes up here again. Three full decades after *Delta Wedding*, Welty again considers domestic life and love in the context of social relationships. In *Delta Wedding* Robbie Fairchild's rivalry with the Fairchild clan for her husband's attention is one example, and community intervention in familial relations recurs in "Lily Daw and the Three Ladies," "Petrified Man," "Asphodel," and other early stories. In *Losing Battles* the tension between family loyalty and the need for privacy reaches a clamorous level, and Welty here answers her posed questions with less ambiguity. The dichotomy between private relations and societal obligations remains a central topic in the novel.

Perhaps more than any other pair in Welty's fiction, Jack and Gloria Renfro in *Losing Battles* grapple with the difficult questions of marital allegiance, insularity and privacy, and the proper balance of familial obligations with communal and social roles. Aside from their financial worries, this dichotomy between private affairs and community is the crucial problem in their marriage. Like Judge Moody's car, balanced precariously on a tree limb, hanging from a cliff, this tension keeps both husband and wife shifting their balance toward marital equilibrium—and not always succeeding.

Jack and Gloria adapt to living "most privately when things are most crowded." They must renew their affection and commitment in the midst of a family reunion. They have their intimate moments, and some naturally occur "in front of the whole family." "First kiss of their lives in public, I bet a hundred dollars," Aunt Cleo announces upon Jack's initial embrace of his wife (73). Other moments find them quietly alone with one another. Nonetheless, their predominant need is for privacy and intimacy, and Jack's long absence in jail makes that need more acute and juxtaposes it to the equally demanding need for a viable family life and social context. Jack hopes for a lasting reconciliation among his family members and Gloria, and she hopes for private life apart from the "clannishness" of his family.

Privacy is of value to Gloria, especially when she finds herself in a large family of new in-laws, whom she does not particularly like, for the duration of Jack's jail term. Early in the novel Gloria's in-laws criticize her characteristic insistence upon her privacy: "'Mind out, Sister Cleo, Gloria don't like to tell her business,' Miss Beulah called" (48). Later, when Aunt Birdie assumes that the entire family will gather to tell Jack about his new baby, born since he went to prison, Gloria brings the whole family up short with a reassertion of her sense of intimacy: "She's my surprise to bring" (69). Even later, when the family begs for the surprise, Gloria stays inside the house and calls out the window that she is "tending to some of my business." Trespassing further into Gloria's territory, "the crowd" of this family grows increasingly intent upon telling the secret of the baby: "'Gloria! What have you got for Jack? Ain't it just about time to show him?' The crowd caught up with her in the kitchen, clamoring to her. 'I'll be the judge,' said Gloria from the stove" (74). What Gloria so carefully judges is a private boundary she feels the need to protect within the larger expanse of the family.

The first intimate moment Gloria shares with Jack is welcome, especially in view of the intrusive and insistent family: "Chewing softly, he kept his eyes on Gloria, and now in a wreath of steam she came toward him. She bent to his ear and whispered her first private word. 'Jack, there's precious little water in this house, but I saved you back some and I've got it boiling'" (75). When Gloria finally shows Jack their baby, the family realizes that by confidential, epistolary means, Gloria has already revealed to Jack, during his jail term, the secret of the baby. The surprise is now the family's, as they find out that Jack knows all: "'Gloria told him what she had. That baby's no more a surprise than I am,' cried Aunt Nanny. 'I'm not afraid of pencil and paper,' said Gloria" (94). With this pronouncement Gloria establishes not only her literacy but also her views about her private sphere with Jack. The family seems disappointed to learn that this baby is no surprise: "'Lady May all along was supposed to be his surprise. Now what is she?' cried Aunt Birdie." Disappointment may reign among the ranks, but Gloria delineates and sharply monitors the distinction between the public and the private, especially regarding the intimate subject of childbirth, as she insists: "she was my surprise to tell" (92).

Conversely, Jack Renfro feels strong familial and social obligations. Reminiscent of George's conflict with Robbie in *Delta Wedding* and his loyalty to his large family, Jack's entreaty to Gloria is to embrace his family: "'Say now you'll love 'em a little bit. Say you'll love them too. You can. Try and you can. . . . Honey, won't you change your mind about my family?' "'Not for all the tea in China,' she declared" (360). Jack wants Gloria to accept and love his family; his vision, like George's, is flexible and all-inclusive: "'Be my cousin,' he begged. 'I want you for my cousin. My wife, and my children's mother, and my cousin and everything. . . . Don't give anybody up. . . . Or leave anybody out. . . . There's room for everything, and time for everybody'" (361–62).

Typically, however, Gloria takes the opposite view: she dreams of devoting herself to the marriage and core family unit. She keeps her mind on "the future" and dreams of a day when she, Jack, and the baby can move to a "two-room house, where nobody in the world could find us" (434, 412): "'Oh, this is the way it could always be. It's what I've dreamed of,' Gloria said, reaching both arms around Jack's neck. 'I've got you all by myself, Jack Renfro. Nobody talking, nobody listening, nobody coming—nobody about to call you or walk in on us—there's nobody left but you and me, and nothing to be in our way'" (431). Jack understandably feels "sudden danger" at these ideas. So the battle lines are drawn.

Michael Kreyling suggests that these questions are "very real to a man of Jack Renfro's mind, in which family means safety, companionship, defense against chaos" (*Eudora Welty's Achievement of Order* 149). John Hardy has pointed out that "even more fiercely than Robbie Reid, Gloria believes that it is possible to marry a man without marrying his whole kin. She has not quite succeeded in convincing Jack. . . . In her own mind, she is still a long way from being taken captive by the tribe" (105). Louise Gossett adds that "Welty doesn't promise escape, for as Gloria looks away from the house to the future, beyond the bright porch she couldn't see anything" ("Eudora Welty's New Novel" 128). Susan V. Donaldson sees the struggle with family, particularly exemplified during the watermelon fight, as "the drive for power and dominance shaping so many of the tales of the noisy Beechams and Renfros" ("Opposing Modes" 38).

The argument, however, remains unresolved. This battle will be neither won nor lost. Gloria wants her privacy from his family, and Jack still maintains, "You just can't have too many, is the way I look at it" (435). Welty commented in an interview that "every instinct" in Gloria wants them to "go and live by themselves," and "Jack, of course, is just oblivious to the fact that there could be anything wrong with staying there and having the best of both" (*Conversations* 305). Welty offers the rationale for each side of the question: "Jack is really a good person, even though he is all the other things. . . . He allows himself to be used by everybody. . . . [But that] comes out of his goodness. . . . Yes, I really like Jack. He's a much better person than Gloria" (306). The struggle defines their relationship, and the marital tension remains high for much of the novel.

Jack and Gloria face a dilemma—not of goodness versus evil or right versus wrong but of the dynamics of togetherness and opposition in marriage, which draws together and pushes apart those who engage and interact over time. Both positions in the argument may have merit, but Gloria simply appears to be selfish. To balance privacy and community, and the competing claims of passion and society, Jack and Gloria must prevent slipping either into isolation or clannishness. To preserve the integrity of their most intimate relationships, they must dodge intrusion and protect their private relations. At the same time the familial and social influence on the couple seems essential in supporting and embracing them as part of a large family. Indeed, the communal context becomes the vital thread without which characters such as Livvie, Robbie, and Gloria risk unraveling the fabric of their marital lives.

The relationship of Jack and Gloria Renfro flourishes, even in view of the challenges they face. The marriage of Jack and Gloria depends for inspiration not upon exotic travels, scandalous infidelity, or fairy-tale fantasy but on a traditional relationship. Like other Welty love stories, this one takes on the structure of a comic love story, with her typical southern setting: the lovers separate and eventually find reunion—with pine needles as their bed.

The seventy-five-page prelude to Jack's arrival is anticipatory strategy. The entrance of the newlywed husband, reuniting with the recent bride and meeting for the first time their new child, prepares the way for both Gloria's and the family's extensive reaction to Jack's homecoming. As if in preparation for a wedding, the "girl cousins" march ceremoniously around Gloria like flower girls, chanting what might easily be a wedding song: "*Down on the carpet you must kneel / Sure as the grass grows in this field*" (29). Time suspends until the lovers are again united. The throng of family parts, as if they were the Red Sea, for the dramatic moment when Jack greets his wife. Welty offers a description of their embrace and kiss: "They divided and there stood Gloria. Her hair came down in a big puff as far as her shoulders, where it broke into curls all of which would move when she did, smelling of Fairy soap. Across her forehead it hung in fine hooks, cinnamon-colored, like the stamens in a Dainty Bess rose. As though small bells had been hung, without her permission, on her shoulders, hips, breasts, even elbows, tinkling only just out of her ears' range, she stepped the length of the porch to meet him. . . . Jack cocked his hands in front of his narrow-set hips as she came. Their young necks stretched, their lips tilted up, like a pair of rabbits yearning toward the same head of grass, and Jack snapped his vise around her waist with thumbs met" (73). With rose imagery—like the "stamens in a Dainty Bess rose"—Gloria exudes sexuality. The stamen of a rose is sexually suggestive, in and of itself. Welty also describes the cactus as the color of "mistletoe," providing Jack with ample excuses for kissing in public (24). Like India in *Delta Wedding*, the onlookers try to see "what there was about a kiss." Poised amid the throngs of family, rejoined, this couple takes center stage and full dramatic power as Welty further explores her question from *Delta Wedding*: "What do you ask for when you love?" (146).

The omniscient point of view Welty chooses provides the first private conversations between a man and wife. Gloria presents her husband with the gift of a new shirt that she has saved relentlessly to buy for him. In the first of many intimate moments between them, she helps Jack dress: "Without ever taking his eyes from her, and without moving to get the old shirt off till she peeled it from his back, he punched one arm down the stiffened sleeve. She helped him. He drove in the other fist. It seemed to require their double strength to crack the starch she'd ironed into it, to get his wet body inside. She began to button him down, as his arms cracked down to a resting place and cocked themselves there. . . . By the time she stood with her back against the door to get the last button through the buttonhole, he was leaning like the side of a house against her. His cheek came down against her like a hoarse voice speaking too loud. . . . She straightened him up and led him back into the midst of them" (78).

Their sexuality is apparent. Along with Jamie and Rosamund in *The Robber Bridegroom* and George and Robbie Fairchild in *Delta Wedding*, Jack and Gloria leave for an afternoon together in the woods. Miss Beulah Renfro, Jack's mother, articulates the moment, from Gloria's perspective: "this minute is all in the world she's been waiting on" (94). The woodland setting is paradisiacal but southern; their woods are replete with bees crawling "like babies into the florets," and the birds move like "one patch quilt": "They walked through waist-high spires of cypress weed, green as strong poison, where the smell of weed and the heat of sun made equal forces, like foes well matched or sweethearts come together. Jack unbuttoned his new shirt. He wore it like a preacher's frock-tailed coat, flying loose. . . . Then side by side, with the baby rolled next to Jack's naked chest, they ran and slid down the claybank, which had washed away until it felt like all the elbows, knees and shoulder, cinder-hot. . . . Keeping time with each other they stepped fast without missing a tie. . . . Jack reached for her" (98).

The pallet is of the soft needles of the southern pine: "The big old pine over them had shed years of needles into one deep bed." The squirrels playing and courting overhead reenact the play among the humans below: "a pack of courting squirrels electrified a pine tree in front of them, poured down it, ripped on through bushes, trees, anything, tossing the branches, sobbing and gulping like breasted doves." Jack approaches Gloria with equal earnestness: his face rushes "like an engine toward hers" (99). Alone at last, the couple enjoys some private time together.

In their other love scenes (during the novel's span of one day) Jack and Gloria continue their reuniting. After accidentally bumping her head on a log, "Without stopping to be sorry for her head," Jack "crammed kisses in her mouth, and she wound her arms around his own drenched head and returned him kiss for kiss" (113). Jack comforts her as she recounts Julia

Mortimer's opposition to their marriage: "He drew her near, stroking her forehead, pushing her dampening hair behind her ears. . . . He went on stroking her. . . . Gloria's tears ran down the face he was kissing" (168). And they reaffirm their promises: "I ain't ever going to laugh at you, and you ain't ever going to feel sorry for me. We're safe." Right now they agree that "being married" means "we're a family" (171).

Emotions run high, but the "deep bed" of pine holds them gently. Jack "held her in his arms and rocked her, baby and all, while she spent her tears. When the baby began to roll out of her failing arm, he caught her and tucked her into the pillow of the school satchel. Then he picked up Gloria and carried her the remaining few steps to that waiting bed of pinestraw" (171). Gloria returns from this brief, second honeymoon looking "like all the brides that ever were," and Jack confirms that she is still looking "just like a bride" (361), even after a family watermelon fight. In the ensuing discussion of Miss Julia's accusations of incest, Gloria reveals that her worst fears are all symbolized in three words: "null and void" (321). What she wants most is to keep this marriage to Jack away from all serious threats.

The moon, always an enchanting force in Welty's love stories, "now at full power" assists Jack as he assuages Gloria's fears with his caring ways (333). The night-blooming cereus—that magical flower—lifts its blossoms triumphantly and nocturnally, as the natural world celebrates this reunion on a midsummer night. The lovers are at their most intimate in the privacy of their bedroom. Under the magical "white trumpets" of the night-blooming cereus, the moonstruck Gloria and Jack entreat one another (in their third love scene of the day) to protect the boundaries, at least for the moment, and allow no one to intrude: "She put her mouth quickly on his, and then she slid her hand and seized hold of him right at the root. And so she convinced him that there is only one way of depriving the ones you love—taking your living presence away from theirs; that no one alive has ever deserved such punishment . . . and that no one alive can ever in honor forgive that wrong, which outshines shame, and is not to be forgiven until it has been righted" (362).

Like Shelley, the keen observer in *Delta Wedding*, the young boy Vaughn in *Losing Battles*, still lying awake nearby, ponders the mysteries of love as he espies Jack and Gloria. He found them earlier in the day in their embrace, "lying deep in the woods together, like one creature" (363). The image recalls Loch Morrison's gazing, in "June Recital," at the lovers in the abandoned house next door and seeing them "like a big grasshopper lighting, all their legs and arms drew in to one small body, deadlike, with protective coloring" (*Golden Apples* 282). Vaughn may see a physical image of love—two people joined as one creature—but he cannot yet comprehend the fuller meaning of the relationship he observes, or people "getting tangled up with each other." To this "moonlit little boy," a version of romantic Jamie Lockhart, the mysterious phenomenon of love is a "danger"—and something for later and farther away. Jack and Gloria, however, have found the end of waiting. They are in the present: their love happens now and cannot be postponed an instant longer. As they drift to sleep by the light of the silvery moon, in their woodland bed of pine straw, Jack and Gloria take their place among Welty's most successful couples, yet they have many battles ahead of them to be lost and won.

CHAPTER 10

"It Was the Old Wood
That Did the Blooming"

The Optimist's Daughter *and* One Writer's Beginnings

The Optimist's Daughter and *One Writer's Beginnings* are, taken together, Welty's tour de force. In them Welty offers her most complex depictions and assessments of love, and her conclusions are profound. Her autobiographical novel and her later memoir are reflective of one another in numerous ways. Michael Kreyling and Suzanne Marrs rightly note the similarity: "Since *One Writer's Beginnings* overlaps *The Optimist's Daughter* so closely, it is impossible not to read the later text back upon the earlier" (*Understanding* 209). Peggy Prenshaw sees a variety of differences in her examination (*Composing* 257).

Love and devotion, the sanctity of privacy, the domestic framework, and the deep commitment that Welty's earlier love stories portray are here again upheld. Love in the face of deep loss and grief, first limned in "A Curtain of Green," is no less painful here, perhaps even more so, but the consolation Welty posits in *The Optimist's Daughter* is different: although the past is dead and deceased loved ones gone, through memory individuals can recapture some of what is lost. She differentiates herself here from William Faulkner, for whom the past and the present are one, so the past is "never dead" (*Requiem for a Nun* 80). In Welty's view, only through memory is the past reachable. Love may overcome death, and memory can ameliorate grief. Her protagonist, Laurel Hand, thinks back to the marriage of her parents, then later to her marriage and late husband. In her three finely delineated portraits of marriage in this novel, Welty considers what emotions emerge as people love (*Conversations* 222).

The rose also takes on its most resonant metaphorical significance in *The Optimist's Daughter*. In the ease and simplicity of their marriage,

Becky and Judge McKelva enjoy a relationship that is "time-honored," like the climbing rose Becky cultivates in her garden and prunes annually on George Washington's birthday. Becky's climber perfectly symbolizes the great flowering and longevity of the McKelva marriage. Marrs see the climber as "the key emblem of memory" (*One Writer's Imagination* 245); Helen Levy writes that "the extended scene in Becky's garden prepares us for Laurel's understanding of her artistic birth," and eventually Laurel "can leave the mother's garden and create her own world" (190, 195).

That Judge McKelva attempts to continue the annual pruning ritual after his wife's death is a testament to his devotion beyond life. As he prunes the old rose, he believes he "started seeing behind me" (5). This problem may signal his impending eye trouble, but on a symbolic level he sees the long, dead past and seeks to reclaim some memories of his wife, who has predeceased him. In the fullness of their lives the couple garnered the respect of all who know them, and most of the community remembers the union as nearly perfect. The history of this first McKelva marriage unfolds through the memories of Laurel as she reaches back into her past to portray her beloved parents and the closeness of their relationship. As he prunes the old rose, the Judge finds that his memories flow freely. The old rose represents his lovely marriage to Becky, their happiness and longevity together, and then is the pathway to reaching her after she is gone to death.

The climbing rose, perennially blooming in the garden, carefully tended by the loving hands of Judge McKelva, in memory of his wife, is the resplendent image of loyalty in marriage, the memory of which is undisturbed by the passage of time: "In some cases, it was the old wood that did the blooming" (115). The "old wood" signifies the old marriage and the old memories, flowering out now in McKelva's mind and heart, as he reaches across time, distance, and death to recall his beloved wife Becky. The comparison between the McKelva marriage and Welty's own parents' marriage is unmistakable, and her depictions—one in novel, the other in memoir—by a devoted daughter commemorate their love. The climbing roses—drawn from the real roses in the Welty garden, tended carefully both by Chestina Welty and her daughter, Eudora, and now carefully restored in that garden at the Welty homeplace—are a reminder of the strength, endurance, and devotion of her parents' marriage, her enduring love for them, and the grace and charm of their southern garden.

Laurel reminisces, seeing behind her, as does her father when his eye trouble first starts. Her hindsight begins as she travels home at the first inkling of her father's illness. The bridesmaids who had long ago attended Laurel's wedding— like Welty's close circle of friends, who called themselves "The Basic Eight"—reiterate that Judge and Becky would "do anything for each other" (126). Tish recalls the Judge's bringing home a beaded crepe dress, with beads "neck to hem," which he had bought for Becky in New Orleans (125). Becky wore it, Tish recalls, "nearly a hundred percent of the time" (126). The "happily married" couple has a relationship "strong as an old apple tree" (180, 114). Like their winter-hardy climbing roses, they "will hardly take a setback" (5).

To understand and honor them, Laurel spends time reminiscing and recollecting the memories of her parents and their marriage. Laurel recalls her childhood nights, comforted by her parent's quiet and secure relationship. The sound of their nightly reading to one another envelops her in feelings of love, security, and pleasure: "When Laurel was a child, in this room and in this bed where she lay now, she closed her eyes like this and the rhythmic, nighttime sound of the two beloved reading voices came rising in turn up the stairs every night to reach her. She could hardly fall asleep, she tried to keep awake, for pleasure. She cared for her own books, but she cared more for theirs, which meant their voices. In the lateness of the night, their two voices reading to each other where she could hear them, never letting a silence divide or interrupt them, combined into one unceasing voice and wrapped her around as she listened, as still as if she were asleep. She was sent to sleep under a velvety cloak of words, richly patterned and stitched with gold, straight out of a fairy tale, while they went reading on into her dreams" (57–58).

In her highly autobiographical novel Welty fictionalizes experiences from her childhood. In the memoir *One Writer's Beginnings* she makes the connection between the two portraits clear: "My mother read to me. She'd read to me in the big bedroom in the mornings, when we were in her rocker together, which ticked in rhythm as we rocked, as though we had a cricket accompanying the story. She'd read to me in the dining room on winter afternoons in front of the coal fire, with our cuckoo clock ending the story with 'Cuckoo,' and at night when I'd got in my own bed" (5).

Welty recalls the feelings of security and delight she felt as a child listening to her parents talk to each other at night. They allowed her once to occupy their double bed when she was sick: "My parents draped the lampshade with a sheet of the daily paper, which was tilted, like a hatbrim, so that they could sit in their rockers in a lighted part of the room and I could supposedly go to sleep in the protected dark of the bed. They sat talking. I was free to listen to every word my parents said between them." The "chief secret" she recalls is "the two of them, father and mother, sitting there as one": "I don't remember that any secrets were revealed to me, nor do I remember any avid curiosity on my part to learn something I wasn't supposed to—perhaps I was too young to know what to listen for. But I was present in the room with the chief secret there was—the two of them, father and mother, sitting there as one. I was conscious of this secret and of my fast-beating heart in step together, as I lay in the slant-shaded light of the room" (20–21).

Even though Welty is in another room, her parents' voices murmuring back and forth to one another give the child not a sense of distance from them but a sense of inclusion: "What they talked about I have no idea, and the subject was not what mattered to me. It was no doubt whatever a young married couple spending their first time privately in each other's company in the long, probably harried day would talk about. It was the murmur of their voices, the back-and-forth . . . that made me bask there at my distance. What I felt was not that I was excluded from them but that I was included in—and because of—what I could hear of their voices and what I could see of their faces" (*One Writer's Beginnings* 20–21).

Within this protected environment Welty developed important feelings of privacy, inclusiveness, and security that would later resonate in her fiction. She was a bona fide part of the family; she is one of three and not simply an unimportant extra to the two main family members—her parents. In *One Writer's Beginnings* she recounts hearing her parents "duet" as they communicated with each other in the morning with humming and whistling a tune as they prepared for the day ahead: "They would begin whistling back and forth to each other up and down the stairwell. My father would whistle his phrase, my mother would try to whistle, then hum hers back. It was their duet." In *The Optimist's Daughter* the marriage of Laurel's parents, like that of Welty's, is the "breath of life" for the child listening intently when "every word is beautiful": "For every book here she had heard their voices, father's and mother's. And perhaps it didn't matter to them, not always, what they read aloud; it was the breath of life flowing between them, and the words of the moment riding it that held them in delight. Between some two people every word is beautiful, or might as well be beautiful" (118).

Laurel recalls more and more details of her parents' marriage as the novel progresses. Michael Kreyling explains that "Laurel is left alone in the Mount Salus house to come to terms with family myth and questions of her own past" (*Understanding* 222). She discovers their courtship letters and photographs, and now she has a history of their romance: "There was a careful record of those days preserved in a snapshot book. Laurel felt along the shelf above the pigeonholes and touched it, the square boards, the silk tassel. She pulled it down to her. "Still clinging to the first facing pages were the pair of grayed and stippled home-printed snapshots: Clinton and Becky 'up home,' each taken by the other standing in the same spot on a railroad track (a leafy glade), he slender as a wand, his foot on a milepost, swinging his straw hat; she with her hands full of the wildflowers they'd picked along the way" (136). Welty again describes her own parents' letters to one another, written during their courtship and engagement—the couple had been separated while Welty's father secured a new job in Jackson: "Their letters had all been kept by that great keeper, my mother; they were in one of the trunks in the attic. I didn't in the end feel like a trespasser when I came to open the letters: they brought my parents before me for the first time as young, as inexperienced, consumed with the strength of their hopes and desires, as *living* on these letters. . . . he wrote more often than any once a day . . . letters that are so ardent, so direct and tender in expression, so urgent, that they seemed to bare, along with his love, the rest of his whole life to me" (*One Writer's Beginnings* 75–76). Laurel's finding her parents' letters after their deaths is revelatory and cathartic for her. She no longer sees them from the child's perspective but from the vantage point of her own adulthood. She can now understand them as they once were: young, vital, romantic, and in love. She finds her mother's openness: a cabinet looks "like a little wall out of a country post office which nobody had in years disturbed by calling for the mail" (134–35). Elizabeth Evans contends that "Laurel's experience forces her to sort through the remaining possessions of her dead parents; and as she relives the memories, she is forced to reassess not only her parents, their marriage, and their shortcomings but also to reassess her own role as the dutiful daughter" (59). The cabinet door is open—Becky never locked it: "There was no key in either keyhole of the double doors of the cabinet. But had there ever been a key?" The scene is reminiscent of Ellen and Battle in *Delta Wedding,* who never locked a door, and Laurel's mother has a similar concept of privacy: "Her mother had never locked up anything that Laurel could remember. Her privacy was keyless. She had simply assumed her privacy" (134). Like the characters Ellen Fairchild and Becky McKelva, for Welty's mother "privacy was keyless."

Although she read the letters from her grandmother to her mother, Laurel does not violate privacy between her parents, so for their letters, with their envelopes "turned saffron" with age and tied with "ribbons that were almost transparent, and freckled now, as the skin of her mother's hands came to be before she died," she demurs (135). She knows instinctively what follows the opening line, "My darling Sweetheart," and having read the one line, she returns the letters respectfully to the desk.

Laurel's father, the Judge, is also a discreet and private man but is not the "great keeper" of letters: "Her mother had written to him every day they were separated in their married lives; she had said so. . . . Where were the letters? Put away somewhere, with her garden picture? . . . They weren't anywhere, because he hadn't kept them. He'd never kept them: Laurel knew it and should have known it to start with. He had dispatched all his correspondence promptly, and dropped letters as he answered them straight into the wastebasket; Laurel had seen him do it. And when it concerned her mother, if that was what she asked for, he *went*" (122–23). Laurel follows her father's example when she burns all these letters and assigns her knowledge of them to memory and to the inviolable past (169).

Presumably, this portrait mirrors Welty's actions in ensuring the ultimate privacy of her parents.

In contrast to the deep love and commitment obvious in the first Mc-Kelva marriage, the second one, between Judge McKelva and Fay Chisom, presents a world of contradictions. Innuendoes about the Judge's "failing vision" allude to the fact that his judgment in marrying Fay has dimmed as well (Tiegreen, "Mothers, Daughters" 193). Even the "bridesmaids" say that other women around town, who would have "jumped" at the chance to marry the Judge, would have been more appropriate choices for his new wife.

Scholars have analyzed Fay's character with appropriately little sympathy for her. Guy Davenport compares her to "Psyche's nasty hateful sister" and says that "in the pecking order of the South," Fay is "white trash." He adds to his colorful assessment that she is one of the "weak-witted, pathologically selfish daughters of the dispossessed" (Davenport, "Primal Visions" 697). Ruth Weston sees her as having taken on the role of outsider (161). Patricia Spacks says that Fay belongs to "the great, interrelated family of those who never know the meaning of what has happened to them" (510). John Hardy has been only somewhat kinder: "Fay's family are only a slightly modernized version of the Peacocks, and all the worse for the updating" (107). He calls her "emotionally retarded but as hopelessly provincial," and yet he sees her as a "pitiable and lonely" character, like Laurel: "Both now are lightening ship for the alien future. . . . Both are pitiable and lonely fugitives from their pasts; both the more pitiably doomed to solitude" (110, 114). Julia Eichelberger sees her as a "selfish and short-sighted" woman who embodies "all that threatens the stability and order of the Southern aristocracy." She adds that Fay's "denunciations of various people and customs that the genteel Mount Salus reveres are usually transparently egotistical, just like her response to her husband's illness ("I don't see why this had to happen to me!" [*Prophets* 130–31]). Ruth M. Vande Kieft notes that "in every way Fay contrasts with Laurel" (*Eudora Welty*, rev. ed. 167). Helen Hurt Tiegreen adds that "Judge McKelva's vision . . . takes him away from the present" (193). Ann Romines sees Fay as "almost a parody of narcissistic modernity" (*Home Plot* 258).

The bedroom again represents the couple who inhabits it. Here the bedrooms and beds contrast the Judge's two marriages. The effects of his decision to remarry, and to marry Fay in particular, come fully into dramatic light in Fay's choice of bedroom decor. Draped in peach satin is the bedchamber, which swims "in pink" light. The pink bedroom color may allude to Faulkner's "A Rose for Emily," with its "valance curtains of faded rose color" and "rose shaded lights," but in any case is an indication of Fay's personality (Weaks 11–12): "Laurel went up, knocked, and opened the door into the big bedroom. Instead of her mother's writing cabinet that used to stand between those windows, the bed faced her. It seemed to swim in a bath of pink light. The mahogany headboard, rising high as the mantelpiece, had been quilted from top to bottom in peach satin; peach satin ruffles were thrown back over the foot of the bed; peach satin smothered the windows all around. Fay slept in the middle of the bed, deep under the cover, both hands curled into slack fists above her head" (60).

Laurel recoils at the thought of her father's relationship with Fay. In the Hibiscus Hotel the bedrooms of the two women are adjoining, separated only by a thin partition. Laurel "shrank from that thin board and from the vague apprehension that some night she might hear Fay cry or laugh like a stranger at something she herself would rather not know" (18). Laurel dreads hearing or seeing evidence of intimacies between Fay and her father. Later in the novel, when Miss Tennyson and Miss Adele enter the house to prepare it for the funeral, the minister's wife notices another revelatory detail—their "bed wasn't made." "I won't describe the way Adele and I found it," Miss Tennyson points out with social condescension (106). As these examples accrue, they indicate the sense of familial betrayal and destruction Laurel feels and articulates when she says to Fay, "You desecrated this house" (173).

Scholars have paid great attention to the bed scene. Kreyling sees the bed as "that contraption" that is "not really a bed" (*Eudora Welty's Achievement of Order* 169). Hardy argues that the peach satin bed evinces the Judge's "more vulgar inclination," which Laurel cannot accept. Fay's presence violates the sanctity of Laurel's memory of her parents' marriage. Hardy adds that "there is nothing to counter the appalling evidence of the pink-satined bed" (117). Eichelberger sees the pink satin as an indication of Fay's "sensual indulgence, and always satisfying such appetites in direct contradiction to the wishes of others or to old traditions" (*Prophets* 131). Axel Nissen further extrapolates that "the *pièce de resistance* of camp incongruity in the novel is, of course, the transformation of the McKelva marital bed—the very symbol of tradition, marital sanctity, and family values—into a camp vision worthy of Liberace": "The headboard of the very same bed in which Laurel was born and Becky died quilted and the entire bed swathed in peach pink satin!" (223). Suzan Harrison points out that "Fay's pink-satin bed serves as a garish reminder of her sexual nature, a transgression of the traditional restraint in the McKelva home" (*Eudora Welty* 121).

The reason for the second marriage is in itself a subject of conjecture. Fay seems childlike to the Judge, albeit with his unclear vision: "So Fay might have appeared, just at the beginning to her aging father, with his slipping eyesight" (76). Missouri corroborates this view that the Judge saw Fay as childlike and as someone on whom the Judge could dote: "He mightily enjoyed having him somebody to spoil." Later she adds, "He always want Miss Fay to have her breakfast in bed" (59). Miss Tennyson and Adele Courtland concur that Clinton "doted" on Fay: "'Oh, indeed he doted on her.' . . . 'Doted. You've hit on it. That's the word,' said Miss Tennyson. . . . 'A man can feel compunction for a child like Fay'" (107). Fay's childlike nature seems appealing to the Judge, but his judgment is faulty or unclear.

Fay seems childlike to Laurel as well. She says Fay is "perhaps . . . forty," but Laurel notes that there is "little of forty in [Fay's] looks except the line of her neck and the backs of her little square, idle hands. She was bony and blue-veined; as a child she had very possibly gone undernourished. Her hair was still a childish tow" (26). Laurel is in her middle forties and thus roughly the same age as Fay (3), but her maturity contrasts directly with Fay's childish appearance and behavior.

Fay thus may seem a surrogate child in the Judge's life, not so much for his wife Becky but for his daughter, Laurel, who lives far away in a city in the North. Welty devotes attention to Laurel's mother's grief over leaving her home and her mother. Now Laurel repeats the pattern in her own life. The community chorus disapproves: "Daughters need to stay put, where they can keep a better eye on us old folks," Miss Tennyson Bullock warns (61), but Laurel disregards them and follows a career in Chicago as a "professional designer of fabrics" (16). "There's not enough Mount Salus has to offer a brilliant mind," Miss Adele adds pointedly (113). Fay's remarks are even sharper: "Oh, I wouldn't have run off and left anybody that needed me. Just to call myself an artist and make a lot of money" (28). Community censure is clear.

The Judge's own words also suggest his need for Laurel when she is away in Chicago, not long before he decides to marry Fay. He writes to Laurel, inviting her to accompany him to England, and suggests that she "knock off, invite a friend for company, and all go see England and Scotland in the spring" (121). Laurel is too busy to answer. The next news Laurel hears is that the Judge "was about to marry Fay." Old Mrs. Pease articulates the situation: "Laurel is who should have saved him from that nonsense. Laurel shouldn't have married a naval officer in wartime. Laurel should have stayed home after Becky died. He needed somebody *in* that house, girl" (115). The community is disapproving, indeed.

These remarks raise a central concern of the novel and one that Welty has addressed earlier, in "Kin": the child's obligation to a father and mother. Becky McKelva faces this same question in her own life as well. In her moments of self-condemnation for failing her parents, Laurel recalls her mother's own pain at the death of her mother. Becky explains that her grandfather's big iron bell was erected in sight of the door of the old house: "If anything were ever to happen, Grandma only needed to ring this bell" and help would come (139). Laurel's mother's words burn in her memory now: "Laurel asked about the bell, her mother replied calmly that how good a bell was depended on the distance away your children had gone" (142). Her mother, too, is disapproving of her daughter's absence.

Both Becky and Laurel have the same lesson to learn. The child cannot save the life of the parent or perhaps "anyone at all" (144). As for Fay, Adele desires to crown Fay "over the head with a good solid piece of something" (115), and Laurel nearly does so with a breadboard later in the novel. Fay was an acceptable choice for the Judge, according to some views. "Rather," Miss Adele summarizes, "she gave him something to live for" (116). Fay's greatest weakness is that "her own life had not taught her how to feel"

(173), especially at this time, when Laurel herself is feeling so deeply. The Judge is "turning between" the two women and "holding onto" both Becky and Fay. Laurel grieves that after death evidence of love seems to disappear "without any sign" (170).

The final two chapters of the novel are Laurel's dark night of the soul. She "faces" her father's library and her mother's sewing room (117), the locations that evoke the most painful memories of each parent. As in "A Curtain of Green," facing love, death, and oblivion govern the most poignant sections of this novel. The central characters lose to death someone they love deeply.

Vande Kieft writes hauntingly that in its "depth and beauty" *The Optimist's Daughter* "comes shrouded in . . . the dark or 'sorrowful' mysteries of life and death, finally impenetrable" (*Eudora Welty*, rev. ed. 177). Harrison further points out, "During her night alone in the house with her memories, Laurel travels toward a mature understanding and acceptance of human intimacy." She adds that Laurel "attempts to come to terms with her past, to find answers to the questions raised by her father's marriage, death, and funeral" (*Eudora Welty* 123, 129). Regarding Laurel's feelings about Phil, Harrison notes, "By the end of this section . . . she is finally free to grieve over the brevity of the marriage" (131).

From her deathbed Laurel's mother, Becky McKelva, voices the same struggle that Mrs. Larkin does in "A Curtain of Green" as she comprehends the futility of asking "compensation," "protest," or "punishment" for the simple fact of mortality and the separation from loved ones that death brings. Becky lashes out and punishes those around her for the bitter fact of mortality. She wounds the people she loves the most—her husband and daughter. "Let them hurt me?" and "Why did I marry a coward?" are mild precursors to her most bitter condemnations of her husband, whom she calls "Liar" and even "Lucifer" (145, 148, 150). Becky's last words to her daughter show her profound disappointment in the human inability to conquer death: "You could have saved your mother's life. But you stood by and wouldn't intervene. I despair for you" (151). Laurel and the Judge must grieve helplessly for her as she dies. They are defenseless against her harsh judgments of them. Laurel attempts to intercede in her parents' "argument of souls" (Welty, *Eye* 7): "Laurel battled against them both, each for the other's sake. She loyally reproached her mother for yielding to the storms that began coming to her out of her darkness of vision. Her mother had only to recollect herself! As for her father, he apparently needed guidance in order to see the tragic" (145).

As she grapples with the end of her mother's life, Laurel recalls her mother's anguish in approaching death. Becky feels "love's deep anger" in her husband's inability to help her die: "What he could not control was his belief that all his wife's troubles would turn out all right because there was nothing he would not have given her" (146). Even Laurel is "turned for a while against her father": "he seemed so particularly helpless to do anything for his wife. He was not passionately enough grieved at the changes in her!" (145). Becky's despair is keen: "Her cry was not complaint; it was anger at wanting to know and being denied knowledge" (148).

The awareness of human frailty and ultimate helplessness is at the root of Becky's disappointment in coping with finalities: "Her trouble was that very desperation. And no one had the power to cause that except the one she desperately loved, who refused to consider that she was desperate. It was betrayal on betrayal" (150). Neither Laurel nor her father could have saved Becky, nor can Laurel later save her father. This reality makes the dying accusations of Becky all the more excruciating. Before her death Becky recalls the lines from her grade school reader that describe people caught in a fate that demands the highest price and against which any effort, though endless, seems pointless:

"*Rising and leaping—*
Sinking and creeping,
Swelling and sweeping—
Showering and springing,
Flying and flinging,
Writhing and ringing . . .

Turning and twisting,
Around and around
With endless rebound;
Smiting and fighting,

A sight to delight in;
Confounding, astounding—" . . .

"And glittering and frittering,
And gathering and feathering,
And whitening and brightening,
And quivering and shivering,
And hurrying and skurrying,
And thundering and floundering." (147)

The battle here is between death and love. Anger, fear, and incomprehension are a part of death and loss.

Optimism and pessimism both appear in the novel in significant ways, and Laurel exhibits both characteristics, presumably inherited or learned from her parents. She is a child of her parents' optimism and pessimism. This dichotomy clearly has roots in the personalities of Welty's parents and of her own.

The personalities of Welty's parents find their way into the novel. Peggy Prenshaw notes: "In *One Writer's Beginnings*, Welty writes of having early formed an impression of her parents as embodying opposing, if complementary, personalities. Welty's relationship to her parent casts much light upon certain persistent themes in her fiction, particularly the existence of the mysterious otherness that lies below the surface of self." She adds, "In *One Writer's Beginnings* Welty traces her perception of doubleness from the example of [her parents]" ("Antiphonies" 234). See further discussion of Welty's depiction of her parents in Prenshaw (*Composing* 258).

Although finding the optimist in these two works is not easy, some clues lead the way. In *One Writer's Beginnings* Welty explains that her mother "suffered from a morbid streak which in all the life of the family reached out on occasions—the worst occasion—and touched us, clung around us, making it worse for her; her unbearable moments could find nowhere to go" (17). Welty describes her father as optimistic in his "general belief in life's well-being." He could not "bear pain very well," however, and after the loss of Eudora's infant brother, no one in the family could mention the name of that child: "I am only certain that my father, who could never bear pain very well, would not have been able to bear it" (19).

In her memoir Welty recalls her parents' identifying themselves as optimist and pessimist. Her mother said to her father: "You're such an optimist, dear," and she often said that to him "with a sigh." Her father answered, "You're a good deal of a pessimist, sweetheart." Her mother had the last word, with pride: "I certainly *am*" (*One Writer's Beginnings* 45). In the novel the Judge initially seems optimistic, but as the novel progresses, his words become increasingly qualified with a scowl or "saturnine" smile. Becky seems optimistic until she becomes ill, but then her mood is dark. She also is the family risk taker: "'Up home, we loved a good storm coming, we'd fly outdoors and run up and down to meet it,' her mother used to say. 'We children would run fast as we could on top of that mountain when the wind was blowing, holding our arms wide open. The wilder it blew the better we liked it.' During the very bursting of a tornado which carried away half of Mount Salus, she said, '*We* never were afraid of a little wind. Up home, we'd welcome a good storm'" (144). Here Becky seems fearless and optimistic of no lightning strike, and yet later in her life, she is fearful and bitter. Overall both parental figures alternate between optimism and pessimism.

The optimism that Judge McKelva displays in the novel during his wife's difficult death wanes after his own illness begins. He becomes more pessimistic over time and toward the time of his death, fatalistic. The Judge's first "admission of self-concern" occurs when he asks Laurel to accompany him to the doctor. "'I've been getting a little interference with my *seeing*, lately. I just might give Nate Courtland a chance to see what he can find.' . . . His admission of self-concern was as new as anything wrong with his health, and Laurel had come flying" (6–7).

The Judge initially makes optimistic statements such as "Well, I'm an optimist" (17, 10). He needed "guidance in order to see the tragic," which suggests a sunnier view of life (145). Laurel notices a new vulnerability in him, however: "he seemed for the first time in her memory a man admitting to a little uncertainty in his bearings" (19). Later he started "being what he scowlingly called an optimist" (150), and he has his "old saturnine look" and later "his saturnine smile" (60, 114). The Judge shifts from optimism to "scowling" optimism and then to the saturnine, if not to abject pessimism.

As the Judge lies in the hospital bed, his new vulnerability becomes apparent. His head is "unpillowed, lengthening," and emphasizes "the elderly, exposed throat," an image that powerfully suggests his vulnerability. He pays the "unbargained-for price for his recovery" and eventually surrenders totally to helplessness and "obedience": "He opened his mouth and swallowed what she offered him with the obedience of an old man— obedience! She felt ashamed to let him act out the part in front of her" (31–32). Laurel feels deeply for his new, strained situation. His growing silence and blindness in his final days in the hospital parallel Becky's own blindness and pessimism: "He had yet to say that he would be all right" (22). Now he is "paying full attention" to death and the fact that "he was dying." His fate is tragic and ironic: the optimist is now at least a stark realist, if not a pessimist.

Fay's optimism is in contrast to Laurel's deep ruminations about death. Fay implies that the Judge's eye troubles are not serious—all of this attention "just for a scratch?"—and she naively believes she can cajole him back to health. She fails to understand his desperate condition and nearness to death. Laurel, however, takes her father's situation very seriously and "comes flying" home at the first sign of his infirmity. She knows that death is "as far a place as you could go with those you loved, and it was where they left you" (151). His daughter, and not his surrogate daughter, hears his call for help.

What it means to survive—outlive—family and loved ones occupies Laurel's thoughts in her turbulent night of the soul as she searches for meaning. "Outliving those you love," she thinks, is a heavy burden. Bereft of parents, siblings, and mate, Laurel looks to the dying and dead to provide answers for her own grief: "What burdens we lay on the dying, Laurel thought, as she listened to the accelerated rain on the roof: seeking to prove some little thing that we can keep to comfort us when they can no longer feel—something as incapable of being kept as of being proved: the lastingness of memory, vigilance against harm, self-reliance, good hope, trust in one another" (146). She concludes: "The fantasies of dying could be no stranger than the fantasies of living. Surviving is perhaps the strangest fantasy of them all" (162–63). Laurel knows that her parents loved each other, and she sees their relationship as sustaining and at times painful. She examines her role in their lives: "Parents and children take turns back and forth, changing places, protecting and protesting each other" (141). She has known the love produced by the "confluence" of these forces, but now, in her loss, she can only weep "for what happened to life" (155).

The marriage Laurel most deeply represses, and for the longest time, the one that must reemerge in her mind, and subject to her close scrutiny, is her own. Like her parents' union, as she recalls, Laurel's marriage with Phil achieved near perfection: "As far as Laurel had ever known, there had not happened a single blunder in their short life together" (162). Phil is long dead, however, and Laurel, though silent about him, still has an agitated spirit: "Even if you have kept silent for the sake of the dead, you cannot rest in your silence, as the dead rest" (130). "What would I not do," she asks herself, "for consolation?" (132). The specter of her dead husband arises now in her full grief. Eventually, after a long night of reminiscing and grieving, the horrifying visage of her husband, Phil, dead and "waiting" like Lazarus, appears before her: "She had gone on living with the old perfection undisturbed and undisturbing. Now, by her own hands, the past had been raised up, and *he* looked at her, Phil himself—here waiting, all the time, Lazarus. He looked at her out of eyes wild with the craving for his unlived life, with mouth open like a funnel's" (154). Of all the specters of death in Welty's fiction—the "featureless" one staring back at Clytie in the rain barrel; the drowned face of Grady's father in the river in "The Wide Net"; or the earth, like a wide face with eyes and mouth of fire, in "No Place for You, My Love"—Phil's is the most terrifying and the most evocative of the dread of death, both for those who must die and those who survive.

Like Eudora Welty, Laurel outlives many of those she loves. She can only look back now, through memory, to assess and reflect on what transpired during their life together. Until Laurel knew Phil, she thought of love "as shelter; her arms went out in a naive offer of safety. He had showed her that this need not be so. Protection, like self-protection, fell away from her like all one garment, some anachronism foolishly saved from childhood" (188). Laurel learns from this experience too. As John F. Desmond notes, she comes to understand that love is more than the kind of protection and the childhood security she knew with her parents (135). Helen Tiegreen comments further that Laurel "has reached the nadir in her search for answers and for the solace she hopes they will bring; now with an insight that has heretofore evaded her, she discovers that the answers are to be found within, '*By her own hands.*' . . . The answers are all there but it is Laurel who has to find and make personal meaning of them" (204).

Laurel learns that love means taking risks and losing the protective shield of childhood. Laurel has known a satisfying marriage, brief and arrested though it was. She finds release in memories: "A flood of feeling descended on Laurel. She let the papers slide from her hands and the books from her knees, and put her head down on the open lid of the desk and wept in grief for love and for the dead. She lay there with all that was adamant in her yielding to this night, yielding at last. Now all she had found had found her. The deepest spring in her heart had uncovered itself, and it began to flow again." In the early morning hours, after a night of emotional turbulence, Laurel lays these ghosts to rest, at least for now, and finds that the "deepest spring" of her heart is flowing again: "For her life, she had to believe, was nothing but the continuity of its love" (160).

For Welty memory is "the somnambulist" and her greatest "treasure": "My own is the treasure most dearly regarded by me, in my life and in my work as a writer." Through memory she crosses time and distance to recall to mind her loved ones for a brief time. "Hindsight," she says, leaves "arrows that I now find I myself have left behind me, which have shown me some right, or wrong way I have come" (107). Julia Eichelberger says that "the result of Laurel's experience, her affirmation of memory, is not passive or detached, for memory, 'the somnambulist,' can deconstruct many of the distortions people make in their attempts to detach themselves from an unsatisfying world. Memory, the human consciousness, is the repository of love, and despite the great harms that humans can commit, memory can 'come back in its wounds from across the world, calling us by our names and demanding its rightful tears' . . . [and] serving as an agent of praxis, of the world's creative transformation" (*Prophets* 165).

Welty writes in *One Writer's Beginnings* that memory in her own life was "attached to seeing, love had added itself to discovery": "Writing fiction has developed in me an abiding respect for the unknown in a human lifetime and a sense of where to look for the threads, how to follow, how to connect, find in the thick of the tangle what clear line persists. The strands are all there: to the memory nothing is ever really lost" (90).

Memory provides a way for Clement Musgrove, Mrs. Larkin, Judge McKelva, Laurel Hand, and others to glimpse—even if only briefly—a lost time. Memory "is vulnerable to the living moment, it lives for us, and while it lives, and while we are able, we can give it up its due." Possessing a "heart that can empty but fill again" provides Welty's characters with the courage not merely to continue "surviving" and "outliving" their lost loved ones but also to honor the loved ones now gone and retain the fragile recollections of them (179).

Laurel's dilemma finally provides an answer to Robbie Fairchild's question, "What do you ask for when you love?" Laurel's return, in the face of loss and grief, to an affirming stance toward the future is a complex response to mystery, loss, and difficulty. For all of her studies of lovelessness, Welty's Laurel reaches through grief back to love, and this transcendence, even given the constraints of mortality, ultimately posits an affirming point of view. Like Mashula's lamp, kindled nightly in anticipation of her husband's return from a lost war long over, and like the sound of Laurel's mother and father's reading nightly to one another or calling up and down the stairs to one another in a duet of singing and whistling, love can offer great sustenance and, through memory, may extend beyond life.

CHAPTER 11

"A Dark Rose"

Eudora Welty's Love Stories

Eudora Welty was a brilliant woman and a gifted artist. During her long writing life she considered a wide range and variety of topics, including politics, poverty, race relations, and rose gardening. In an impressive number of her stories and novels, however, she turned her pen to the subject of relationships and especially love. In these writings she investigated numerous perspectives and analyzed ambiguities and mysteries that she observed, sensed, or knew. Like her character India in *Delta Wedding*, who rises on tiptoe to determine "what there was about a kiss," the author continually ponders matters of the heart. The love relationship, the search for one, or the consequences of life without it motivates a number of her important characters. Her portraits are rarely simplistic, and she does not eschew difficult, painful, or even terrifying topics. Walker Percy misjudged her in his comment that she wrote "white ladies' fiction" (Tolson 377). Her thinking runs much deeper than this particular description allows, but Percy did admire Eudora Welty (see, e.g., Lawson and Kramer).

Structurally, Welty's stories about relationships generally portray a marriage or friendship at some particularly significant moment or juncture. Generally, the point of view is female and the narrator single, romantically unattached, and unfulfilled. The temptation to see this perspective as essentially autobiographical is hard to resist. Variations exist, however, and some stories occur in the perspectives of young boys or adult males who discover love or look back on it: Loch Morrison, R. J. Bowman, Eugene and Ran MacLain, Tom Harris, and, in "Flowers for Marjorie," Howard are examples. In "No Place for You, My Love" the constant alternation of perspectives from the male to female point of view provides a clear and realistic depiction of the meeting and attraction of two people, from the standpoints of both involved, as they come to know and experience each other.

Welty frequently chooses the omniscient narration by which to reveal the most intimate and shared moments of private interactions and feelings. After a novel-length marital dispute, in one scene Robbie Fairchild clearly expresses the strength of her devotion to her husband in *Delta Wedding*: "Then she was glad there was nothing at all, no existence in the world, beyond George asleep. . . . Any moon and stars there were could rise and set over his enfolding, unemanating length. The sun could lean over his backside and wake her" (148). As in the case of Loch Morrison, who espies lovers with his telescope in *The Golden Apples,* Welty views intimacy at close range. Internal monologue reveals the inner world of those who talk to themselves when their partners are away for a while or permanently gone. Loners contemplate their hopes and dreams to themselves, as R. J. Bowman does in "Death of a Traveling Salesman": "Come and stand in my heart, whoever you are," he thinks, "and a whole river would cover your feet and rise higher and higher and take your knees in whirlpools and draw you down to itself, your whole body, your heart too" (*Curtain of Green* 243). Bowman's judgments, misjudgments, and longings become evident. Welty gauges the degree of privacy and the intensity of feeling.

In prefiguring emotional crises (and resolution) or foreshadowing other fates, Welty's meteorological awareness proves instructive; for her the weather, along with the position, color, and intensity of the moon (and its light), is an indicator of the psychic state of those in the human world below. Changes in seasonal cycles and colors foreshadow the alterations her characters will undergo. Love in the human world reflects movements and change in the natural world, and vice versa.

From her first story, "Death of a Traveling Salesman," Welty writes of the "pervading and changing mystery" people discover in responding to others. The quality of a relationship is one of Welty's frequent subjects. The mysteriousness of what makes relationships work is the heartbeat of much of her writing. The secret may simply lie in the identity of the lover, which can be shrouded in one or another of various indecipherable veils or masks; the search for a lover may prove elusive and mysterious; or the attempt, as in "Circe," to fathom the indefinable idea of love may be futile. Love is not usually comprehensible to those who experience it. "What do you ask for when you love?" is a lasting question that Welty poses and must answer. Her characters who can confront and embrace mystery—and who are curious to know more of it—are those who tend to know fulfillment. William Wallace in "The Wide Net," for instance, strains to understand and find the secret to a mystery. Finally, in the last scene he looks out from the porch as his wife does, and he is able to see where she sees and know more of her perspective. In a highly ambiguous ending to that story, one interpretation is that the couple endures a marital spat and makes up happily at the end. An alternative reading may be that William Wallace is dying or dead. If so, when Hazel looks down at him at the end of the story, she may be holding her dying husband in her arms. In either case he grows in awareness and knowledge until the end.

Welty's presentation of love includes varied types and levels, and the stories of happy domestic loves have brooding counterparts in tales of murder, rape, and lovelessness. Her own words in describing *Losing Battles* apply to much of her writing on this topic: "I wanted to show that the relationships run the whole gamut of love and oppression. Just like any human relationship has the possibilities of so many gradations of affection, feeling, passion, resistance, and hatred" (*Conversations* 221–22). These infinite "gradations" form the basis of much of her most impressive fiction.

From her early stories through her first comic novels, later and more meditative stories, and last novels, Welty considers the many "alternatives and eventualities" in the world of relationships. Some couples know the "ancient promise of communication" between two people and the deep and time-honored commitment that is possible between partners such as Ellen and Battle Fairchild or Becky and Judge McKelva. The sharp pain that loss and death force people to confront, however, is never far removed. Portraits of those who know and then lose or relinquish love are among Welty's most poignant and painful. Laurel Hand is a deeply compelling figure partly because she has both known and lost a marriage which was nearly perfect in its wholeness, enriching and educating for both its members, both challenging and safe, and is also stamped with the author's autobiographical mark as she plunged into love, then had to relinquish it.

Grief and loss, though complex emotions, are for Welty ultimately affirming in some ways. Laurel Hand chooses a regenerative path when she recognizes the importance of "outliving" her grief both for parents and husband. Like Hamlet, she must cope with the deaths of all of them by the end of *The Optimist's Daughter*. Even though for her, and for Mrs. Larkin, memory—the somnambulist—is often nightmarish, it still becomes the main mechanism by which love sustains itself through time, especially when the future is an insensitive and crude newcomer like Fay Chisolm. The memory of love shines like Mashula's polished lamp in the dark night of the soul and offers hope for renewal, even though that renewal may not be coming.

Eudora Welty's own personal love relationships appear autobiographically in her fiction. In "Death of a Traveling Salesman," which she wrote during the period in which she was seeing John Robinson, she seems to have been considering how the seemingly simple facts of marriage and childbearing can seem so difficult and for some, including her, ultimately elusive. Her own ruminations about her prospects for marriage and children most likely inform this portrait.[1] Welty's relationship with Robinson also figures in the writing of *Delta Wedding*, which she penned after a visit to his family in the Delta, while he was away during World War II. In *The Optimist's Daughter* Welty appears to grieve for, memorialize, but then at long last put to rest her memories of the relationship with Robinson, who is the mostly likely model for the character of Philip Hand. The marriage of Phil and Laurel, so carefully drawn with much detail in the draft stages of the novel, elided later by Welty, ends with Hand's death (Wolff, "'Among Those Missing'"). That finality may be a fictional rendering of her close relationship with Robinson, which ended when he revealed to her, after long years of friendship and courtship, that he was homosexual. That novel, too, bears the mark of her deeply important relationship with Kenneth Millar, the other very long and meaningful relationship Welty had that, like the one with Robinson, would not end in marriage. The beautifully written section of the novel about confluence alludes to the coming together of her parents, with an emphasis on the hope of love, perhaps owes to Millar's suggestion and personal influence. What Welty saw of love in others, and what she knew of it herself, contributes to the aching poignancy of her love stories.

The dark rose is the quintessential metaphor for the dichotomies that Eudora Welty portrays. Her outlook is often, and perhaps ultimately, posi-

tive and filled with quiet possibilities, like the almost inaudible, falling petals of a rose. The dark rose, equally evocative of beauty and sadness, as well
as the mysterious qualities of love, complicates and deepens Welty's view.
The rose appears—as Welty's distinctive signature—in most of her stories
and novels, imparts symbolic power, and places her in the age-old tradition of love literature. Her assertion, across stories and novels, is that love
may fail with dark consequences, wear thin under the gossiper's chisel, or
meet the ultimate challenge of the bridegroom, death; nonetheless, love is
still "banked up somewhere," as Edna Earle claims. The dark portraits find
little comfort, but the more exalted ones lift the most turbulent nights of
the soul toward light.

When I first met Eudora Welty—the year she came to Emory University to receive an honorary degree, in 1982—I found her to be friendly
and willing to talk about her work. I was fortunate that we subsequently
became friends, and that friendship grew over a period of nineteen years,
until her death. When I worked in her rose garden, in the heat of a July
day, at her home in Jackson, Mississippi, I extricated the old climbing
rose from the clutches of a dense thicket of wild honeysuckle. Afterward,
when I returned to the house, Miss Welty rewarded me with unforgettable
words: "My thanks to you go back many years." In return, Miss Welty, I offer this book to you, a rose given in friendship and gratitude for your enchanting work. My thanks to you go back many years.

Sally Wolff
EMORY UNIVERSITY

Notes

1. See also Welty's delight in the hibiscus in her garden expressed in Eichelberger, *Tell about Night Flowers* 70.

2. Susan Haltom, the professional gardener who has restored the Welty garden, has said that this rose was not Banksia, or "Lady Banks," but "the climbing Cecile Brunner, a monstrously vigorous climber with small light pink blossoms." When she first started helping Miss Welty and later documenting and restoring the garden, she noticed that "that rose had many canes, twenty feet long, that were intertwined with the board fence. It was the only rose visible along the fence in 1994. This fence separated the Welty yard and the Johnsons', and some years later, when the Johnsons' oak tree was cut down, the Lady Banks sprang up a few feet closer to the house along with another unknown rose. Lady Banks blooms yellow and only in April. There exists a white, fragrant form of Lady Banks, but the Weltys have the yellow unscented form." Perhaps the day that I was in the yard, Miss Welty remembered the "Banksia" but in a different position in the yard (Haltom, personal correspondence with Sally Wolff, January 29, 2008).

INTRODUCTION

1. See Scott Romine's thoughtful discussion of the interplay of place and community in southern literature in *Narrative Forms of Southern Community*; see also Wagner-Martin.

CHAPTER ONE

1. Eudora Welty alludes to Flannery O'Connor's story "Good Country People."

2. See also a varying account of Welty's source for this story in Marrs, *One Writer's Imagination* 29–30.

3. See Barreca's study of the twinning of sex and death in literature, especially of the Victorian era: "Sex and death provide an important matrix of possibilities . . . to produce an ineradicable alignment of sexuality and mortality in nineteenth-century poetry and fiction" (1).

4. Marrs has noted also that "The Wide Net" was further inspired by "anecdotes John Robinson had told her" (*Eudora Welty* 80).

5. See Prenshaw, "Persephone" 153; Smith 73; and Kloss 53.

CHAPTER THREE

1. Shakespeare, Sonnet 116, "Let Me Not to the Marriage of True Minds Admit Impediments," *Complete Works* 1472.

2. Elaine Wolff is the mother of Sally Wolff. Elaine met Eudora Welty in Jackson, Mississippi, at a conference in the 1990s. The day was blustery, and during lunch the weather service issued a tornado warning for Jackson and the surrounding area. Although a tornado did not touch down in Jackson that day, Elaine gave Miss Welty her suggestion as high winds sped past the stalwart, old downtown Jackson hotel in which we were all huddled, and Miss Welty's reply came as the winds whistled in the background.

CHAPTER FIVE

1. In *Absalom, Absalom!* Faulkner draws an analogy between baking and morality: "the ingredients of morality were like the ingredients of pie or cake and once you had measured them and balanced them and mixed them and put them into the oven it was all finished and nothing but pie or cake could come out" (263). Although it is possible that Welty alludes to this passage, she also was a good cook, as was her mother, and so the recipe analogy may be her own.

CHAPTER SIX

1. For further discussion of these and other roses named in Welty's works, see a series of articles on "Roses in Welty's Garden" by Robert Burns, *Eudora Welty Newsletter,* Winter 2003, Summer 2004, Winter 2004, Summer 2005, and Winter 2005.

CHAPTER SEVEN

1. See, e.g., McHaney, "Falling into Cycles" 172–89; see also Mark's extensive treatment of mythological and feminist characteristics of the volume, in *Dragon's Blood.*

CHAPTER NINE

Welty was well acquainted with the Dainty Bess rose. In her letters she tells her friends when the Dainty Bess is blooming in her garden. See Eichelberger, *Tell about Night Flowers* 25, 103, 123.

1. Binding notes that "*Losing Battles* is dedicated to Welty's brothers—as *The Optimist's Daughter* was to be to Chestina Andrews Welty. These losses—in complex ways—stand behind both novels, giving them not just their darkness but their overall depth, their immensity of understanding. There are qualities of the heart in *Losing Battles* that were not even present in *The Golden Apples*" (233).

CHAPTER ELEVEN

1. See Marrs, *Eudora Welty*, for further information about the relationships with Robinson and Millar.

Works Cited and Consulted

Allen, John Alexander. "The Other Way to Live: Demigods in Eudora Welty's Fiction."
In *Eudora Welty: Critical Essays.* Edited by Peggy Whitman Prenshaw, 26–55. Jackson: University Press of Mississippi, 1979.

Appel, Alfred, Jr. *A Season of Dreams: The Fiction of Eudora Welty.* Baton Rouge: Louisiana State University Press, 1965.

Arnold, St. George Tucker. "The Raincloud and the Garden: Psychic Regression as Tragedy in Welty's 'A Curtain of Green.'" *South Atlantic Bulletin* 44 (January 1979): 53–60.

Barreca, Regina, ed. *Sex and Death in Victorian Literature.* Bloomington: Indiana University Press, 1990.

Barthes, Roland. *A Lover's Discourse.* New York: Hill & Wang, 1978.

Bayley, John. *The Characters of Love: A Study in the Literature of Personality.* London: Constable & Co., 1960.

Beauvoir, Simone de. *The Second Sex.* Edited and translated by H. M. Parshlev. New York: Knopf, 1968.

Binding, Paul, *The Still Moment: Eudora Welty, Portrait of a Writer.* London: Virago Press, 1994.

Bolsterli, Margaret Jones. "Mythic Elements in 'Ladies in Spring.'" *Notes on Mississippi Writers* 7 (Winter 1974): 69–72.

———. "Woman's Vision: The Worlds of Women in *Delta Wedding, Losing Battles,* and *The Optimist's Daughter.*" In *Eudora Welty: Critical Essays.* Edited by Peggy Whitman Prenshaw, 149–56. Jackson: University Press of Mississippi, 1979.

Bouton, Reine Dugas, ed. *Eudora Welty's* Delta Wedding. Amsterdam, N.Y.: Rodopi, 2008.

Brooks, Cleanth. "The Past Reexamined: *The Optimist's Daughter.*" *Mississippi Quarterly* 26, no. 4 (1973): 577–87.

———. "The Tradition of Romantic Love in *The Wild Palms.*" *Mississippi Quarterly* 25, no. 3 (1971): 265–87.

Brown, Homer O. "The Errant Letter and the Whispering Gallery." *Genre* 10 (Winter 1977): 573–99.

Works Cited

Browning, Elizabeth Barrett. "Sonnets from the Portuguese." *The Poetical Works of Elizabeth Barrett Browning*. Edited by Ruth M. Adams. Cambridge Edition. Boston: Houghton Mifflin, 1974.

Burns, Robert. *Eudora Welty Newsletter*. Atlanta: Department of English, Georgia State University, 2003–2005.

Burrows, David J., Frederick R. Lapides, and John T. Shawcross, eds. *Myths and Motifs in Literature*. New York: Free Press, 1973.

Buswell, Mary Catherine. "The Love Relationships of Women in the Fiction of Eudora Welty." *West Virginia University Philological Papers* 13 (December 1961): 94–106.

Carson, Gary. "Versions of the Artist in *A Curtain of Green:* The Unifying Imagination in Eudora Welty's Early Fiction." *Studies in Short Fiction* 15 (1978): 421–29.

Clark, Charles C. "*The Robber Bridegroom:* Fantasy and Realism on the Natchez Trace." *Mississippi Quarterly* 26 (Fall 1973): 625–38.

Cochran, Robert W. "Welty's Petrified Man." *Explicator* 27, no. 4 (December 1968): 25.

Complete Works of William Shakespeare, The. General editor, Alfred Harbage, 951, 1472. Baltimore: Pelican Books, 1969.

Corcoran, Neil. "The Face That Was in the Poem: Art and 'Human Truth' in 'June Recital.'" *Delta* 5 (November 1977): 27–34.

Costello, Brannon. "Playing Lady and Imitating Aristocrats: Race, Class, and Money in *Delta Wedding* and *The Ponder Heart*." *Southern Quarterly* 42, no. 3 (Spring 2004): 21–54.

Crews, Elizabeth. "Cixous' New Woman: Laura and Shelley in Eudora Welty's *Delta Wedding*." In *Eudora Welty's Delta Wedding*. Edited by Reine Dugas Bouton, 65–78. Amsterdam, N.Y.: Rodopi, 2008.

Curley, Daniel. "Eudora Welty and the Quondam Obstruction." *Studies in Short Fiction* 5 (Spring 1968): 209–24.

Daniel, Robert. "Eudora Welty: The Sense of Place." In *South: Modern Southern Literature in Its Cultural Setting*. Edited by Louis D. Rubin Jr. and Robert D. Jacobs, 276–86. Garden City, N.Y.: Doubleday, 1961.

Davenport, F. Garvin, Jr. "Renewal and Historical Consciousness in *The Wide Net*." In *Eudora Welty: Critical Essays*. Edited by Peggy Whitman Prenshaw, 189–200. Jackson: University Press of Mississippi, 1979.

Davenport, Guy. "Primal Visions." *National Review* 22 (June 1972): 697.

———. "That Faire Field of Enna." *The Geography of the Imagination*, 250–71. San Francisco: North Point Press, 1981.

Demmin, Julia, and Daniel Curley. "Golden Apples and Silver Apples." In *Eudora Welty: Critical Essays*. Edited by Peggy Whitman Prenshaw, 242–57. Jackson: University Press of Mississippi, 1979.

Desmond, John F., ed. "Pattern and Vision *in The Optimist's Daughter." A Still Moment: Essays on the Art of Eudora Welty.* Metuchen, N.J.: Scarecrow Press, 1978.

Devlin, Albert J. "Eudora Welty's Mississippi." In *Eudora Welty: Critical Essays.* Edited by Peggy Whitman Prenshaw, 157–78. Jackson: University Press of Mississippi, 1979.

Donaldson, Susan V. "'Contradictors, Interferers, and Prevaricators': Opposing Modes of Discourse in Eudora Welty's *Losing Battles.*" In *Eudora Welty: Eye of the Storyteller.* Edited by Dawn Trouard, 32–43. Kent, Ohio: Kent State University Press, 1989.

———. "Gender and History in Eudora Welty's *"Delta Wedding." South Central Review* 14, no. 2 (Summer 1997): 3–14.

Drake, Robert, Jr. "The Reasons of the Heart." *Georgia Review* 11 (Winter 1957): 420–26.

Eichelberger, Julia. *Prophets of Recognition: Ideology and the Individual in Novels by Ralph Ellison, Toni Morrison, Saul Bellow, and Eudora Welty.* Baton Rouge: Louisiana State University Press, 1999.

———. *Tell about Night Flowers: Eudora Welty's Gardening Letters, 1940–1949.* Jackson: University Press of Mississippi, 2013.

———. "'The Way for Girls in the World': Laura's Escape from Drowning in *Delta Wedding.*" In Eudora Welty's *Delta Wedding.* Edited by Reine Dugas Bouton, 47–63. Amsterdam, N.Y.: Rodopi, 2008.

Eisinger, Chester E. "Traditionalism and Modernism in Eudora Welty." In *Eudora Welty: Critical Essays.* Edited by Peggy Whitman Prenshaw, 3–25. Jackson: University Press of Mississippi, 1979.

Evans, Elizabeth. "Eudora Welty and the Dutiful Daughter." In *Eudora Welty: Eye of the Storyteller.* Edited by Dawn Trouard, 57–68. Kent, Ohio: Kent State University Press, 1989.

Faulkner, William. *Absalom, Absalom!* New York: Random House, 1936.

———. *Requiem for a Nun.* 1950. New York: Random House, 1975.

Fialkowski, Barbara. "Psychic Distances in *A Curtain of Green:* Artistic Successes and Personal Failures." In *A Still Moment: Essays on the Art of Eudora Welty.* Edited by John F. Desmond, 63–70. Metuchen, N.J.: Scarecrow Press, 1978.

Fiedler, Leslie A. *Love and Death in the American Novel.* New York: Criterion Books, 1960.

Fuller, Danielle. "'Making a Scene': Some Thoughts on Female Sexuality and Marriage in Eudora Welty's 'Delta Wedding' and 'The Optimist's Daughter." *Mississippi Quarterly* 48, no. 2 (Spring 1995): 291–319.

Gossett, Louise Y. "Eudora Welty's New Novel: The Comedy of Loss." *Southern Literary Journal* 3, no. 1 (Fall 1970): 122–37.

———. *Violence in Recent Southern Fiction*, 98–117. Durham, N.C.: Duke University Press, 1965.

Goudie, Andrea. "Eudora Welty's 'Circe': A Goddess Who Strove with Men." *Studies in Short Fiction* 13 (Fall 1976): 481–89.

Gretlund, Jan Nordby, and Karl-Heinz Westarp. *The Late Novels of Eudora Welty*. Columbia: University of South Carolina Press, 1998.

Griffith, Albert. "The Numinous Vision: Eudora Welty's 'Clytie.'" *Studies in Short Fiction* 4, no. 1 (Fall 1966): 80–83.

Gross, Seymour. "Eudora Welty's Comic Imagination." In *The Comic Imagination in American Literature*. Edited by Louis D. Rubin Jr., 319–28. New Brunswick, N.J.: Rutgers University Press, 1973.

Haltom, Susan. "In Welty's Garden." *Eudora Welty Newsletter* 24, no. 1 (Winter 2001): 1–5.

Hardy, John Edward. "Marrying Down in Eudora Welty's Novels." In *Eudora Welty: Critical Essays*. Edited by Peggy Whitman Prenshaw, 93–119. Jackson: University Press of Mississippi, 1979.

Harrell, Don. "Death in *The Bride of the Innisfallen*." *Notes on Contemporary Literature* 3 (September 1973): 2–7.

Harrison, Suzan. *Eudora Welty and Virginia Woolf: Gender, Genre, and Influence*. Baton Rouge: Louisiana State University Press, 1997.

———. "'The Other Way to Live': Gender and Selfhood in *Delta Wedding* and *The Golden Apples, Mississippi Quarterly* 44 (Winter 1990–91): 49–68.

Hawthorne, Nathaniel. *The Scarlet Letter*. Centenary Edition, 1:258–59.Columbus: Ohio State University Press, 1962.

Helterman, Jeffrey. "Gorgons in Mississippi: Eudora Welty's Petrified Man." *Notes on Mississippi Writers* 7 (Spring 1974): 12–20.

Hemingway, Ernest. "The Short Happy Life of Francis Macomber." *The Short Stories*, 11–42. 1938. New York: Scribner Classics, 1997.

Hollenbaugh, Carol. "Ruby Fisher and Her Demon-Lover." *Notes on Mississippi Writers* 7 (Fall 1974): 63–68.

Huculak, Matt. "Song from San Francisco: Space, Time, and Character in Eudora Welty's 'Music from Spain.'" *Mississippi Quarterly* 59, nos. 1–2 (2005): 313 (16).

Janeway, Elizabeth. "*The Optimist's Daughter*." *Saturday Review* 55, July 1, 1972, 60.

Johnston, Carol Ann. *Eudora Welty: A Study of the Short Fiction*. New York: Twayne, 1997.

Jones, Alun R. "A Frail Travelling Coincidence: Three Later Stories of Eudora Welty." *Shenandoah* 20, no. 3 (Spring 1969): 40–53.

———. "The World of Love: The Fiction of Eudora Welty." In *The Creative Present: Notes on Contemporary American Fiction*. Edited by Nona Balakian and Charles Simmons, 173–92. Garden City, N.Y.: Doubleday, 1963.

Joyce, James. "Araby." *Dubliners: Text and Criticism*. Edited by Robert Scholes and A. Walton Litz, 29–35. Rev. ed. New York: Penguin, 1996.

Kloss, Robert. "The Symbolic Structure of Eudora Welty's 'Livvie.'" *Notes on Mississippi Writers* 7 (Winter 1975): 70–82.

Kreyling, Michael. *Eudora Welty's Achievement of Order*. Baton Rouge: Louisiana State University Press, 1980.

———. *Understanding Eudora Welty*. Columbia: University of South Carolina Press, 1999.

Ladd, Barbara. "'Coming Through': The Black Initiate in *Delta Wedding*." *Mississippi Quarterly* 41 (Fall 1988): 541–52.

———. *Resisting History: Gender, Modernity, and Authorship in William Faulkner, Zora Neale Hurston, and Eudora Welty*. Baton Rouge: Louisiana State University Press, 2007.

Lawson, Lewis A., and Victor A. Kramer. *Conversations with Walker Percy*. Jackson: University Press of Mississippi, 1985.

Levy, Helen Fiddyment. *Fiction of the Home Place: Jewett, Cather, Glasgow, Porter, Welty, and Naylor*. Jackson: University Press of Mississippi, 1992.

Lief, Ruth Ann. "A Progression of Answers." *Studies in Short Fiction* 11 (Summer 1965): 343–50.

Mark, Rebecca. *The Dragon's Blood: Feminist Intertextuality in Eudora Welty's* The Golden Apples. Jackson: University Press of Mississippi, 1994.

Marrs, Suzanne. *Eudora Welty: A Biography*. Orlando: Harcourt, 2005.

———. *One Writer's Imagination: The Fiction of Eudora Welty*. Baton Rouge: Louisiana State University Press, 2002.

McDonald, W. U. "Eudora Welty's Revision of 'A Piece of News.'" *Studies in Short Fiction* 7 (Spring 1970): 232–47.

McHaney, Thomas L. "Eudora Welty and the Multitudinous Golden Apples." *Mississippi Quarterly* 26 (Fall 1973): 588–623.

———. "Falling into Cycles." In *Eudora Welty: Eye of the Storyteller* Edited by Dawn Trouard, 173–89. Kent, Ohio: Kent State University Press, 1990.

McWhirter, David. "Secret Agents: Welty's African Americans." In *Eudora Welty, Whiteness, and Race*. Edited by Harriet Pollack, 114–30. Athens: Athens: University of Georgia Press, 2013.

Milton, John. *Complete Poems and Major Prose*. Edited by Merritt Y. Hughes. Indianapolis: Odyssey Press, 1957.

Mortimer, Gail. *Daughter of the Swan: Love and Knowledge in Eudora Welty's Fiction*. Athens: University of Georgia Press, 1994.

Nissen, Axel. "Queer Welty, Camp Welty." *Mississippi Quarterly* 56, no. 2 (Spring 2003): 209–30.

Oates, Joyce Carol. "The Art of Eudora Welty." *Shenandoah* 20 (Spring 1969).

———. "Eudora's Web." *Atlantic* 225 (April 1970): 118–22.

Owen, Jim. "Phoenix Jackson, William Wallace, and King MacLain: Welty's Mythic Travelers." *Southern Literary Journal* 34, no. 1 (Fall 2001): 29–43.

Phillips, Robert L. "Patterns of Vision in Welty's *The Optimist's Daughter*." *Southern Literary Journal* 14 (Fall 1981): 10–23.

Pitavy-Souques, Danielle. "Of Suffering and Joy: Aspects of Storytelling in Welty's Short Fiction." In *Eudora Welty: Eye of the Storyteller*. Edited by Dawn Trouard, 142–50. Kent, Ohio: Kent State University Press, 1989.

Polk, Noel. "Cultural Patterns in Eudora Welty's Delta Wedding and 'The Demonstrators.'" *Notes on Mississippi Writers* 3 (Fall 1970): 51–68.

———. *Faulkner and Welty and the Southern Literary Tradition*. Jackson: University Press of Mississippi, 2008.

———. "Water, Wanderings, and Weddings: Love in Eudora Welty." In *Eudora Welty: A Form of Thanks*. Edited by Louis Dollarhide and Ann J. Abadie, 95–122. Jackson: University Press of Mississippi, 1979.

Pollack, Harriett, ed. *Eudora Welty, Whiteness, and Race*. Athens: University of Georgia Press, 2013.

———. "On Welty's Use of Allusion: Expectations and Their Revision in 'The Wide Net,' *The Robber Bridegroom*, and 'At the Landing.'" *Southern Quarterly* 29, no. 1 (Fall 1990): 5–31.

Prenshaw, Peggy Whitman. "The Antiphonies of Eudora Welty's *One Writer's Beginnings* and Elizabeth Bowen's *Pictures and Conversations*." In *Welty: A Life in Literature*. Edited by Albert J. Devlin, 225–37. Jackson: University Press of Mississippi, 1987.

———. *Composing Selves: Southern Women and Autobiography*. Baton Rouge: Louisiana State University Press, 2011.

———, ed. *Eudora Welty: Critical Essays*. Jackson: University Press of Mississippi, 1979.

———, ed. *Eudora Welty: Thirteen Essays*. Jackson: University Press of Mississippi, 1983.

———. "Persephone in Eudora Welty's 'Livvie.'" *Studies in Short Fiction* 17 (Spring 1980): 149–55.

Pugh, Elaine Upton. "The Duality of Morgana: The Making of Virgie's Vision, the Vision of *The Golden Apples*." *Modern Fiction Studies* 28 (Fall 1982): 435–51.

Romine, Scott. *The Narrative Forms of Southern Community*. Baton Rouge: Louisiana State University Press, 1999.

Romines, Ann. *The Home Plot: Women, Writing, and Domestic Ritual*. Amherst: University of Massachusetts Press, 1992.

———. "The Powers of the Lamp: Domestic Ritual in Two Stories by Eudora Welty." *Notes on Mississippi Writers* 12, no. 1 (Summer 1979): 1–16.

Ross, Virginia, and Sally Wolff. "Conversations with Eudora Welty and William Maxwell." *South Atlantic Review* 64, no. 2 (Spring 1999): 128–45.

Rougement, Denis de. *Passion and Society.* London: Faber & Faber, 1939.

Rubin, Louis D., Jr. "Everything Brought Out in the Open: Eudora Welty's *Losing Battles.*" *Hollins Critic* 7 (June 1970): 1–12.

Schmidt, Peter. *The Heart of the Story: Eudora Welty's Short Fiction.* Jackson: University Press of Mississippi, 1991.

Slethaug, Gordon E. "Initiation in Eudora Welty's *The Robber Bridegroom.*" *Southern Humanities Review* 7 (Winter 1973): 77–87.

Smith, Julian. "'Livvie'—Eudora Welty's Song of Solomon." *Studies in Short Fiction* 5 (Fall 1967): 73–74.

Spacks, Patricia Meyer. Review of *The Optimist's Daughter. Hudson Review* 25 (Fall 1972): 508–10.

Thoreau, Henry David. *Philosophers of Freedom: Writings on Liberty by Henry David Thoreau.* Edited by James Mackaye. New York: Vanguard Press, 1930.

Thornton, Naoko Fuwa. *Strange Felicity: Eudora Welty's Subtexts on Fiction and Society.* Westport, Conn.: Praeger, 2003.

Tiegreen, Helen Hurt. "Mothers, Daughters, and One Writer's Revisions." In *Welty: A Life in Literature.* Edited by Albert J. Devlin, 188–211. Jackson: University Press of Mississippi, 1987.

Tolson, Jay. *Pilgrim in the Ruins: A Life of Walker Percy.* New York: Simon & Schuster, 1992.

Trouard, Dawn, ed. *Eudora Welty: Eye of the Storyteller.* Kent, Ohio: Kent State University Press, 1989.

Vande Kieft, Ruth M. *Eudora Welty.* New York: Twayne, 1962.

———. *Eudora Welty.* Rev. ed. New York: Twayne, 1987.

———. "'Where Is the Voice Coming From': Teaching Eudora Welty." In *Eudora Welty: Eye of the Storyteller.* Edited by Dawn Trouard, 190–204. Kent, Ohio: Kent State University Press, 1989.

Virgil. *The Aeneid of Virgil: A Verse Translation.* Translated by Rolfe Humphries. New York: Charles Scribner's Sons, 1951.

Wagner-Martin, Linda. "'Just the Doing of It': Southern Women Writers and the Idea of Community." *Southern Literary Journal* 22, no. 2 (Spring 1990): 19–32.

Wall, Carey. "Virgie Rainey Saved." In *Eudora Welty: Eye of the Storyteller.* Edited by Dawn Trouard, 14–31. Kent, Ohio: Kent State University Press, 1989.

Warren, Robert Penn. "The Love and the Separateness in Miss Welty." *Kenyon Review* 6 (September 1944): 246–59.

Weaks, Mary Louise. "The Meaning of Miss Emily's Rose." *Notes on Contemporary Literature* 11 (November 1981): 11–12.

Welty, Eudora. *Conversations with Eudora Welty.* Edited by Peggy Whitman Prenshaw. Jackson: University Press of Mississippi, 1984.

———. *A Curtain of Green.* Garden City, N.Y.: Doubleday, Doran & Co., 1941.

———. *Delta Wedding.* New York: Harcourt, Brace, & Co., 1945.

———. *The Eye of the Story: Selected Essays and Reviews.* New York: Random House, Vintage Books, 1979.

———. *The Golden Apples.* New York: Harcourt, Brace, 1947.

———. *Losing Battles.* New York: Random House, 1970.

———. *One Writer's Beginnings.* Cambridge: Harvard University Press, 1984.

———. *On Writing.* New York: Modern Library, 2002.

———. *The Optimist's Daughter.* New York: Random House, 1969.

———. *The Ponder Heart.* New York: Harcourt, Brace, 1954.

———. *The Robber Bridegroom.* Garden City, N.Y.: Doubleday, Doran, & Co., 1942.

———. *The Wide Net and Other Stories.* New York: Harcourt, Brace, 1943.

Westling, Louise. *Women Writers: Eudora Welty.* London: Macmillan Education, 1989.

Weston, Ruth. "American Folk Art, Fine Art, and Eudora Welty: Aesthetic Precedents for 'Lily Daw and the Three Ladies.'" In *Eudora Welty: Eye of the Storyteller.* Edited by Dawn Trouard, 3–13. Kent, Ohio: Kent State University Press, 1989.

———. *Gothic Traditions and Narrative Technique in the Fiction of Eudora Welty.* Baton Rouge: Louisiana State University Press, 1994.

Wolff, Sally. "'Among Those Missing': The Disappearance of Phil Hand from *The Optimist's Daughter.*" *Southern Literary Journal* 25, no. 1 (Fall 1992): 74–88.

———. "The Domestic Thread of Revelation: An Interview with Eudora Welty." *Southern Literary Journal* 27, no. 1 (Fall 1994): 18–24.

———. "Some Talk about Autobiography: An Interview with Eudora Welty." *Southern Review* 26, no. 1 (1990): 81–88.

Yaeger, Patricia. "'Because a Fire Was in My Head': Eudora Welty's Dialogic Imagination." *PMLA* 99, no. 5 (October 1984): 955–73. [Reprinted in Albert J. Devlin, *Welty: A Life in Literature* (Jackson: University Press of Mississippi, 1987), 139–67; *Mississippi Quarterly* 39, no. 4 (1986): 561–86; and Carol Ann Johnston, *Eudora Welty: A Study of the Short Fiction* (New York: Twayne, 1997).]

———. *Dirt and Desire: Reconstructing Southern Women's Writing 1930–1990.* Chicago: University of Chicago Press, 2000.

Index

Absalom, Absalom! (Faulkner), analogy between baking and morality in, 202n1

African Americans, treatment of in Welty's work, 103

Allen, John Alexander, 22, 110

"Araby" (Joyce), 67

Arnold, St. George Tucker, 53

As You Like It (Shakespeare), 94, 96

"Asphodel" (Welty), 2, 67, 92, 123, 169; Cora in, 83; Don McInnis in, 129, 143; Don's sexualized image in, 85; Irene in, 83; marriage of Sabina and Don in, 83, 84–85, 86; phallic and Edenic imagery in, 84; Phoebe in, 83, 85, 86; ritualistic storytelling (the telling of Sabina's story) in, 83, 84, 85; role of the baskets of food in, 84; Sabina's death, denial of love, and alienation from communal life in, 86–87; Sabina's outrage at the post office in, 86; symbolic nature of the "frieze of maidens" on the columns of Asphodel, 83; the worship of wildness in, 83–87

"At the Landing" (Welty), 46–51, 125; Billy Floyd in, 46, 47, 48–49; dream of Jenny in, 50; dualities of love in, 51; Edenic references in, 47, 48; force and power of the river in, 46–47; Jenny's "Mona Lisa" smile in, 46; Jenny's smile in, 50–51; loss of Jenny's innocence in, 48–49; meeting of Floyd and Jenny in, 47–48; moon imagery in, 50; rape of Jenny Lockhart in, 46, 50–51

Beauvoir, Simone de, 114; analysis of the Zeus-Danae myth by, 130

Boatwright, James, 2

Bolsterli, Margaret, 163

Bride of the Innisfallen, The (Welty), 2, 127, 146; focus of on human relations, 166; focus of on the mysteriousness of identity in, 166–67

"Bride of the Innisfallen, The" (Welty), 146; the bride as a harbinger of the future in, 153; future and secret joy in, 152–53; various critical opinions of, 152

Brooks, Cleanth, 2, 4, 12

Brown, Homer, 81

Buswell, Mary Catherine, 2, 3, 129–30

Carson, Gary, 68

"Circe" (Welty), 146, 153–57, 196; apprehension of human qualities by Circe in, 156–57; bedroom scenes of Circe and Odysseus in, 155–56; Circe's apparent hatred of men in, 154–55; dehumanizing of men by Circe in, 155; Elpenor in, 156; human feelings of Odysseus in, 156; inability of Circe to grieve in, 156, 157; magical powers of Circe in, 154, 155; Odysseus's power to resist Circe in, 155; secrecy and the mystery of the unknown as central topics in, 153–54; tragic and comic elements in, 154

"Clytie" (Welty), 9, 22, 53, 147; Clytie's seeking comfort in water/rain in, 66;

"Clytie" (*continued*)
descent of Clytie into mental distraction in, 64–65; disturbing nature of Clytie's fate in, 52–53; as an "elegy for love," 64; Gerald and Rosemary in, 65; Gerald's view of love in, 65; imagination and madness in, 63–66; Mr. Bobo in, 65–66; narrator's naïve conception of love in, 70–71; Octavia in, 64; rose imagery in, 69–70; theme of judgment in, 64; tragic fate of Clytie in, 52; Welty's impetus for writing "Clytie," 63

Cochran, Robert, 88

Collins, Carvel, 150

communal life, as a fundamental social component of life in Welty's fiction, 5

Composing Selves: Southern Women and Autobiography (Prenshaw), 189

Corcoran, Neil, 3

Costello, Brannon, 116

Crews, Elizabeth, 115

Curley, Daniel, 12, 61, 129

Curtain of Green, A (Welty), 7

"Curtain of Green, A" (Welty), 53, 63, 64, 177; alienation of Mrs. Larkin from the community surrounding her in, 53–54; as a biographical portrait of Chestina Andrews Welty, 54, 57; grief of Mrs. Larkin in, 53–54, 187; isolation of Mrs. Larkin in, 55–56; Mrs. Larkin's loss of consciousness in, 57; physical activity of Mrs. Larkin in, 56–57; psychic pain of Mrs. Larkin in, 56; the role of rain in Mrs. Larkin's emotional life in, 57

Davenport, Garvin, 40, 49, 85

Davenport, Guy, 130; on the character of Fay Chisom in *The Optimist's Daughter*, 183

"Death of a Traveling Salesman" (Welty), 1, 2, 3, 9, 51, 196, 198; "ancient communication" in, 33–40; Bowman in, 7, 30, 119–20, 195, 196; Bowman's arrogance in, 34; Bowman's crucial symbolic association of with the town of Beulah in, 35; Bowman's hallucination in, 33–34; Bowman's self-understanding in, 38; Bowman's sense of security in, 34; children in the story juxtaposed to Bowman's empty life, 37–38; "dark cradle" metaphor in, 38, 39; Harris in, 7; image of Bowman's car as a cradle in, 37, 38; insecurity and security as themes in, 34; loving marriage of Sonny and his wife in, 35–36, 102; Welty's relationship with John Robinson as crucial background to the story, 38–39

Delta Wedding (Welty), 2, 74, 82, 94, 100, 102–18 *passim*, 127, 171, 198; Aunt Mac in, 113–14; Aunt Mashula Hines in, 103, 104, 105, 113, 114, 125, 194; Aunt Shannon in, 113; Bluet in, 103, 117; boundaries separating George and Robbie from their family and community (Shellmound) in, 109–10; communality and family love in, 110–11; complex/intense relationship of George and Robbie Fairchild in, 107, 108, 174; concern with love and marriage in, 103; cotton imagery in, 104–5; Dabney's fear of sexuality in, 112; Dabney's sexuality in, 112; death of Denis Fairchild in, 102; devotion of Ellen to her children and marriage in, 103–4; George Fairchild in, 3, 163; Gloria Renfro in, 100; ideas from Welty's earlier works that occur in, 118; India in, 112, 117, 195; intense emotionality of Robbie in, 107–8; Jim Allen in, 106; Laura in, 116; Laura's brooch in, 117; Little Ranny in, 117–18; marriage of Ellen and Battle Fairchild in, 102, 103, 105, 168, 182, 197; marriage of George and